THE ADVENTUROUS
MALE

THE ADVENTUROUS
Male

CHAPTERS IN THE HISTORY OF THE WHITE MALE MIND

Martin Green

THE PENNSYLVANIA STATE UNIVERSITY PRESS

University Park, Pennsylvania

Library of Congress Cataloging-in-Publication Data

Green, Martin Burgess, 1927–
    The adventurous male : chapters in the history of the white male
mind / Martin Green.

        p.   cm.
    Includes bibliographical references and index.
    ISBN 0-271-00875-X
    1. White men—Psychology.   2. Adventure and adventurers.
    3. Masculinity (Psychology)   I. Title.
    HQ1090.G74   1993
    904′.01′9—dc20   92-26085

Published by The Pennsylvania State University Press,
Suite C, Barbara Building, University Park, PA 16802-1003

Dedicated to
Diane Carmody Wynne
with gratitude and affection

It is the man who provokes danger in its recess, who quits a peaceful retreat, for peril and labour, to drive before a tempest or to watch in a camp. . . . It is the ADVENTURER alone on whom every eye is fixed with admiration, and whose praise is repeated by every voice.

—John Jawkesworth, in his London periodical *The Adventurer*, which began publication in 1752

The Word Adventures carries in it so free and licentious a Sound in the Apprehensions of People at this Period of Time, that it can hardly with propriety be apply'd to those few and natural incidents which compose the History of a Woman of Honour.

—*The Female Quixote*, by Charlotte Lennox (London, 1752)

Contents

Introduction

The concept of adventure is both familiar and popular, but it is not one we often think about at all exactly. I notice that when I tell people I am writing about adventure they smile and relax. The word acts as a signal, not of intellectual work, or difficulty, or risk, but of easy enjoyment or complacent nostalgia.

One sign of this is that everybody wants to name his or her own cause or group adventurous, however much they suspect the violence and gender bias of traditional adventure tales or political adventurism. For instance, many feminists disapprove of "adventure heroes," in books and in real life, but feel free to claim some truer idea of adventure for their own cause. The word still signifies a positive value—that of shared memories or future comradeship—and is so user-friendly that it can be applied on opposite sides of most controversies.

I myself try to treat the idea realistically, meaning both that I link it to actual events and that I note their grimmer moral aspects. I try to avoid the too frothy and fun-filled meanings ("two hundred pages of sheer adventure") and thus also the more metaphorical uses of the word ("my adventures with Marcel Proust"). At the same time, I give to adventure meanings other people may call metaphorical. I find the idea all over the place in our culture, hidden under more serious-sounding or more technical-sounding terms—in the theory and practice of capitalism, of science, of war. I believe the mental world built by the white nations is characterized—that is, signalized, if not differentiated from all other cultures—by its adventurousness as much as by anything else.

The idea has many facets, and the chapters in this book will each discuss one of them. The sequence of the chapters is a descriptive rather than a logical one, if logic means any approach to the cause-and-effect rigor of physics. I am turning this idea over and over, feeling its facets, estimating its dimensions—asking, for instance, "is adventure an idea of the size of liberty or equality, or of the shape of nationalism or imperialism?"

It therefore happens, and it may help the reader to expect, that in many of the chapters I try first to make a connection between some other, more familiar term and this one, in order finally to establish a web of such connections, of which the spider is adventure. In this Introduction that other word will be "power," or potestas.

It may also be helpful to say that I recognize an adventure landscape, as well as adventure narratives. In many books, and so outside books also, we feel our minds worked on by the adventure ethos embodied in a landscape (a desert island, a dangerous neighborhood, a city in revolution) even when our expectation of adventure *action* is denied or mocked. There is also an adventure philosophy, which may be embodied in a personality, and that personality may be either historical or fictional, and either active or—sometimes—sedentary. For instance, Long John Silver, in Robert Louis Stevenson's *Treasure Island*, was based on the real-life figure of W. E. Henley (who was, of all things, Stevenson's literary adviser). Both Henley and Silver were incarnations of adventure. In the presence of such individuals, we sneer at prudence and laugh at scruple—or think we ought to.

There is also an adventure sociology or anthropology, a way of looking at social groups or whole societies rather unlike the ways of "serious politics." To see social types in their colorfulness and contrastiveness, as picturesque castes rather than economic classes, in an aesthetic panorama, is to see them in adventure terms, even when those looked at are unadventurous in themselves. Adventure is always in some degree aesthetic because it is linked to pleasure and excitement rather than to moral argument.

Thus, the idea of adventure, even when we have excluded the trivial loose usages of the word, is a subtle and complex thing. But it is primarily associated, and for good reason, with the ideas of frontier and empire, as I have argued in earlier books. Let me give three examples of adventure thinking (not great thoughts, but habits of mind) from twentieth-century writers of the British Empire in India. Sara Jeannette Duncan's Anglo-Indian heroine in the story "A Mother in India" thinks, on the ship to India,

> the look of wider seas and skies, the casual, experienced glance, the touch of irony and of tolerance, how well I knew it and how well I liked it! Dear old England . . . seemed to hold by comparison a great many soft, unsophisticated people, immensely occupied about very peculiar trifles. How difficult it had been, all the summer, to be interested! These of my long acquaintance belonged to my country's Executive, acute, alert, with the marks of travail on them. Gladly I went in and out of the women's cabins and listened to the argot of the men; my own ruling, administering, soldiering little lot.[1]

It is a land of adventure to which this woman gladly goes, leaving the homeland behind with relief.

Maud Diver expresses the same imaginative preference for a land of adventure over a country where law is fully established. In her biography of Honoria Lawrence she evokes a sense of how and why the nineteenth-century English went out to India: "From copious Georgian and early Victorian families—from country vicarages, where money was scarce and children plentiful—brother followed brother to India." This was, we note, a pilgrimage not for all English men and women but for the upper class or, even more limited, the clerisy. (Joseph Conrad makes the same assumption in *Lord Jim*.) But what matters to us is its connection with adventure, which Diver asserts: "The racial spirit of adventure [was] quickened, no doubt, by the narrow bounds and piously rigid discipline of the period. In effect, it may almost be said that the dullness of British homes has been the making of the British empire."[2]

The third, and more recent example comes from Paul Scott's *Raj Quartet*. When Susan Merrick admits she has seen her husband wearing Pathan dress, she explains, "I'm sorry if it sounds melodramatic, but

---

1. Sara Jeannette Duncan, *The Pool in the Desert*, 9–10.
2. Maud Diver, *Honoria Lawrence*, 25.

this is a very melodramatic and violent country. If you're a police officer and take your job seriously you can't just sit in an office like a deputy commissioner. You have to get out into the bazaars and listen to what people are saying. You have to do all sorts of things that so-called pukka members of the *raj* pretend don't have to be done."[3] Here the key word is "melodrama"—all India is a melodramatic country—another concept, like adventure, alternative to moral realism, which is the aesthetic mode appropriate to England, the home country. (We might note, to show the bi-gender character of the idea, that all three of these testimonies are in a woman's voice.)

Eros and Potestas

I will define adventure abstractly as I have before in discussing the adventure tale, calling it a series of events that outrage civilized or domestic morality and that challenge those to whom those events happen to make use of powers that civil life forbids to the ordinary citizen, powers restricted (in a home country) to the police, the secret services, the army. For in the prototypical case, to engage in adventure means to engage in violence, but associated with violence are certain kinds of virtue, like leadership, cunning, endurance, courage, and so on. Adventure shows us heroes, men acting with power.

Perhaps the central virtue in that list is courage—meaning, when we are discussing adventure, what is called the physical kind. If one means moral courage, one could hardly argue that the adventure tale deals any more in that quality than the serious novel. Has Robinson or d'Artagnan any more moral courage than Dorothea Brooke or Emma Woodhouse? It is difficult to know what such a question means. But if we are thinking of "physical courage," we know a lot about the adventurers' prowess in that field, and little about the heroines' prowess—or that of the men in their novels. While, in the twentieth century, we hear Stephen Dedalus— that portrait of the artist—declaring he is a coward, and we hear James Joyce telling us Stephen is more authentic a poet than Buck Mulligan, who *is* courageous.

That kind of courage is important. Most people's self-respect, and

3. Paul Scott, *A Division of the Spoils,* 510.

nearly all men's, depend upon possessing some share of that quality. It is a real flaw in the moral authority of much modern literature that it avoids the topic, and a real reason to read adventures is to learn from their treatments of that topic. On the other hand, treating that quality simply as a moral virtue is not very satisfactory. It introduces that unhelpful division into physical and moral, and it is a kind of half-truth, moralistic propaganda on behalf of adventurers.

Defining courage exclusively as a virtue (at least if one understands virtue in a morally transcendent way) makes it something that shows itself negatively, a way of responding to other people's initiatives. We are shown our hero not being afraid, not backing down from a threat, not crying out under torture—always reacting to an enemy's initiative. Such a figure is a paradox—the nonviolent person who is better at violence than his enemies—a very familiar paradox in, for instance, Hollywood Westerns. In a more distinguished way, Tolstoy depicts this virtue—force without aggression—in, for instance, Captain Khlopov in the early story "The Woodfelling." But this nonviolent violence must surely be a half-truth, or a whole lie, from the point of view of moral philosophy. What are the brave man's own initiatives likely to be?

If one turns the image over, to find the positive corresponding to this negative virtue, what one faces is a person's ability to impose his or her will on a dangerous situation, including the other people involved. That person transforms the situation into a field for his or her action, whether the situation is a burglary or a drowning or a mugging. (If one acts courageously in someone else's field of action, that is a different kind of courage. One might call it the martyr's kind, not the adventurer's.) The virtue then comes into play as the ability to overcome the others' resistance, their aggression, both physical and psychological. In other words, courage is a concomitant of force, moral and physical.

The idea of adventure is therefore closely tied to this other idea, which I want to call "potestas" (from the Latin word for "power"), using it in contrastive parallel with "eros," because potestas covers a field as large and complex as eroticism, and in some ways similar. Like the latter term, potestas describes a set of relationships, but the latter have to do with force not love, domination not desire.

Love is an extraordinarily various concept, or field of meaning. One thinks of sexual desire, affection, *caritas,* the love of God, the love of one's children, the love of one's leader. The word comes to mean nothing—covering too many things—and yet everything. It's still love that makes the world of ideas go around. Power, or potestas, is the same kind of concept, and if the reader, in the pages to come, protests against its endless extension, and the protean fluidity I ascribe to it, he or she must recall the similar aspects of eros. The fact that far more books have been written about the latter is only another reason to pay attention to the former.

There are many connections between eros and potestas. Most notably, to look like an adventurer is to have a form of sexual glamour, especially for men. The tanned face and muscled body are erotic not only for what they are, biologically, but for what they signify, in social identity. The tanned man is both the servant of nature, not culture, and the frontiersman or adventurer. That the tan may, in a given case, have come entirely out of a bottle proves the sign was misleading, but not that it wasn't a sign. The tan works more definitely in this way on a man—on a woman it may mean rather a gilding of the lily—but the point is just that the two connect. This is then a crossing of adventure and the erotic. But such a crossing is no guide to the serious meanings of either term—it is metaphorically as well as literally a cosmetic use of both.

As recent studies of rape and other things have shown us, in sexual behavior both sets of relationships get expressed, and often confused. Male-female relationships have traditionally been a matter of potestas as much as of eros, whether admittedly or not. This crossing *is* a guide to serious meanings.

But the two fields are in many ways opposite, and remote from each other. In the world of literature, the gulf between the two is shown in the career of D. H. Lawrence, who, having written some of the greatest of erotic fiction, tried to make power the subject of his writing in the 1920s, in *Aaron's Rod, Kangaroo,* and *The Plumed Serpent.* Here, one might say, he was venturing on the subject matter of his great antagonist, Rudyard Kipling, and he was as at ill at ease in the field of power as the older man had been in the field of love.

At the climax to *Aaron's Rod,* Lilly, who represents Lawrence, says to his disciple Aaron, "Well then, there are only two great dynamic urges in life: love and power." The other man replies, "Love and power? I don't see power as very important." (Aaron represents the reader, the average sensitive man.) "You don't see because you don't look," replies Lilly, and in the remaining few pages of the book Lawrence/Lilly tries to make *us* look at power in relation to politics and culture.[4] For instance,

4. D. H. Lawrence, *Aaron's Rod,* 284.

four pages later, Lilly says, "We've exhausted our love-urge, for the moment. . . . It was the great dark power-urge which kept Egypt so intensely living for so many centuries. It is a vast dark source of life and strength in us now" (p. 288). And however little we may want to swallow Lawrence's practical prescriptions on this point, as an analytical tool his or some other theory of power reveals so much as to be necessary in any description of our society.

In potestas, as in eros, there are a thousand forms and transformers of the original drive—in this case, of the will to power; transforming it into pleasure and into pain, into assertion and submission, forms that elude all the individual's attempts at discipline and denial. Potestas, like eros, seems to act like an electric shock or poisonous acid, transmitted by the touch or eye. And the classical image of a god is appropriate in this case too. It is as difficult to pluck out the darts of Mars as the arrows of Cupid, once they have struck.

In both cases, moreover, when one person either desires or dominates another, a reciprocal action occurs whereby the second person either resists, or accepts the position of being desired or dominated, or, on the other hand, seeks the position of desiring or dominating a third. (As this phrasing suggests, the two systems go together often. One often both desires and dominates the same other.)

We find the cult of potestas everywhere, but it is reflected with special vividness in American rather than British films and fiction—for instance, in the mystery story, where the American style has differed so much from the British. If we let Agatha Christie and Dorothy Sayers represent the latter, and Raymond Chandler and Robert Parker the former, the difference is obvious. In American stories of this kind, potestas or potency is being asserted all the time, gun to gun or eyeball to eyeball, in competition and confrontation. The truly potent man rarely needs to be violent, until the end of the story, and the definition and cult of potency can become very subtle. But the *excitement* of potency (in this sense, which is quite distinct from the erotic sense, however mixed together they may get in life) is what charges every page.

Some adventure tales we of course associate with the feeling of freedom, and even especially freedom in personal relationships, freedom *from* competition and confrontation. Perhaps the supreme example is *Robinson Crusoe*, where the hero is so free that there is nobody else on his island. If this is an essential example of adventure (as it *is*), how can we associate the idea of adventure with that of potestas? One answer is that Crusoe dominates his island, in various ways. But the main answer is that he dominates Friday. And Crusoe *needs* Friday, emotionally; he dreams of "getting a savage into my possession" even before luck brings him one. And this example is exemplary. Whenever a hero achieves freedom in an adventure, someone else loses it, sooner or later. Domination, like love, is a reciprocal system.

So far I have used the traditional language of personal relationships, but there are group and political forms. One vivid example of political potestas, though in a sinister or pathological form, is George Orwell's *1984,* and the historical events Orwell was referring to. At one of the story's climaxes, O'Brien tells Winston Smith that the Party seeks power for its own sake, not for this or that good or bad reason. Power, to the Party, is not a means but an end. In that idea, political potestas is revealed in all its lurid glory, and the figure of O'Brien, and all the famous features of the story, from Big Brother to the torture chambers, fit into that scheme. But, as *Aaron's Rod* can remind us, not all aspects of potestas are limitedly sinister.

The greatest writer in English about potestas—though not in realistic so much as in mythical, legendary, poetic, and humorous terms—was probably Rudyard Kipling. He was obsessed with the subject and shows us dozens of ways—often subtle and paradoxical—in which authority makes itself felt, in which people rejoice in being dominated, in which power is passed down a long chain, in which punishment is gladly accepted, in which values like sensibility and individuality are self-sacrificed to potestas. Men, in Kipling's stories, are essentially conductors of power: it is inflicted on them, and they inflict it on others; it is their fate to first suffer it, rebelliously, and then impose it, righteously. As we read about Mowgli, about Kim, about Stalky, about the Road and the Bridge and the Wall, about the parts of a ship learning to work together, about the British in India and the Romans in England and intelligence officers in disguise, and above all, perhaps, about army NCOs (noncommissioned officers) who in every army translate power from its initial well-bred officer tones into the bullying roar the common soldier hears, we are listening to one great choral hymn to potestas.

It is no accident that Kipling began his career by writing about India, for it is in adventures on the various social frontiers, in the situations of danger and lawlessness, that the cult of potestas flourishes. Where law is fully established, it takes on *itself* the actions and sanctions of potestas, which thus become in some ways mechanized, systematized, impersonal. Where law is feeble, being already in decay or not yet established, men (and women, but men more prominently) exert power over each other in the splendid, intoxicating, or toxic, forms of potestas. That is what every Western movie tells us.

Common sense, at least masculine common sense, assents to Kipling's and the Western's teaching. But there are many dissents, especially among intellectuals; one of that group's constitutive traits is a dislike of potestas, at least when experienced at the receiving end. One powerful dissent that seems to be intrinsic and absolute is found in Jean-Paul Sartre. In his autobiography, *Les mots* (The Words), he claims he has no superego—and so he is a nonconductor of power. He speaks of his "incredible levity," his lack of all normal gravity, in every sense. "I am not a leader, nor do I aspire to become one. Command, obey, it is all one. The bossiest of men commands in the name of another—his father—and transmits the abstract acts of violence which he puts up with. Never in my life have I given an order without laughing, without making others laugh. It is because I am not consumed by the canker of power."[5] He would be no leader, on an adventure.

Thus Sartre completely repudiated his heritage of potestas, seeing it primarily as a reciprocal system. "There is no good father, that's the rule. Don't lay the blame on men but on the bond of paternity, which is rotten" (p. 11). Because his own father died when he was two and he grew up in his grandfather's home, where his mother was still a daughter, with no power, the boy Sartre escaped the almost universal bondage of power.

This recoil from potestas (and so from adventure) is common among writers, many of whom are refugees from that system. James Joyce depicts the same psychology in his autobiographical characters. Stephen Dedalus in *Portrait of the Artist as a Young Man,* and in *Ulysses,* is set free from the reciprocal system by his father's having abandoned the moral dignity of manhood. (Simon Dedalus continued to claim the privileges of manhood, but he had no *right* to them.) And Stephen turns away from his contemporaries when he sees that they assert the power, the potestas, of manhood, in its graceful as well as its grosser forms. For instance, he thinks, they protect women from insult and save them from drowning, as he does not; they are manly—capable of adventure and action. When they (Cranly in the major instance) argue with Stephen about his unmanliness, he declares, "I cannot strive against

5. Jean-Paul Sartre, *The Words,* 12–13.

another," and decides to go into exile from Ireland alone. For all their cynical talk, they hold by the adventure virtues, and so they cannot be his comrades.

In Joyce's autobiographical play, *Exiles,* Richard Rowan declares (as Joyce did in life), "I cannot be severe with a child," so his wife must impose the discipline on their son. He cannot be a masterful father, or husband. Both he and Leopold Bloom, though jealous husbands, fearful that they have been cuckolded, renounce or never feel the masculine lust for revenge—that classic form of potestas—on either the woman or the other man. When a friend speaks of taking Richard's wife, Bertha, from him, Richard says, "That is the language I have heard often and never believed in. Do you mean by stealth or by violence? Steal you could not in my house because the doors were open; nor take by violence if there were no resistance."[6]

Taken on to the political plane (as Joyce takes the theme, briefly, in *Ulysses*), this nonresistance of evil must remind us of Tolstoy. As a young man, born into a military caste family, Tolstoy entered whole-heartedly into the systems of desire and domination. At past the age of fifty, he began to try to disentangle himself therefrom. His eldest son's tutor, Alekseev, became to him a model of meekness and innocence. And in his last years Tolstoy wrote stories—for instance, "Ivan Durak" (Ivan the Fool)—in which he held such figures up to admiration.

One of the most striking cases was his long story *Father Sergius,* in which the eponymous central character is one we are bound to associate with Tolstoy himself. He begins life distinguished by "marked ability and tremendous pride" and a hot temper.[7] As a cadet at the imperial court, close to the emperor Nicholas I, the culminating figure in all Russia's system of potestas, Sergius feels a passionate love for the czar, but discovers that the girl he wants to marry had been the czar's mistress and that their match has been promoted as a way to pension her off. Sergius is about to play a shameful part in a system of potestas, to become that inert body on which a greater man steps toward further conquests—a means for the czar to intensify his potency. In revulsion from everything he has so far desired, Sergius leaves the court and the service. He enters a monastery and strives to become "industrious, abstemious, meek, gentle, pure, and obedient" (p. 511).

6. James Joyce, *Exiles*, 78.
7. Leo Tolstoy, *Father Sergius*, 500.

Despite his sincerity of intention, he finds that his moral efforts feed his masculine pride still further. And so he is unhappy and dissatisfied and for many years lost, until he remembers a poor relation, Pashenka, whom he had known as a boy when she was always the victim of his and his brothers' pranks. He seeks her out again and finds her now living with her daughter and grandchildren but still "somehow insipid, insignificant, and pitiful" (p. 560). Her daughter and son-in-law get on badly, and Pashenka "did everything in her power to smooth things over, to prevent reproaches, to prevent ill-feeling" (p. 563). Her efforts were all ineffectual. Nevertheless, Sergius says to himself, "Pashenka is precisely what I ought to have been, and what I have not been. I lived for man, pretending to live for God; but she lives for God, imagining that she lives for man" (p. 572).

Tolstoy uses conventionally moralistic language here, but the contrast between Sergius and Pashenka—and that contrast is the point of the whole story—is between someone entangled in the system of reciprocal domination and someone free from it, or involved only passively, as its victim. It is a contrast that prefers the victim to the hero, and that latter is what Sergius is, whatever happens to him.

Pashenka is a fool, a holy fool, like Ivan Durak. Sergius is a leader, and has the virtues, as well as the vices, of leadership. And thus, though things happen to Pashenka, she has no adventures; only Sergius has adventures, because adventure is the name for, among other things, those series of events and ideas in which potestas is pursued, achieved, developed.

Part
1

ADVENTURE
AND MASCULINITY

THIS BOOK DEALS not only with the idea of adventure, but also with a body of thought, conscious or not, like an uncharted landscape in which adventure is situated. Adventure itself is like a mountain in that landscape, and if you look to its left you can see a system of hills running up to this one and, to the right, others running away. So you can see the whole landscape in adventure terms. Of course, starting from a different peak, you could make a different chart, but some element of the arbitrary is at the starting point of every logic. On one edge of this adventure landscape we find violence, and on the other we find play—near opposites though those concepts are. Each of the next two chapters relates adventure to one of those concepts.

Playfulness and violence are always the two faces of adventure. Thus, adventure is often accused of leading us toward *real* violence, making us enjoy the latter, by means of its *playful* violence, its tales sugarcoated with bravery and hairbreadth escapes and happy endings. But if we believe that people must learn how to manage force, individually and in groups, must become at ease with it imaginatively, then this is adventure's social danger but also its social strength.

The main point I want to *argue* in these chapters is simply the neglected importance of adventure as a concept. That concept is important in understanding both genders and all phases of life, so this section could have been called "Adventure and Personhood" or "Adventure and Humanity." But adventure is a concept so signally linked to manliness, and so dialectically linked to male citizenship (so co-extensive or constitutive, and yet so contradictive, of that other concept), that it seemed well to announce these links in the title of Part One.

A few lines by adventure writer Jack London, in a book written in 1913, will tie things together for us suggestively. After saying how dreary most adults' lives seemed to him when he was a boy in Oakland, California, he says: "In the saloons life was different. Men talked with great voices, laughed great laughs, and there was an atmosphere of greatness. . . . My head filled with all the wild and valiant fighting of the gallant adventures on sea and land."[1] This book, *John Barleycorn*, is a tract against drink, written in adulthood, but London still makes the connection between adventure, masculinity, and greatness.

1. Jack London, *John Barleycorn*, 46.

1

Adventure, Manhood, Citizenship

Although adventure is so important, there are vested interests in our thought-world, our thinking, that minimize and trivialize our experience of it. Thus, if we began by defining adventure in accordance with mainstream literary or philosophical or political-science thought, we should soon find ourselves contrasting it with something else (serious fiction, traditional philosophy, actual politics) that better deserves our attention. Those ideas are the instruments and products of the established disciplines of thought, and adventure will seem whimsical next to them. In order to escape that mutilation, I begin with a sort of speculative anthropology practiced primarily in France, which may at first seem to us far from the centers of respectable thought, the kind guaranteed as serious. The words these writers use are "violence" and "liminal areas" rather than "adventure," but I shall assume that the close connections between all three concepts will quickly become obvious.

Georges Bataille says we must think of cities and citizenship as based on the purposes and values of work, which means the denial of all activities hostile to work, such as both the ecstasies of eroticism and those of violence (i.e., adventure). "The [civilized] community is made up of those whom the common effort unites, cut off from violence by work during the hours devoted to work."[1] And work, it follows, initiates the social or civic contract. We should think of this last not in Rousseau's terms but as the tacit agreement that requires the good citizen to give up many possibilities of immediate individual fulfillment in return for mutual respect and productivity and deferred gratification. (It will be obvious how this idea accords with late Freudian and post-Freudian philosophy.)

But the forbidden activities persist in the liminal areas of social and psychological life. The repressed drives do not cease to exist or to inspire action. They continue to seem intensely valuable to most people, and they always have their spokespersons, practitioners, and even philosophers. Moreover, the social contract itself is a very complex document, full of riders and exemptions. Society, even at its most official, does not totally forbid those activities; we all know of social castes consecrated to them (professional soldiers and prostitutes are the most obvious examples) and of *limines* where loyal citizens can sample those pleasures. There are stretches of both space and time that give a local habitation and a name to those *limines,* places where respectable citizens (as long as they are *being* respectable) feel ill at ease, like red-light districts and hunting woods and battlegrounds, and times like the years of young manhood before marriage. Many novels and movies work by arousing and exploiting that uneasiness and excitement.

Marcel Detienne analyzes the hunting myths of Atalanta and Adonis to show how hunting, for example, takes place in such a permissive space where social laws can be flouted. A fundamentally adventurous activity that leads to bloodshed and meat-eating, hunting is linked to war, another activity that is morally reproved but imaginatively endorsed by civilized culture. Both hunting and war are contrasted with the normative activity, the *work,* of agriculture: "Situated at the intersection of the powers of life and the forces of death, the hunter's space constitutes at once that which is beyond the farmer's fields and their negation."[2]

Women have much less often than men been assigned the freedoms of adventure (this is a typical case of the "double standard") and men are therefore quite generally associated with violence. Testimony to this is a passage from a work of literary theory by W. P. Day quite remote from my own in its main concerns: "Violence is, of course, the natural

1. Georges Bataille, *Erotism: Death and Sensuality,* 47–48.
2. Marcel Detienne, *Dionysos Slain,* 24.

expression of the masculine in its purest form, the application of force
to the world to assert its power and identity."[3]

This radical proposition is perhaps put to us so confidently, not to say
blithely, because the larger argument surrounding it is offered as legendary or mythical, with its immediate references remote from actual
contemporary behavior: "The knight and the warrior [are] gone; that
form of heroism [has] disappeared. . . . Men who [have to be] businessmen or office-workers or bureaucrats could not really imagine themselves questing knights. The aristocratic warrior became the professional
soldier, who in a way was only another businessman or bureaucrat" (p.
82). Norman Mailer teaches us how shortsighted is this reliance on a
psychic barrier separating past from present. In *Why Are We in Vietnam?*
our businessmen *do* imagine themselves as hunters, and modern professional soldiers do behave like warriors. Men need to imagine themselves
in the terms of adventure.

Starting from this point, we can soon see how crucial a concept
adventure is (it is the way, the truth, and the life of all liminal experience)
and how many other concepts it relates to. However, the work of these
French anthropologists has analyzed, above all, erotic experience. In the
thought of Georges Bataille, therefore, the concept of violence tends to
have a metaphorical character. This is not one hundred percent true,
because it is literally violent and sadistic sex he discusses, but he does
not make us think of those other, nonerotic forms of violence that are
so crucial to adventure and potestas.

Bataille is the most interesting of these thinkers, and his *Death and
Sensuality* deserves a good deal of our attention. First, he develops the
idea of work, which, he tells us, has made man what he is. The opposite
of the workday is the holiday (carnival time), when reality is suspended
to allow for the satisfaction of our "wild impulses." Our everyday work
and even our serious thought "demands rational behavior where the wild
impulses . . . are frowned upon. . . . These impulses confer an immediate
satisfaction on those who yield to them. Work, on the other hand,
promises to those who overcome them [the impulses] a reward later on."
The opposite of work and reason is violence and excess—that which
exceeds our needs and our moral bounds. "Most of the time work is the
concern of men acting collectively, and during the time reserved for
work the collective has to oppose those contagious impulses to excess in

3. William Patrick Day, *In the Circles of Fear and Desire*, 80.

which nothing is left but the immediate surrender to excess, to violence, that is."[4] Bataille's key word is "violence," meaning both the literal fact and its violation of our moral feelings, the two occurring in the one action.

We can find similar ideas and concerns in Roland Barthes and Susan Sontag. Barthes says violence is "an unusual word that creates a kind of panic of responses in us. [The "us" refers to men and women of letters or intellect.] This kind of impasse finally develops a religious dimension."[5] Sontag has often reacted against the liberal, modern presentation of sex as playful and innocent by depicting it as violent. Thus, in "Approaching Artaud" she points out how Artaud "regarded eroticism as something threatening, demonic. . . . Virginity is treated as a state of grace, and impotence or castration is presented . . . as more of a deliverance than a punishment."[6]

More generally, Sontag is interested in the difference between "goodness" and the adventurous, morally ambiguous qualities that most of us (overtly or not) prefer to be known for. In her "Project for a Trip to China," she makes China the symbol of simplicity and goodness: "What doesn't put me off, imagining it on the eve of my departure for China, is all that talk about goodness. I don't share the anxiety I detect in everyone I know about being *too* good. . . . [A little later, however, she makes it seem that she does share that anxiety.] But to be good one must be simpler. Simpler as in a return to origins. Simpler as in a great forgetting."[7] Goodness, simplicity, and truth go together. We prize them but are not satisfied by them alone. "The truth is simple, very simple. Centered. But people crave other nourishment besides the truth. Its privileged distortions, in philosophy and literature. For example" (p. 26 [*sic*]). Here literature and philosophy are seen to go with breaking the social or the intellectual contract, to be forms of transgression, distortions of simple truth. They are intellectual adventures, the imaginative equivalent of the literal adventures I am discussing. They would have to be sacrificed in Communist China, she suggests, the land of goodness and simplicity and truth.

Another alternative to adventure, another social embodiment of civic virtue, though here named as "religion," is represented by the nonviolent

4. Bataille, *Erotism*, 41.
5. From a 1978 interview quoted in Roland Barthes, *The Grain of the Voice*, 307, 309.
6. Susan Sontag, *Under the Sign of Saturn*, 27.
7. See Susan Sontag, *I, Etcetera*, 22.

philosophy of Tolstoy and Gandhi (the one story by Tolstoy that Gandhi translated into Gujarati was "Ivan the Fool"). That philosophy came into being because they saw violence as occupying a central position in history, and they were attempting to change the main currents of history, to change "human nature." When Gandhi said, as he often did, that Western or modern civilization was based on violence, we can best understand him if we think of violence in this sense of adventure, as well as in the most obvious sense. Most other world-views deal with the moral problem of violence by treating it as peripheral or only intermittently important. Unlike Tolstoy and Gandhi, the worldly philosophers try to make it occupy less rather than more space in the mind than common sense assigns it—they try to make it go away by ignoring it.

The major strategy of modern political philosophy—the alternative to the study of force as central—is the study of work and its profits as central, analyzing the way the means of production and exchange are controlled and the way justice is distributed between the classes, and so on. From this point of view (it is used by both the capitalist and the Marxist), force is simpy the means by which action is taken. Violence is certainly in some sense to be deplored, this view's spokespersons say, but nothing is gained by concentrating our thoughts and feelings on that focus.

The German sociologist Georg Simmel was also interested in adventure, but he also saw it as primarily erotic. In an essay entitled "The Adventurer" (1911), he defines adventure rather as Bataille and Detienne do, as something dropped out of the continuity of life.[8] But he insists that one type of experience—the erotic—tends to appear in this form more than any other: "Our linguistic custom hardly lets us understand by 'adventure' anything but an erotic one" (p. 195). What can this custom be but an intellectual taboo on literal adventure, operating beneath the conscious level?

The taboo's results are widespread. The same idea lies at the root of Suzanne Roth's historical study *Les aventuriers au XVIII siècle*. She discusses as adventurers a variety of "marginal" types of that period, semi-official ambassadors, half-pay officers, the writers of librettos, of occasional poems, of dilettante works of history—all of them implicitly opposed to social order and alien to the hierarchy of responsibility. They are of many types, but Roth's central examples are Casanova and

8. See Georg Simmel, *On Individuality and Social Forms*, 187.

Cagliostro, Beaumarchais and Saint-Germain. The adventures their names signify are above all those of eros, those that Simmel says our very language compels us to associate with the word. My contention is that this is far from compulsory, and indeed is intellectually nonsensical. Adventure has more to do with potestas, with force and violence, than with eros.

The idea of violence is linked to another idea that plays a large part in Bataille's scheme: the concept of taboos as positive forces, constitutive of culture. Taboos are necessary, he says, from several points of view. They save us from violence, the element of destruction: "Violence is what the world of work excludes with its taboos."[9] But the latter operate against more than the literal meanings of violence—for instance, against all sexuality not licensed and officially approved. " 'Thou shalt not kill'; 'Thou shalt not perform the carnal act except in wedlock.' Such are the two fundamental commandments found in the Bible, and we still observe them" (p. 42). The power of taboo has also its intellectual effects, as we saw implied in Sontag's essay. Bataille says:

> Taboos acted on behalf of science in the first place. [We should perhaps recall that *science* means more in French, that in English "science" is close to "knowledge."] They removed the object of the taboo from our consciousness by forbidding it, and at the same time deprived our consciousness—our full consciousness, at any rate—of the movement of terror whose consequence was the taboo. But the rejection of the disturbing object, and the disturbance itself, were necessary for the clarity, the untroubled clarity, of the world of action and of objectivity. Without the existence of prohibitions in the first place, men would not have achieved the lucid and distinct awareness on which science is founded. Prohibitions eliminate violence, and our violent impulses (those which correspond with sexual impulsions?) destroy within us that calm ordering of ideas without which human awareness is inconceivable (p. 38).

That is why, as both Barthes and Lionel Trilling tell us, there is a special antipathy between the intellectual and violence.

Thus, taboos are truth. They must not be regarded, the way modern

9. Bataille, *Erotism*, 42.

thought so often does, as just mistaken, as something to be transcended by the sophisticated. They do not just inhibit or, to use Bataille's word, prohibit life. "The truth of taboos is the key to our human attitude. We must know, we can know that prohibitions are not imposed from without" (p. 38). They are part of our essential identity. The anguish of mind we feel at violating taboos (even in adventure, if we take it seriously) is what religion calls the experience of sin and accompanies adventure's excitement. (Let me suggest here, as an example, that even Robinson Crusoe felt that anguish on leaving home, in the most peaceful and work-oriented of all adventure tales.)

In the world of art, in the grand sense, this conflict between social morality and adventure is often asserted, but its significance is somewhat obscured, or indeed inverted. Artists like to see themselves as "adventurers" in some of the sillier and more "glamorous" senses, though also in the serious senses. They like to separate themselves from "social conventions," to make themselves the champions of these tabooed experiences. But the best take the idea seriously—today, notably, Norman Mailer and Philip Roth. In his novels and essays, Mailer has continually asserted the irrationalist or adventurous thinking of our social outcasts, but also of our men in power, and he declares a close connection between erotics and sin or violence.

Roth implies the same. His hero in *Portnoy's Complaint* finds himself, on a visit to Israel, sexually impotent because the girl who attracts him is, politically, not sinful. She is virtuous—that is, she believes in her country and her life there, and therefore in the social function of her sexuality—and this virtue, this innocence, by contagion, defeats his desire. (Sontag, while making her remarks about goodness, says everyone fears it will bring with it a loss of energy and individuality: "in men, a loss of virility."[10]) When Portnoy, in his anger and frustration, talks of "fucking away" at the Israeli girl, "She shivered with loathing. 'Tell me, please, *why* must you use that word all the time?' 'Don't the boys say 'fuck' up in the mountains?' 'No,' she answered condescendingly, 'not the way that you do.' 'Well,' I said, 'I suppose they're not as rich with rage as I am. With contempt.' "[11] Rage and contempt are forms of violence, and all three go together. The Israelis are fighters, on occasion, but they are not engaged in violence, as we have defined the word. They

10. Sontag, *I, Etcetera*, 22.
11. Philip Roth, *Portnoy's Complaint*, 270.

are not engaged in sin. Portnoy is, from this point of view, more the adventurer. The two concepts, sex and sin, are linked together in this sociopolitical sense of sin.

Roth's point is not quite the same as Bataille's, because his two characters differ significantly whereas Bataille sees everyone as alike in this guilt. But does Roth really believe in the innocence the girl claims? It is not really part of the world of his novel, but something pointed to on the periphery. In any case, his story depicts a strong connection between violence and violation in the sexual case, and that connection is even easier to see when we substitute the pleasures of hunting and war for those of love. The pleasures of adventure are inseparable from sin, ultimately, however long one may put off that realization. The Israeli soldiers will one day have to see their fighting as violence, not just as patriotic duty.

When man began to work, Bataille says, he escaped from the realm of violence to some extent by renouncing violence in principle.[12] But that renunciation was partial as well as principled: "In fact men have never definitively said 'no' to violence" (p. 62). So sin is an essential part of civilized life. "Organized transgression together with the taboos make social life what it is" (p. 65). One form of organized transgression is patriotic war, and there are many others. Even organized religion is based on breaking the rules rather than on the rules themselves; feast days, the crown of religious life, are also escapes into license. They are holidays that make inroads on the world of virtue, of order (p. 68).

Only China as Sontag imagines it in her "Trip to China" (or, as I would say, Tolstoy and Gandhi, the prophets of nonviolence) constitutes an exception. All the others, in various ways, rely on the inroads of license and the adventures of the *limines*—hence the paralysis or revulsion that overcomes most people at the thought of virtue and order. Bataille's idea is developed to illuminate our experience of eroticism, but we can easily enough extend its application to cover traditional adventure—to cover, for instance, the violent action of *The Three Musketeers*. (We need, of course, to unwrap that action, stripping off the plumes and diamonds and swordplay and laughter in which the author disguises it.) Indeed, Bataille applies taboo that way himself: "The taboo within us . . . is general and universal. . . . Its shape and its objects do change; but whether it is a question of sexuality or death,

12. Bataille, *Erotism*, 43.

violence, terrifying yet fascinating, is what it is levelled at" (pp. 50–51). Adventure is therefore taboo for all who hold *strictly* to the social contract.

But does anyone do so? I need hardly argue that the binding force of that contract, that negative, is not felt fully by all. Quite apart from those special castes mentioned before, licensed for war or for orgy, there are various underclasses of the poor, and other minorities, who see the rules of society as not binding on them, as merely imposed on them— that is part of the fascination those classes have for artists. And then most people, even of the respectable and responsible classes, have allowed themselves certain exemptions from the rules they largely uphold and enforce, so adventure exists for them and among them too.

These exemptions were, I said, tacitly acknowledged for men, not women, but that is not always true. In the idea-realm of the Great Goddess, made the site of art by writers like D. H. Lawrence, that rule is reversed. Such writers present women as having an *easier* access to freedom and "wild impulse." Thus women too, in certain ways, are adventurers, which seems plausible enough.

"Sexuality and death," says Bataille, "are simply the culminating points of the holiday nature celebrates, with the inexhaustible multitude of human beings" (p. 61). Nature figures here as the irresponsible opposite of civilization or society, and we can extend the idea of "death" to cover war and adventure, for the approach to death—to inflicting it as well as suffering it—is the secret lure of adventure, though usually hidden in stories for boys. These two points signify to Bataille, in economic terms, "the boundless wastage of nature," opposed as they are to society's urge to live on, to cheat death, its drive to conserve and economize. Excess thus has its economic meaning too. Wastage and extravagance are even built into our religions (with exceptions like Tolstoy and Gandhi again) in hidden and yet well-known places. "The violence of war certainly betrays the God of the New Testament, but it does not oppose the God of the Old Testament in the same way" (p. 63). The desire to kill is not alien to us, and among the underclasses (those who effectively deny the social contract) it leads as lively an existence as sexual appetite does (p. 72).

Violence, and therefore adventure, is an element, hidden or disguised, but entwined with others that seem opposite, in all our experience. And yet it retains its power to shock and horrify us wherever it is revealed. "The origins of war, sacrifice and orgy are identical; they spring from the existence of taboos" (p. 116). And Bataille's introduction begins: "Eroticism, it may be said, is assenting to life up to the point of death." The same formula can be applied to adventure. Of course, these things are not true of adventure in the sense of a spontaneous and small-risk breaking with routine—the spice of life, the spice of personality—any more than they are true of playful and affectionate sex. But when people decide to intensify those spices, to increase the doses, these truths soon appear on the horizon of their thought.

The Adventure Writer

In the age of conscious imperialism at the end of the nineteenth century, when there was a cult of adventure, America had several notable adventure writers. Stephen Crane, Jack London, Richard Harding Davis, and John Reed earned their living, typically, as war correspondents. (Kipling, their intellectual father, was a war correspondent in the Boer War in South Africa.) Their lives, crystallized as they were lived into stories and episodes of social myth, were powerful agents of adventure propaganda. The most brilliant example of the type, at least as measured by world reputation, was Ernest Hemingway, of the next generation, who was most effective as a describer of action, an *implicit* celebrant of violence, adventure, and masculinism. But in one or two places he was their worthy analyst and theorist also, in a style quite like that of the moralists just cited.

Thus, in *Death in the Afternoon* (1932) Hemingway discusses the bullfight, in which adventure and art are fused: "Bullfighting is the only art in which the artist is in danger of death, and in which the degree of brilliance in the performance is left to the artist's honor";[13] moreover, the death in question is one that he, the artist, inflicts as well as (potentially) suffers.

Hemingway spells out the connection between his own writing career and his interest in these subjects. When he began to write, he said, "The only place where you could see life and death, i.e. violent death, now that the wars were over, was in the bull-ring and I wanted very much to go to Spain to study it. I was trying to learn to write, commencing with

13. Ernest Hemingway, *Death in the Afternoon*, 91.

the simplest things, and one of the simplest things of all and the most fundamental is violent death" (p. 2). His interest was not just that of a spectator; he identified with the bullfighter, seeing himself in the ring and seeing his own literary art in would-be similar terms. In *The Sun Also Rises* (1926), Romero the toreador is the perfect artist, whom Jake Barnes and even Hemingway can only admire, and that is partly because Romero's art is adventure: he puts his life at risk everytime he performs. Hemingway tried to make his writing seem an adventure in something like the same sense. (Hemingway's master, Kipling, had the same philosophy of art. His interest in bullfighting and in the Roman army's cult of Mithras, which involved a bull-sacrifice, is also worth noting.)

Early in his book, Hemingway declared that *Death in the Afternoon* would be a "serious book on an unmoral subject" (p. 4) and says on the first page: "I suppose that from a modern moral point of view, that is, a Christian point of view, the whole bullfight is indefensible; there is certainly much cruelty, there is always danger, either sought or unlooked for, and there is always death" (p. 1). Those are its attractions, for him. His own morality, he says, is not modern but antique, not Christian but aesthetic, which means that his adventure is fused with art perfectly: "I believe that the tragedy of the bullfight is so well ordered and so strongly disciplined by ritual" that aestheticism merges into spirituality (p. 8). But this is a spirituality strikingly unlike that of Tolstoy and Gandhi, or that of the traditional civic contract:

> The truly great killer must have a sense of honor and a sense of glory. . . . Killing cleanly and in a way which gives you aesthetic pleasure and pride has always been one of the greatest enjoyments of a part of the human race. Because the other part, which does not enjoy killing, has always been the more articulate and has furnished most of the good writers we have had a very few statements of true enjoyment of killing . . . the feeling of rebellion against death which comes from its administering. Once you accept the rule of death thou shalt not kill is an easily and a naturally obeyed commandment. But when a man is still in rebellion against death he has pleasure in taking to himself use of the Godlike attributes; that of giving it (pp. 232–33).

This is the world of adventure, one forbidden us by the civic contract— which for Hemingway, as for Bataille, is identified with Christianity:

"These things are done in pride and pride, of course, is a Christian sin and a pagan virtue" (p. 233).

Hemingway much admired Blaise Cendrars, 1887–1961, the French adventure writer, and so did Henry Miller, Hemingway's contemporary, as we shall see. Miller explored the transgressions of sex, as Hemingway did those of literal violence. Cendrars was their precursor, and in a sense their master. The two Americans went to Paris in the 1920s partly to learn how to combine the values of art with those of violence, but the Frenchman may be said to have gone wandering through America earlier, with the same purpose. America was the land of adventure, and so of the adventure writer. Cendrars had in fact there met the outlaw Al Jennings, who gave Cendrars his gun—a powerfully symbolic act, the memory of which Cendrars treasured. (Jennings, known to Theodore Roosevelt and his fellow adventure-lovers, became a close friend of famous short-story writer "O. Henry." The lineage of adventure writing is full of these connections, and of the swapping of guns and pens.)

Blaise Cendrars made an important contribution to aesthetic modernism in France, both in literature and in painting, in the decades immediately before and after the Great War. He is especially associated with dada and surrealism but is said also to have brought certain elements of modernism to several other artist-intellectual groups; he "discovered" the American elements of infatuation with speed and machinery and a new brutality of tone. But—or "This was because"—he was also an adventurer, in a way that distinguished him from his colleagues in those enterprises. He early began wandering through Russia, China, and America, involved in one adventure after another.

As adventurer, Cendrars was a model to many other writers. Henry Miller, in *The Books in My Life* (1951), made Cendrars the central figure and took his epigraph from him. Miller writes to Cendrars: "You have roamed far, you have idled the days away, you have burned the candle at both ends. . . . *To live* is your primary aim, and you *are* living and will continue to live both in the flesh and in the roster of the illustrious ones."[14] Cendrars was, Miller says, the man D. H. Lawrence wanted to be. Miller signs his letter not as Cendrars's peer but as his devotee and disciple. There were many such tributes in the *Mercure de France* issue in Cendrars's honor in 1962. He was saluted as a literary conquistador who had dominated life, wrecked its limits, its normal

14. Henry Miller, *The Books in My Life*, 80.

rules, its monotony, and had done so not by his dreams, like romantic writers, but by his deeds.

As one might expect, however, Cendrars himself was uneasy in the role of a man of letters, as indeed were Kipling and Hemingway. Cendrars bluntly scorned such literary colleagues as Gide, Cocteau, Breton, and Valéry and was indifferent to Sartre and Picasso. Rimbaud and Villon were his ancestral authors. In *Moravagine* (1926) he says that what he has always held most in disgust is literature.[15] On the other hand, he understood that word mystically rather than empirically; he himself was always a writer and a reader, in love with language and with thought. In the same book he says he finally realized he had always been a contemplative, contemplating his actions as he performed them, like an inverted Brahmin (p. 133).

Cendrars served in the Foreign Legion and volunteered in the Great War. One of his books about that experience, published in 1918, was entitled *J'ai tué* (I Have Killed). The title draws our attention indirectly to our habit of setting the act of killing at a distance from the acts of reading and writing; we find it difficult to believe that someone can *write* those words, at least in sincerity and not as a literary ploy. Cendrars insists, "I killed first. I have the sense of reality, poet as I am. I acted. I killed. Like one who wants to live."[16] However, the note of existential anguish is matched by other notes. Cendrars described the men in his company much in the adventure language of Theodore Roosevelt describing his regiment in *Rough Riders*, the language of lusty enjoyment.

Cendrars was therefore like Roosevelt and Kipling (like the latter in his uneasiness as a man of letters and in his enthusiasm for the colonies), as well as a modernist. In *Rhum: L'aventure de Jean Galmont* (1930) he wrote: "Life in the colonies is the greatest school of energy and courage."[17] In the colonies one is free; one has no master. Life is all adventure. We think of such declarations as being part of a nineteenth-century, pre–Great War, rhetoric, but Cendrars was a modernist.

Rhum is the biography of an adventurer (a man defined by that word throughout the book) who died in Guyana in 1928, poisoned. Cendrars dedicated the story to young people tired of literature, "to prove to them that a novel too can be an act." Jean Galmont had been a gold

15. See J.-C. Lovey, *La situation de Blaise Cendrars*, 161.
16. Ibid., 133.
17. Blaise Cendrars, *Rhum: L'aventure de Jean Galmont*, 126.

prospector, a trapper, and a trafficker in rum and rosewood before turning to politics. Cendrars met him in 1919, when he was supposed to be very rich. One chapter is titled "Aventure," and that word is the motif of the book. "He [Galmont] was the man of adventures: and adventure is not what one imagines, a novel. It is not taught in a novel. . . . It is always something lived" (pp. 58–59). Thus Cendrars worked out a Nietzschean philosophy. In his book *Bourlinguer* (1948)—the title means the art of wandering—he says that there is no truth, only action, action that obeys a million different motives: "Life is not a dilemma. [It is not "true".] It is a free act. And action liberates. That is why God is the Creator."[18]

The narratives of Hemingway and Cendrars (and Roth and Mailer) together with the analyses of Bataille, Detienne, and Sontag, should be enough to convince us how deep and widespread the interest is even today in the ideas I have associated with "adventure," though it is in some sense a hidden interest.

This line of thought—philosophically developed by Nietzsche—is of course more ambitious and more somber than that used by the spokespersons for adventure in nineteenth-century middlebrow England. There the talk was more simply joyful—of the waves tossing your boat, the struggle to reach the mountaintop, the last-minute saving of your comrade, the cunning that encompasses the villain's destruction. The audience aimed at was usually boys, and the declared intention was to reinforce the official morality, not subvert it, by adding the spices of adventure. That is no less true an adventure discourse, or only somewhat less true, than the line of thought cited, but the latter seems more likely to catch the contemporary reader's attention—if only by scandalizing.

18. Quoted in Lovey, *La situation de Blaise Cendrars*, 246.

2

Adventure, Boyhood, Play

Boyhood is that phase of life at which the ideology and propaganda of adventure have traditionally been directed, and traditionally the best people, young and old, men and women, delighted to remain "boys at heart." I use the past tense in that sentence and in all of this chapter, instead of the present tense that predominated in the last one, because my approach this time will be, roughly, historical, while last time it was, even more roughly, philosophical. Throughout this book there will be something of that alternation, which will bring with it also an alternation of national source, for the philosophical ideas will often have a French or German origin, while the historical and fictional examples of action will come mostly from England or America.

If the sponsor for "adventure," the associated and more familiar term, was violence in the previous chapter, in this one it will be "play." (The disparateness between the two reminds us of the shifting dimensions of the realm of adventure—one of the likenesses between potestas and eros.) Play characterizes the writers of this period in many ways: Rudyard Kipling's *Just So Stories* and J. M. Barrie's *Peter Pan* are strikingly playful in verbal and stylistic matters, for instance—on the edge of nonsense. But what matters most here is the merging or interaction of play with adventure as substance, as subject-matter.

If some philosophers exalt adventure under the name of violence, many philistines diminish it under the name of play. Of course, the linking of all three concepts is a complacent commonplace and was even more widespread in the past, for instance, in nineteenth-century England. It was said that the Battle of Waterloo had been won for England on the playing fields of Eton, where the officer class learned courage, cunning, and endurance, the virtues of violent adventure. In *Stalky and Co.*, Kipling worked out that idea in considerable detail. And Sir Henry Newbolt's poem with the refrain "Play up, Play up, and play the game!" linked the school cricket field with the "sands of the desert," which are sodden red with the blood of a soldier's square that broke.

That particular linkage of play and war, that complex image or conceptual brooch, is no longer allowed in polite circles, but its elements are still present, disguised. That which is forbidden in seriousness is permitted in playfulness, and associated with play are games, pretense, joking, fantasy, and the tone of voice in which we talk to children and to animals. In those tones we make certain assertions that we retract as we make them; as Salman Rushdie says, "Once upon a time: it was so and it was not so." Between the one and the other, adventure and fantasy slip back into our lives. Better put, between the one and the other we slip out of the social contract, out of moral realism, back into adventure and fantasy. Rushdie, however, refers us to the realm of art. We shall be looking instead at the realm of literal and active play, of social (socially permitted and encouraged) play.

The examples will come largely from the age of conscious imperialism at the turn of the nineteenth century, when the cult of adventure was most developed. Throughout this book, in fact, I shall take most of my examples from that period. However, although imperialism was openly professed for only a short time, and then was energetically repudiated, ideas that emerged then into the light ran on, and still run on, underground.

This is true of many kinds of discourse, but I shall concentrate on literary adventure. The adoption of adventure material by ambitious artists in the late nineteenth century was a starting point for developments that characterize later thinking, and even our contemporary thinking. I shall show that this is true of, for instance, poststructuralism and magic realism.

The main alternative congeries of opposed ideas we might call moral or political realism, and we might associate it, at the level of theory, with

F. R. Leavis and Raymond Williams and British culture criticism. Kipling has always been anathema to that school. It is worth noting that in Williams's *Culture and Society* this period, 1880–1920, is called an interregnum, a blank or featureless time between episodes of action. But in fact, I suggest, it was when a great new idea was born, and subsequent history has been a conflict between those two ideas.

When I say there was a cult of adventure, I mean something analogous to a church's exhibition of a sacred object to the faithful at an appointed place and time, usually performed by priests in suitable vestments and accompanied by solemn chanting and exhortation. When displayed in the wrong way, in "bad taste," as the national flag is displayed to the boys in *Stalky and Co.*, such display becomes deeply repugnant to the devout. The cult of national or imperial adventure (in literature, say *Puck of Pook's Hill*) is different in its materials from religion, and freer in its treatment, with more inventiveness, variety, and humorousness, but similar in its fundamental purpose to reawaken the congregation's commitment to certain memories and values. In *Stalky and Co.*, for instance, the sense of the sacred is preserved by being disguised, quite deceptively, with irony and even blasphemy.

I have already, in earlier books, discussed the adventure tale itself as the carrier of ideology, and in Part Two of this book I discuss the institutions of adventure, but there were in this period a hundred other sources of adventure images. In England they ranged from music hall songs and biscuit tins to the pictures of famous sportsmen on cards given away with packets of cigarettes, which boys collected and developed in play. A recent volume of cultural history, *Propaganda and Empire* (edited by John M. MacKenzie, 1984) gives an interesting account of this cultural phenomenon with regard to Great Britain and the British Empire.

One personal and literary account of that adventure propaganda is Cyril W. Beaumont's autobiographical *Flash-Back* (1931). At the time he wrote this book, Beaumont was an aesthete, a lover of the ballet and the decorative arts. He had put his childhood behind him, or apparently so. His book has a preface by Sacheverell Sitwell, who says, "I should call this book an almost perfect example of a Jules Verne childhood. I wonder whether Jules Verne is still read by children."[1] During the 1920s, aesthetes and dandies like these two had persuaded themselves that the

---

1. Sacheverell Sitwell, "Preface," in Cyril W. Beaumont, *Flash-Back*.

adventure ethos in which they had been brought up was infinitely quaint and forever past.

We can take Jules Verne's name to represent all the writers of the enormous genre of adventure, although he was of course more interested in science and technology than most of them. Sitwell describes Verne's theme as "one man in all the luxury of command of a whole jungle of machinery," the word "jungle" suggesting the parallel between Verne and the forest adventure-writers, like Arthur Conan Doyle and Henry Stanley (p. xi). Beaumont tells us he was given a copy of *Twenty Thousand Leagues Under the Sea* for his twelfth birthday, and, having made his brother Bryan his engineer, he and Bryan acted out together the preparation of meals on the submarine, the care of the engines, the underwater life on the ocean floor, and so on. Science and technology became a living myth for them. Beaumont makes us see how the scenes described by the writer were taken over by the readers in mimetic play and driven home into their imaginations.

Sitwell piously hopes that Beaumont's book will teach the lesson that the former adventure and romance of war has been destroyed by technology. But that is mere piety. Adventure must always be said to belong to another place or time. Despite their irony and aestheticism, the two men still display an enthusiasm for adventure (locating it in the historical and psychological past, of course), and the enthusiasm is oriented as much toward Napoleon and his armies—and their uniforms—as toward Verne and his machines (p. x).

This is of major importance. Napoleon was, indeed is, the most gigantic single European figure uniting adventure with historical fact in modern times. The feeling of Englishmen for him is part of their adult love of history, even intellectual and artistic history. Sitwell says, "It might be argued that the whole output of painters and writers in France during the nineteenth century was due in part to the shadow of Napoleon falling on them in their childhood." And he tells us that Beaumont is still interested in the Napoleonic campaigns, although now his interest is fanciful and aesthetic. "I think he is just the same, now, as he was then (p. viii).

Beaumont also lists the books he had in his bedroom as a boy. Adventure themes dominated, several of them Napoleonic: the novels of Stanley Weyman, Dumas, Henty, Doyle, Verne, Wells, and the memoirs of such soldiers as Marbot and Coignet, the histories of Motley, Prescott, and Parkman, and detective stories by Poe, Doyle, Gaboriau, and so on.

He also had in his room a bomb picked up on the battlefield of Strasbourg mounted as an inkstand, two prints of pictures by Lady Butler (the semi-official painter of the late Victorian army), and one print of Delaroche's *Napoleon*. In his toy theater he put on productions of patriotic plays, such as *Henry V* and *Richard III*. He read the Robin Hood Library and played at being Robin Hood, and he and friends acted out the Britons versus the Boers in the contemporary Anglo-Boer War.

These motifs were popular in other Western countries too. In *Life Studies*, Robert Lowell talks of his own indoctrination with just these ideas and images in his American boyhood, as late as the 1920s. His father, he tells us, "had an unspoiled faith in the superior efficiency of northern nations" and "modelled his allegiances and humor on the cockney imperialism of Rudyard Kipling's swearing Tommies, who did their job."[2] Moreover, the boy Lowell seems to have been brought up in an atmosphere of Napoleonism. He delighted in the family portrait of a uniformed ancestor called Major Mordecai Myers because this man looked like "such a fellow as Napoleon's mad, pomaded, son-of-an-innkeeper-general, Junot, Duc d'Abrantès" (p. 12). And his mother often replayed for him her memory of Sarah Bernhardt playing the title role in *L'aiglon,* the Edmond Rostand play about Napoleon's son (p. 13).

This cult was above all embodied in Lowell's toy soldiers—things to play with, of course, and described by him in playful tones, but recognizably a cult:

> My real *love,* as Mother used to insist to all new visitors, was toy soldiers. For a few months, at the flood tide of this infatuation, people were ciphers to me—valueless except as chances for increasing my armies of soldiers. Roger Crosby, a child in the second grade of my Brimmer Street School, had thousands—not mass-produced American stereotypes, but hand-painted solid lead soldiers made to order in Dijon, France. Roger's father had a still more artistic and adult collection; its ranks—each man at least six inches tall—marched in glass cases under the eyes of recognizable replicas of mounted Napoleonic captains: Kléber, Marshal Ney, Murat, King of Naples.

2. Robert Lowell, *Life Studies,* 16.

The young Lowell managed by cunning exchanges to cheat his friend out of some "gorgeous, imported Old Guards, Second Empire 'red-legs,' and modern *chasseurs d'Alpine* with sky-blue berets" (p. 13). These he was obliged to return, but he consoled himself with his own soldiers, with the military portrait of Major Myers, and with drawing his father's dress sword (Mr. Lowell wore a naval uniform) in and out of its scabbard.

Cyril Beaumont talks of reading about Crécy and Agincourt and imagining the armor and the jousting: "The recital of those famous deeds never fails to quicken the pulse and fire the blood."[3] In *Brideshead Revisited,* written during World War II, Evelyn Waugh's representative, Charles Ryder, reflects on the difference between himself and Hooper, an Englishman of the commercial class whose pulse never did quicken to hear about those famous deeds. They served together in the war, but Ryder tells us Hooper condemned army practices by saying, "They wouldn't get away with that in business." He has commercial, or H. G. Wells, values. Ryder says:

> Hooper was no romantic. He had not as a child ridden with Rupert's horse or sat among the camp fires at Xanthus-side; at the age when my eyes were dry to all save poetry—that stoic, red-skin interlude which our schools introduce between the fast-flowing tears of the child and the man—Hooper had wept often, but never for Henry's speech on St. Crispin's Day, nor for the epitaph at Thermopylae. The history they taught him had had few battles in it but, instead, a profusion of detail about humane legislation and recent industrial change. [This is history as Wells would have it taught.] Gallipoli, Balaclava, Quebec, Bannockburn, Roncevales, and Marathon—these, and the Battle in the West where Arthur fell, and a hundred such names whose trumpet-notes, even now in my sere and lawless state, called to me irresistibly across the intervening years with all the clarity and strength of boyhood, sounded in vain to Hooper.[4]

In the military romanticism of Ryder (and Waugh) we see the long-term effects of the adventure and war propaganda on people who as

---

3. Beaumont, *Flash-Back,* 10.
4. Evelyn Waugh, *Brideshead Revisited,* 14–15.

young men in the 1930s, in peacetime, would have spoken of such things in the same tones of dismissal as Beaumont and Sitwell. In wartime, Ryder and his creator turn back to adventure stories. Waugh does the same in his *Officers and Gentlemen* trilogy (1955). Graham Greene, in *The Heart of the Matter* (1948), also shows sophisticated characters, including the writer's representatives, who revert to boyhood reading, and to adventure virtues, to carry them through the testing experiences of World War II.

The playing with toy soldiers was an important part of this adventure propaganda, for Beaumont and Lowell, and we find the same, much earlier, in the life of the Brontë sisters. Their brother Branwell was given twelve wooden soldiers in June 1826, and, having played with them for three years, the siblings started to write plays about them. After 1831, Emily and Anne withdrew to work on the Gondal stories (somewhat more realistic), but Charlotte and Branwell continued to write war-adventure stories about Angria and Glass Town until 1839. Their father loved armies and battles and idolized Wellington, as another Irishman and Tory like himself.

Thus contemporary history and contemporary literature were blended into adventure material. Charlotte took as her heroes the Duke of Wellington and two sons she ascribed to him, while Branwell invented one called Alexander Percy. (This character was originally a Byronic villain-hero called Rogue.) Later Charlotte took Mary Percy as her heroine and wrote about love themes—Mary was torn between father and husband, and Branwell wrote about war, debates, and business deals. Branwell had been given a *Description of London* in 1828. Charlotte's literary sources are said to have been the Bible, Bunyan, Milton, Scott, *The Arabian Nights,* and *Blackwood's Magazine*. Geography books and magazines gave them both words and ideas like Fezzan, Ashanti, Dahomey, Niger, the Gambia, Senegal, and the Mountains of the Moon. *Blackwood's* ran many articles on African and Arctic exploration and on the Peninsular War. The Brontës' characters usually had names taken from the newspapers.

A play they wrote in 1826 was entitled "Young Men," and in it twelve adventurers sailed on "The Invincible" in 1793 and settled on the east coast of Africa. Fernando Po, which had been described in *Blackwood's* in June of that year, became their Glass Town, which Wellington was elected to rule. "The Islanders" (1827) began with a varied group of British heroes—Wellington, Scott, Bentinck, Lockhart, Leigh Hunt, and

John Bull, all on an island of fifty miles circumference.[5] We have reason to assume that other families, who did not come to be famous in literature and so to be biographized in detail, read, invented, and/or enacted similar adventures.

Nineteenth-century historical novels for children, at least those written for boys, were usually also adventures. They provided scenarios for games and amateur theatricals. We hear about Kipling as a boy playing at an adaption of Scott's *The Pirate* while staying with his Burne-Jones relatives. It was in the course of the nineteenth century that middle-class children came to expect a book for Christmas—in fact, children's books became as much a part of the Victorian Christmas as plum pudding. In 1888 Edward Salmon said that forty years before there had been no such flood of Christmas books for boys and girls.[6] And one thing that made children's books different from adults' books was that they were expected to lead to play.

The first stories composed specifically for nineteenth-century children were written by Evangelical writers, with Protestant but often also imperial implications. One later didactic example is the Methodist minister W. H. Fitchett's *Deeds That Won the Empire* (often mentioned by anti-imperialist writers as the source or food of their childhood imperialism). In the 1860s, novels about the Middle Ages that were essentially adventure tales were written for boys, under the influence of Scott. Thus, J. G. Edgar wrote *Cressy and Poitiers* in 1863, and Francis Davenant wrote *A Story of King Richard II's Days* in 1865. Edgar had set himself the task of covering the history of England from William the Conqueror to William of Orange in a series of stories for boys, just as Scott and Cooper did for adults. G. A. Henty took up that ambition when Edgar died in 1864, according to Salmon (p. 63). No doubt some of these stories formed part of the inspiration for Mark Twain to write his mocking story of King Arthur.

Edward Salmon said the best humorous writers for children were American. American stories for boys also seem to have focused more on self-help, with titles such as *From Log Cabin to White House*. The English equivalent for that was *From Powder Monkey to Admiral* (1883) and Kingston's series from *The Three Midshipmen* to *The Three Admirals* (1873–77), and the *Boys' Own Paper* felt it should argue in a note that such promotions could happen in the modern English navy.

5. See *Early Writings of Charlotte Brontë*, ed. Christine Alexander, 83.
6. Edward Salmon, *Juvenile Literature as It Is*, 32.

Salmon's book summarized the result of a questionnaire sent out to schools in 1884. Some 2,000 answers were received, allegedly from all levels of society. Out of 790 boys who answered, 223 said their favorite author was Dickens, 179 said W.H.G. Kingston (a boys' author), 128 said Scott, 114 said Verne, 102 said Marryat, and so on. Among the favorite single books read by boys, *Robinson Crusoe* led with 43 votes, *The Swiss Family Robinson* got 24, and Dickens's titles came after. Among magazines, the *Boys' Own Paper* had a long lead, with 404 votes. Among poets, Scott was the favorite: *The Lady of the Lake* got 99 votes, *Marmion* had 65, and *The Lay of the Last Minstrel*, 37. Some of Macaulay, such as "Horatius at the Bridge" and the "The Spanish Armada," were popular, as was Tennyson's "Charge of the Light Brigade," another adventure poem. Popular biographies for children were those of Nelson and Wellington, Cook and Stephenson, Livingstone, Stanley, and Columbus.

More than 1,000 girls answered the same questionnaire, and their preferences put Dickens, and then Scott, way ahead of the mere adventure writers. But if we look at individual titles, we may be surprised to see a boys' adventure book, Kingsley's *Westward Ho!* with 34 votes, ahead of such girls' stories as Susan Warner's *Wide Wide World,* with 29 votes, and *Little Women,* with 21. Indeed, Salmon says, "If we covered the country we would probably find that as many girls as boys read *Robinson Crusoe, Tom Brown's Schooldays,* and so on," because girls' books lack stirring plot and lively movement (p. 28). Salmon believed American girls' books were better than British girls' books.

At the turn of the century, as we have seen, the linkage of adventure to patriotic and imperial values became more direct. Boys' magazines had Union Jacks and Prince of Wales feathers at their masthead, and cover pictures of big game, and color charts of navy ships and regimental badges, flags, and so on. Kipling wrote verses for Fletcher's *School History of England* in 1911, which meant that adventure and children's writing received more official sponsorship and patronage.

Thus, we find propaganda for empire and adventure in children's books of the period even when the writer had left-wing views, as was the case with Edith Nesbit. And we can follow the translation of religious values into adventurous ones in the autobiographies of John Buchan and his sister Anna. John Buchan delighted in the copies of Bunyan's *Holy War* and *Pilgrim's Progress* his minister father gave him as a boy, because the boy took the military action to be the substance of the story—he took the spiritual meaning to be allegorical. And when he had to teach a class of slum boys in his father's Glasgow parish, he held their interest by telling them adventure tales, in which nominal missionaries performed deeds of daring. Anna Buchan (also a popular novelist of the 1920s and 1930s) describes one of her heroines doing just the same when foster-mothering some children, in order to get around the traditional prohibition of secular fiction on Sundays; her foster children act out the stories they read. And in *Huntingtower* John Buchan depicts Glasgow boys like those he had taught involved in contemporary adventure-tale adventures with an exiled Russian princess. This is almost explicit game-playing.

Playful Writers

In France, Sartre's autobiography offers us an interesting example of boys' adventure reading. As a child, Sartre adored "the books in the Hetzel series," and he cites Jules Verne's *Les enfants du Capitaine Grant,* Cooper's *Last of the Mohicans,* and Dickens's *Nicholas Nickleby.* It is an Anglo-Saxon nineteenth-century tradition he met.

> I owe to those magic boxes—and not to the balanced sentences of Chateaubriand—my first encounters with Beauty. When I opened them, I forgot about everything. Was that reading? No, but it was death by ecstasy. From my annihilation there immediately sprang up natives armed with spears, the bush, an explorer with a white helmet. . . . The New World seemed at first more disturbing than the Old; there were murder and pillage; blood flowed in torrents. Indians, Hindus, Mohicans, Hottentots carried off the girl, tied up her old father, and swore he would be tortured to death. It was pure Evil. But it appeared on the scene only to grovel before Good. Everything would be set to rights in the next chapter. . . . Moreover, death itself was asepticized. One fell to the ground, arms outstretched, with a little round hole under the left breast, or, if the rifle had not yet been invented, the guilty were "run through with a sword." . . . At last I had what I needed: an Enemy who was hateful, though, when all was said and done, harmless, since his plans came to naught, and even,

despite his efforts and diabolical cleverness, served the cause of good. . . . From these magazines and books I derived my most deep-seated phantasmagoria: optimism.[7]

His love for those books never ended, Sarte tells us: "Even now, I read the 'Série Noire' more readily than I do Wittgenstein" (p. 48). However, it is the Anglo-Saxon countries that must receive most of our attention.

In America, the most famous example of the playful literary propaganda for adventure is Mark Twain's *Tom Sawyer,* and the other books about bad boys at the end of the nineteenth century, by W. D. Howells, T. B. Aldrich, and so on. To tell a tale about boys playing at adventure was a way to praise and spread the latter, as well as a way to re-play it nostalgically and humorously. The mockery of adventure by writers like Twain is in effect little more than a disinfectant, employed to reassure the reader that he is in adult company as he reverts to boyhood. But I will discuss the two English writers who most brilliantly embody the act of play in their stories.

Richard Jefferies (1848–87) wrote a book called *Wood Magic* (1881) with partly animal characters playing out a military or adventurous story—a precursor for the *Jungle Books* but also for Kenneth Grahame and T. H. White. The story carries an adventure ethos, unabashed. When the autobiographical central character, Bevis, reproaches a chaffinch for wicked fighting, the latter replies, "My dear Sir Bevis, I do not know what you mean by wicked. But fighting is very nice indeed, and we all feel so jolly when fighting time comes."[8] This is of course what Jefferies and his hero want to hear. Bevis indeed is frankly a bully. The chaffinch says, "You and Mark are fond of each other, but you hit him sometimes, don't you?" "Yes, that I do," said Bevis very eagerly. "I hit him yesterday. . . . It is very nice to hit someone" (p. 24). This is the cult of *potestas* frankly depicted.

The chaffinch concludes by relating aggression to art and romance. "If you can't sing you have no business to fight, and besides, . . . we do the fighting because the ladies love to see it, and kiss us for it afterwards. I am the knight of this tree!" (p. 24). In the last chapter the wind converses with Bevis and tells him about the man who lies buried in a hill nearby, the remains of a Saxon encampment; the Saxon becomes a

7. Sartre, *The Words,* 46–47.
8. Richard Jefferies, *Wood Magic,* 23.

presence to Bevis. This interest in death is part of Jefferies's interest in his own organic life, and that idea was picked up by W. H. Hudson, among others.

Even more striking as a case of play-writing and play-reading is the same author's *Bevis,* published the following year. In the peaceful English countryside of their childhood, Bevis and Mark play games that reflect their country's military and imperialist adventures. They discover the New Sea (a pond) and spend ten days on the New Formosa (an island in the pond). Detailed advice is given, just as in *Robinson Crusoe,* but here it is about swimming and American snap-shooting—and, interesting, native skills. They learn how to make a raft, a spear, a blowpipe, and other native weapons. The boys move in and out of their fantasies, their play, and the author moves in and out of participation in them, without any embarrassment.

The chapter titles reveal the relationship to national or international adventure—geographical, historical, or legendary: chapter 3, "Mississippi"; chapter 5, "By the New Nile"; chapter 11, "The New Catamarans"; chapter 16. "The Battle of Pharsalia"; chapter 20, "The Pinta"; chapter 26, "The Cave"; chapter 27, "The Hut"; chapter 32, "Morning in the Tropics"; chapter 34, "Kangaroos"; and so on. When they anticipate a battle, they cry out to each other, " 'Flashing swords! The ground will shake when we charge.' 'Trumpets!' 'Groans!' 'Grass all red!' 'Flocks of crows!' 'Heaps of white bones!' "[9] Later they are described (like Kipling's schoolboys) as savages gloating over their prey. But this is combined with an "innocent" individual exultation in exercise. Bevis shouts with delight, runs like the wind, bathes in the nude. "Wild" is a favorite word. "The sunlight poured upon them, and the light air came along; they bathed in air and sunbeam, and gathered years of health like flowers from the field" (p. 91).

In *The Story of My Heart* (1883) Jefferies spells out a kind of animism, pantheism, and sun-worship in which Hudson followed him: "I spoke to the sea; though so far, in my mind I saw it, green at the rim of the earth and blue in deeper ocean; I desired to have its strength, its mystery and glory. Then I addressed the sun, desiring the soul equivalent of his light and brilliance, his endurance and unwearied race."[10] This is the embrace of nature as opposed to culture, which we noted before.

9. Richard Jefferies, *Bevis,* 102.
10. Richard Jefferies, *The Story of My Heart,* 4–5.

Jefferies sees his own flesh and blood as materially the same as the sun, wind, or sea. He identifies with the latter: "Let my soul become enlarged; I am not enough; I am little and contemptible. I desire a greatness of soul" (p. 11). There is a surprising sensual paganism here too: "To be shapely of form is so infinitely beyond wealth, power, fame, all that ambition can give, that these are dust before it" (p. 26). This is another, and stronger, overlapping of eros and potestas.

However, though Jefferies was a remarkable writer, he has always remained a little out of the mainstream and never sold in large numbers. In England the most striking testimony to the social effectiveness of such adventure writing, its power to shape the imagination of readers, comes in the form of Kipling and tributes to Kipling. Philip Mason—though in adulthood a critic of imperialism—says in his book on Kipling that at the age of fourteen he was an idolatrous fan, having identified himself in turn with Mowgli, then Kim, then Beetle.

We note the importance of games in all three of the books Mason alluded to; they exemplify in fact three different functions of play. The *Jungle Books* invite child readers to play mimetically at being Mowgli, Bagheera, or Shere Khan. In *Kim,* on the other hand, "real people" play games. An obvious instance is Kim's Game, which was in fact taken out of the book and played by Kipling's audience. Then *Stalky and Co.* is about boys adapting adventure fantasies into realistic school-life form.

After that age, Mason says, the attraction faded, and as a young man he came to dislike Kipling strongly. Then he got over that dislike. Such a development bears all the marks of a profound educational experience— adventure shaping a reader's mind more powerfully than serious literature often does. Mason sums up:

> Perhaps no one has had so deep an influence on a whole generation of a certain class as he did. Here was someone who understood the life they were brought up to, their mistrust of politicians and intellectuals, their inarticulate devotion to a cause, the training they had endured, the tenseness that lay beneath the apparently insensitive outer crust, the tenderness they longed to lavish on dogs and children, their nervous respect for those mysterious creatures, women—so fragile compared with themselves, and yet so firmly authoritarian as nurses and mothers.[11]

11. Philip Mason, *Kipling: The Glass, the Shadow, and the Fire,* 307.

Although it proceeds by negations, that is quite a generous sketch of the character molded by adventure-reading, seen from outside.

C. E. Carrington says his main qualification for writing a biography of Kipling is one that he shared with thousands of his readers: that he learned to read with the *Just So Stories,* and the *Jungle Books,* and he went to school with *Stalky and Co.,* read history with *Puck of Pook's Hill,* and discovered *Plain Tales from the Hills* as his first adult book.[12] (Note that in *Puck of Pook's Hill,* as in the other three books, the action begins with and through children playing. They are acting out *A Midsummer Night's Dream* when the immortal Puck makes himself known to them.) In 1914, Carrington says later, he formed his ideas of army life from *Barrack Room Ballads* and "The Brushwood Boy," and the story of a centurion's life in *Puck of Pook's Hill* "strengthened the nerve of many a young soldier in the dark days of 1915 and 1941" (p. 296). George Orwell described his own career of feelings about Kipling in a similar series of changes.

In his preface Carrington says, "Looking back, I find no other writer who has seen through the eyes of my generation with such sharpness of observation. I owe far more to Kipling than to some of the great classic figures of literature." That, no doubt, was partly because Kipling's truths were very unlike the truths of "literature," as represented by, say, Matthew Arnold and George Eliot, so that he was not a "classic figure." "There is no other writer, great or small, whose work I know so well, and I have been often astonished to find how many others, of all ages, knew him as well as I did." They did so surely because of the range of opportunities Kipling gave them, his solicitations to his readers as children, to act out his imaginings, in play. They *knew* him.

Serious writers, whether like George Eliot or like D. H. Lawrence, do not invite us to act out their stories in the form of literal games. Kipling was a cultic writer in that sense (as were fellow aesthetes, such as Stevenson and Barrie). His other cultic themes, besides boyhood and adventure, included laughter, horseplay, and the beauty of sumptuous landscapes and country houses. Kipling invites us to join him and his characters in almost hysterical laughter, in bullying horseplay, and in luxurious delight in old manor houses and the historical legends they evoke—behind which, of course, stands the sacred and secret grail of class, race, and national pride.

12. C. E. Carrington, *The Life of Kipling,* v.

It is also worth saying that although Kipling's primary impact was on a group of readers who can be defined narrowly in social, temporal, and educational terms, as Mason and Carrington do, his impact has also been strong on many others, including some of the later writers who most reviled him. I have tried to demonstrate that literary history argument elsewhere. What matters here is that he could so powerfully use literature, via play, to promote the social cult of adventure; and of related ideas, like boyishness, practical jokes, disguise as a "native," the secret service, guerrilla warfare.

These historical examples must seem a far cry from the cultural anthropology theories of Chapter 1, which came to us (at least in Bataille's case) associated with the cult of de Sade and violent pornography. Even Kipling must seem intellectually naive and morally conservative (in the vulgar sense of morals) in that comparison. On the other hand, we need not reflect long before realizing that boys' adventure tales had probably more social effect than those other books, in the way of promoting real violence and real shedding of blood. But what is important to us is the convergence of both sorts of discourse on the subject matter of adventure.

Part

2

THE INSTITUTIONS OF ADVENTURE

CHAPTERS 3 THROUGH 8 present instances of the cult of adventure in its more practical forms. The more intellectual forms are discussed in Part Three. This distinction, however, has not been easy to keep in focus over my wide range of material, and I must ask the reader's indulgence if he or she finds it blurred in places.

In Parts Two and Three adventure is presented as allied to all sorts of other ideas and as lending its dynamic to mutually opposed sides. For this reason, it will be in some ways hard to sum up: Is it right-wing or left-wing? moral or amoral? rationalist or irrationalist? Such questions are not going to be fruitful. What *is* fruitful is to ask, Where does adventure appear in modern ideology—in however disguised and shifting a form—and how close is it each time to the moral centers and dynamism of that ideology?

The general idea of this can be suggested by quoting from J. A. Hobson's *Imperialism* (1902), a brilliant book written in reaction against the jingoist propaganda of Kipling and his allies. Because part of that propaganda was the cult of adventure, Hobson shows us the connections between adventure and imperialism, and the vested interests of certain social classes and institutions. "The potency of this factor," he says, meaning imperialist sentiment, "is, of course, largely due to the itch for glory and adventure among military officers upon disturbed or uncertain frontiers of the Empire. . . . The [armed] services are of course imperialist by conviction and by professional interest."[1] Adventure, empire, and glory go together "[for] the aristocrats and the wealthy classes, who seek in the services careers for their sons. To the military services we may add the Indian Civil Service. [The wealthy see every new conquest as] affording more openings for their sons as ranchers, planters, engineers, or missionaries" (p. 46). These are all adventure professions. Hobson reminded his readers that James Mill described the empire as "a vast system of outdoor relief for the upper classes."

I shall be looking at institutional connections in a similar way, without

1. J. A. Hobson, *Imperialism*, rev. ed., 45.

investigating the institutions themselves. The title of Part Two is not a promise of a systematic survey of such organizational forms as football teams and clubs, youth hostels and hiking groups, or indeed army companies and regimental messes. Such a survey would be worth conducting, but I approach the topic from another angle.

The adventure enthusiasm is at its most concentrated and poignantly interesting in an individual or a small group. When incorporated into a large organization and embodied in rules, it is likely (though not certain) to suffer some dilution or frustration. In fact, what I offer in this book are mostly striking individual experiences and expressions of adventure feeling, some analyzed and defined, some implicit and unselfconscious. Within this part those expressions derive more from organized or semi-organized social forms.

3

Travel and Exploration

Our first example is clearly not a fully organized social activity. The travels and explorations that concern us were individual or small-group enterprises. This is part of what made them adventures. They drew on various kinds of support—for instance, from private patrons and government bodies in the eighteenth century, and from missionary societies and newspapers in the nineteenth century. But once out of sight of his native land, the explorer was on his own, to a significant degree. We will therefore take for granted the sense in which such an individual explorer and traveler was part of commercial exploitation and official empire— the solitary hero, or more likely the small group, merely preceding the government official—adventure in that more acute form being just a preface to political or state adventurism. Instead, we will study the way individual travelers described the psychological expansion they felt as they traveled.

François Le Vaillant, writing of South Africa around 1800, reflected, "Proud of his origin, man thinks it an indignity that people should beforehand dare to number his steps. I . . . never thought myself completely free, but when surrounded by the rocks, forests and deserts of Africa." Referring to one particular tribe, he wrote: "By the freedom of my will, which commanded them with sovereign sway, and by my complete independence, I really perceived in man the monarch of all animated beings, the absolute despot of nature."[1]

This was partly, in this case, because Le Vaillant saw his own freedom reflected in that of the free and brave Gonaquas. But it was also partly because exploring in general gave him a special relationship to "origin" and "nature" (which meant an escape from his own culture). Never before had he experienced "the full value of existence."[2] He felt he was close to a great creative force. More than a hundred years before, Montaigne had described the Brasil Indians he saw in France as fresh from the hand of God. Similarly, a hundred years later, one of adventure writer Rider Haggard's first published articles, for *The Gentleman's Magazine*, described a "Zulu War Dance" and said it was like coming face to face with Nature—Nature as she was on the morrow of the Creation.

By means of this familiarity with the divine act of creation, the Western traveler became himself creative and divine, or at least legendary and heroic. In the Renaissance, William Spengemann says, the voyager was seen as a modern chevalier: "He was brave, resourceful, magnanimous, proud, and curious."[3] In Elizabethan England, Hakluyt spoke of the voyager's "vertuous heroicall mind" and honorable purposes. We can follow that line of thought through the centuries. An important step forward in the career of adventure was taken in the eighteenth century, when Captain Cook made his three famous voyages of discovery. These were, among other things, works of propaganda for the Enlightenment and for Protestantism, Protestant replays of Columbus's great voyages. The latter were over before most people were aware of their importance, but Cook's were designed *as* heroic ventures in knowledge as well as in action. There was keen competition to sail with Cook, especially on his last voyage, when almost everyone aboard was keeping a journal.

All this is summed up, and related to our topic, by the naming of Cook's ships: the *Endeavour,* the *Discovery,* the *Resolution,* and the *Adventure*. This was the moral profile displayed by Enlightened Europe at its most self-conscious—not the names of saints or kings, but of virtues: endeavor, discovery, resolution, and adventure. These are all

1. François Le Vaillant, *Travels in the Interior Parts of Africa, 1780–1785,* 1:132, 133, quoted in Peter Knox-Shaw, *The Explorer in English Fiction,* 20.
2. Quoted in Knox-Shaw, *Explorer in English Fiction,* 20.
3. William Spengemann, *The Adventurous Muse,* 27.

members of the family of adventure virtues, and obviously unlike other families, such as the one that includes compassion, patience, humility, selflessness. And these names were given on the occasion of those voyages. The *Endeavour,* for instance, had until then been called *The Earl of Pembroke,* but that name spoke of a feudal and socially static landowning aristocracy. It was the moral virtue of endeavor, theoretically available to every freeborn mind, that had to be invoked.

As for the nineteenth century, Oswald Spengler, at the end of his world history, written at the very beginning of the twentieth century, said that Western man had a discoverer's soul, that his passion was to discover what is hidden. "The Faustian inventer and discoverer is something unique. The power of his will, the radiance of his vision, the steely energy of his practical purposes, must be uncanny and incomprehensible to anyone from another culture seeing them, but they are in the blood of all of us. Our whole culture has a discoverer's soul" (we might add the word "adventurer" without distorting Spengler's idea).[4]

Spengler was summarizing and echoing the nineteenth-century explorers' language about their own energy, which they presented against the background, implicit or explicit, of "simple savages" or "oriental despotisms." Henry Stanley, for instance, described the physical and moral exuberance that for him went with exploring:

> That impulse to jump, to bound, to spring upward and cling to branches overhead, which is the characteristic of a strong green age, I gave free rein to. Unfettered for a time from all conventionalisms, and absolved from that sobriety and steadiness which my position as a leader of half wild men compelled me to assume in their presence, all my natural elasticity of body came back to use. I dived under the obstructing bough or sprang over the prostrate trunk, squeezed into almost impossible places, crawled and writhed like a serpent through the tangled undergrowth, plunged down into formidable depths of dense foliage, and burrowed and struggled with frantic energy among shadowing pyramids of vines and creepers, which had become woven and plaited by their numbers into a solid mass.[5]

4. Oswald Spengler, *The Decline of the West,* 2:501.
5. Henry Stanley, *Through the Dark Continent,* 219–20.

These images suggest a Tarzan-like atavism, and this is obviously a style, of words and deeds, that many writers for boys could and did imitate from Stanley in their stories.

When, on his search for Livingstone, Stanley was told that the other man's camp was just ahead, his quest achieved, he grew wildly enthusiastic. "And I—what would I not have given for a bit of friendly wilderness, where, unseen, I might vent my joy in some mad freak, such as idiotically biting my hand, turning a somersault, or slashing at trees, in order to allay those exciting feelings that were well-nigh uncontrollable. My heart beats fast, but I must not let my face betray my emotions, lest it shall detract from the dignity of a white man appearing under such extraordinary circumstances. . . . So I did what moral cowardice and false pride suggested was the best thing."[6] The Western adventurer, seen in the usual confrontation with natives, is both wildly excited and impassively judicious.

Stanley's chapter titles were menus of adventure. Chapter 15 of *Through the Dark Continent* (1878) announces: "Mutiny in the camp—Again among the cataracts—Frank's body found—The fall of the Edwin Arnold River—Tired out!—Wholesale desertion—More cataracts—'Goodbye, my brother; nothing can save you!'—Rushing blindly on—Saved again!—The *Jason* found." Sir Richard Burton's passages of description, even when they did not name the idea of genesis, even when they did not include adventure action, produced the same effect with their rapturous vividness: "Above was the normal mottled, vapoury sky of the rainy zone, fleecy mists, opal-tinted, and with blurred edges, floating on milky blue depths."[7] He tells how the calabar

> stretches its stumpy, crooked arms over the clustering huts. The tree is at once majestic and grotesque; the tall conical column of spongy and porous wood, covered with a soft, glossy rind, which supplies half Africa with bast, will have a girth of forty to fifty feet . . . topped with snowy blossoms, like the fairest and lightest of water-lilies, and hung about with four or five hundred gourds; ovals somewhat larger than a cocoa-nut, dressed in green velvet with the nap on, and attached by a long thin cord, like tassels which wave with every breath of the zephyr, its appearance is striking as it is novel. (pp. 2–3)

6. Quoted in Alan Moorehead, *The White Nile*, 110.
7. Richard Burton, *Zanzibar*, 2:50.

The readers are bound to feel how far short of Burton's their own perceptions fall and to look forward to becoming adventurers themselves, to inhabiting a realm where they too will see and smell and hear and know like that.

Even a largely sedentary intellectual like Darwin wrote at the end of his "Naturalist's Voyage Round the World": "I do not doubt that every traveler must remember the glowing sense of happiness which he experienced, when he first breathed in a foreign clime, where the civilized man had seldom or never trod." It is believed, Darwin said, that the love of the chase is inherent, "a relic of an instinctive passion." "If so," he continued, "I am sure the pleasure of living in the open air, with the sky for a roof and the ground for a table, is part of the same feeling; it is the savage returning to his wild and savage habits."[8]

"Nature" is the word that conceals and connects with the idea of adventure in all these cases. The idea of adventurous travel was thus linked to the feeling of a return to the source, to genesis, even when the traveler was a distinguished scientist. Alexander von Humboldt said in 1808 that a free and vigorous setting stimulated a spirit of adventure and that distant, richly endowed lands conveyed the sense of the earlier ages of mankind.

Modern men and women of letters, especially those of the current generation, are usually skeptical about this feeling of genesis. In his *Explorer and English Fiction*, Peter Knox-Shaw says that, in the post-Freudian world, genesis-enthusiasm is well understood to be the dream-work of the daylight self. The study of such excitements becomes the province of psychology or philosophy, and the experiences the travelers report are treated as symptoms. For his study of travel writing, Dennis Porter takes the title of his *Haunted Journeys* from Baudelaire's "Le Voyage," which includes also "The only true travelers are those who leave / For leaving's sake." Travel is really a psychological phenomenon, a way of relating to what one leaves behind; even including the traveler's "observations" and "experiences," it is a phenomenon of pathology. But people of another, more active temperament have never understood things so. And in earlier centuries their enthusiasm was corroborated by the outside world of geography and history and culture.

"In the Victorian age," says Alan Moorehead in his history *The White Nile,*

8. Quoted in Dennis Porter, *Haunted Journeys*, 190.

explorers' books exerted an extraordinary power over people's minds: they supplied the drama and the entertainment that now very largely belongs to the documentary cinema and television, and although such magazines as *Blackwood's* were widely circulated, there was as yet no illustrated press to compete with them; they had the quality of science fiction. Few publications have captured people's imaginations or influenced political policy like Livingstone's three works on South and Central Africa, or Stanley's account of his Congo travels, or Gordon's journals, which, for a time, focused the attention of all England upon Khartoum and the Sudan.[9]

The adventurous story of exploration was then a politically powerful force as well as adventurously entertaining.

These authors often pleaded moral causes of the day, such as the abolition of slavery, "and since the appeals were interlarded with themes of bravery and high adventure the response was enormous" (p. 62). Moreover, there were many other excitements incidental to reading travel books: one might read of the author in the newspapers, one might hear of his death before reading about the voyage on which he died, jealous rivals might have contradicted his stories, and so on. The meetings of the Royal Geographical Society were occasionally confrontational. Thus, an author's several books, and indeed "all these books, taken together, are in the nature of installments in a long serial" (p. 62).

In the legend of General C. G. Gordon, the language used by him and about him was implicitly chivalric—another variant of the adventure rhetoric. The editor of the 1888 edition of Gordon's journals says, "Gordon's lonely ride into the slavers' camp at Shaka had fired the ex-Khedive's imagination,"[10] and the general himself, discussing his decision to stay with his Sudanese troops, says, "I do not dictate, but I say what every gentleman in Her Majesty's Army would agree to—that it would be *mean (coûte que coûte)* to leave men who (though they may not come up to our ideas as heroes) have stuck to me, though a *Christian dog in their eyes,* through great difficulties" (p. 106).

Gordon's editor also says of the journals, "They breathe the kindliest

9. Moorehead, *The White Nile,* 61.

10. Introduction to Charles Gordon, *The Journals of Major-General Charles G. Gordon, C.B., at Khartoum,* xix.

wisdom, the most prudent philanthropy; and it would be well if those whose lot is thrown in barbarous lands would take them for a constant guide" (p. x). They were also especially recommended to working-class boys, and a number of "Gordon Clubs" were set up to promote their circulation—the journals would implicitly teach such boys upper-class values at their best and correct misapprehensions. The dangerous legend that Gordon had "disobeyed orders," the editor tells us, "has become a common phrase among the working classes in the North of England, when they are either speaking of or are spoken to about General Gordon." He continues, "Now I sincerely trust and believe that the Journals will be read eagerly by the working classes; they cannot occupy their leisure time better than in reading them, and, indeed, in learning much of them by heart" (p. xxx).

Richard Burton, one of the greatest of the explorer writers, declared that the many-authored serial Moorehead spoke of had in his time lost its earlier popularity. "In the heroic ages of Bruce and Mungo Park, Denham and Clapperton, Hornemann and Caillié," he wrote, "African travel had a prestige which, after living through a generation, came, as is the fate of all things sublunary, to a natural end. The public, glutted with adventure and invention, . . . learned to nauseate the monotonous tale of rapine, treachery, and murder, of ugly and unsavoury savagery, . . . of bleared misery by day and animated impurity by night, and of hunting adventures and hairbreadth escapes." But the sordid can be taken up into the romantic, and in fact reinforce it. Burton himself admits that the attraction of travel persists: "Yet African travel still continues to fulfill all the conditions of attraction . . . remoteness and obscurity of place, difference of custom, marvellousness of hearsay; events passing strange yet credible; sometimes barbaric splendour, generally luxuriance of nature, savage life, personal danger."[11] And of course the glamour of exploration, of hunting adventures and hairbreadth escapes, continues to be felt even today.

Burton also stressed the semi-military character of travels like his. The traveler is "his own general, adjutant, quartermaster, and commissariat officer. . . . These African explorations are campaigns on a small scale, wherein the traveler, unaided by discipline, has to overcome all the troubles, hardships, and perils of savage warfare" (pp. 224–25). Stanley, who did in fact command small armies in the biggest of his African

11. Burton, *Zanzibar*, 139–40.

expeditions, gives a similar account. In *Through the Dark Continent* he says, "You are constantly engaged, mind and body; now in casting up accounts, and now traveling to and fro hurriedly to receive messengers, inspecting purchases, bargaining with keen-eyed relentless Hindi merchants, writing memoranda, haggling over extortionate prices, packing up a multitude of small utilities, pondering upon your lists of articles, wanted, purchased, and unpurchased."[12] This gave explorers the air of playing at war, engaging in it semi-innocently and semi-comically.

Sir Samuel Baker was more concerned to depict the explorer as the advance guard of civilization. In his introduction to *Albert N'Yanza* he says: "The explorer is the precursor of the colonist; and the colonist is the human instrument by which the great work must be constructed— that greatest and most difficult of all undertakings—the civilization of the world."[13] Baker had decided early in life to find the source of the Nile or die in the attempt. "From my youth I had been inured to hardships and endurance in wild sports in tropical climates" (p. 1). He portrays the experience of writing, and even of reading, his book, in similar terms: "I must take the reader of these volumes by the hand, and lead him step by step along my rough path from the beginning to the end; through scorching deserts and thirsty sands; through swamp, and jungle, and interminable morass; through difficulties, fatigues, and sickness, until I bring him, faint with the wearying journey, to that high cliff where the great prize shall burst upon his view—from which he shall look down upon the vast *Albert Lake,* and drink with me from the Sources of the Nile!" (p. viii)

Baker was perhaps the most Victorian of the nineteenth-century adventurers, accompanied everywhere, as he was, by his wife. Theirs was an adventure as domestic as a Dickens novel. Baker was also the most exuberantly hearty, confident that he embodied the values he so completely endorsed and giving us to understand that he habitually enforced those values on gigantic natives, in Tom Brown style, by the manly science of pugilistics: "Stepping quickly on board, and brushing a few fellows on one side, I was obliged to come to a physical explanation with the captain ["a gigantic black"] which terminated in a delivery of the oars" (p. 30).

Thus, the concept of adventure was given a rich moral resonance and

12. Stanley, *Through the Dark Continent,* 54.
13. Samuel Baker, in introduction to *Albert N'Yanza,* 1:xxi.

a realization, a vivid body of images, for nineteenth-century readers of voyages. And the latter were not only the philistines. The Romantic poets drew widely on travelers' accounts, and American transcendentalists, like Thoreau, read them with enthusiasm all their lives.

4

Sports and Holidays

"Sports and holidays" is a category similar to "travel and exploration," but it offers a milder dose of danger, a more limited scope of action. One kind of both sport and holiday adventure at the end of the nineteenth century particularly attractive to men of imagination was mountaineering, most typically in the Alps, with the Himalayas challenging the boldest. As compared with grouse-shooting, for example, this was an idealistic form of sport and an adventure popular with intellectuals. One figure prominently associated with the Alpine kind was Leslie Stephen, father of Virginia Woolf. In the nineteenth century the Alps were associated with poetry and idealism, and climbing was the way to interact with the mountains and imbibe their essence.

The contrast and mutual alienation between Stephen and his daughter, in this matter as in others, will remind us of how tied to the pre-1914 world all the forms of idealistic adventure were. It was Woolf who gave Stephen's biographer the anecdote about how embarrassingly he chanted adventure ballads as he walked around the house or even on busy streets, a habit she ascribes to Mr. Ramsay in *To the Lighthouse*. That chanting was a sign of, a source of, the egotistic masculinism she hated in her father. It was a kind of rehearsal of mountain-climbing.

Kipling, who wrote such ballads, also made important use of mountaineering in *Kim*. The descriptions of walking and climbing are one of his most effective ways of praising the beauty and greatness of Indian geography. They are also one of the more subtle ways of infecting the reader with the excitement of psychological imperialism. But perhaps most important, the Lama's prowess as a hearty mountaineer reconciles the Kipling reader to his otherwise outlandish spirituality, reconciles East with West.

Kipling's main heir, John Buchan, himself planned to climb Mount Everest in the Himalayas in 1914 (the outbreak of war preventing that), and in 1920 Buchan published a cultic book called *The Last Secrets*, which gathers evocative passages about mountain climbing as a form of both adventure and idealism. (Buchan's title refers to the last-kept of the Earth's secrets, which a series of adventurers have sought out.) For instance, Francis Younghusband wrote: "The sight of climbers struggling upwards to the supreme pinnacle would have taught men to lift their eyes to the hills . . . to something pure and lofty and satisfying. . . . They will have a proper pride in themselves, and a well-grounded faith in the capacity of spirit to dominate material."[1] Théophile Gautier said of mountaineers, "They are the will protesting against blind obstacle, and they plant the flag of human intelligence on the inaccessible."[2] And Hilaire Belloc put it this way: "From the height of Weissenstein I saw, as it were, my religion. I mean humility, the fear of death, the terror of height or of distance, the glory of God, the infinite potentiality of reception, whence springs that divine thirst of the soul."[3]

It makes sense that Buchan, the mountaineer, was not—definitively not—a literary modernist. Writers who *were* modernists, such figures as Virginia Woolf, D. H. Lawrence, James Joyce, and Marcel Proust, were not to be pictured conquering the Alps. One might say that Buchan was a literary antithesis to D. H. Lawrence, and some of the most eloquent post-1918 reactions against this mountaineering idealism one finds in Lawrence's writing about the Alps, in various places—for instance, at the end of *Women in Love* and in "The Captain's Doll."

On the other hand, the reaction of writers like Lawrence and Woolf did not simply end the popularity of mountain-climbing even among literary people, but rather altered the implicit ideology that accompanied the activity—and that accompanied adventure in general. A comparable

---

1. Quoted in John Buchan, *The Last Secrets*, 267.
2. Quoted in ibid., 267.
3. Ibid., 268.

activity was sailing, and an interesting figure to consider as representing that activity is the French adventurer Alain Gerbault. (In discussing this topic we can escape the limits of the Anglo-Saxon late nineteenth century and take examples from France and Germany in the eighteenth and twentieth centuries.) Gerbault and his love of the South Sea Islands are discussed in my book *The Robinson Crusoe Story*.

If we understand sports in the narrower sense of competitive athletics and physical skills, we find in them an ambivalent character, from our present point of view. Though they have an aspect of adventure in the way they are opposite to productive work and study and in the risk or at least stress to which they submit the body (by which they glorify it), they are also eminently social in their forms of organization. Nothing better exemplifies the civic contract than a sports day, whether at the school or the national level.

We usually connect the development of sports as a social phenomenon with nineteenth-century England. In fact, however, the theory of the educational value of sports can be traced to eighteenth-century Germany. Johann Bernhard Basedow (1724–90), inspired by Rousseau's *Emile*, recommended all-around education. His model school, the Philanthropinum, founded in 1774, gave importance to bathing, skating, wrestling, jumping, and climbing. The traditional games, of useless fun, were replaced by these new ones, which were self-improving—exuberant versions of the order, sobriety, and constructiveness that were the basis of the success of the bourgeois class.[4]

When another Philanthropinum was founded in Schnepfenthal one of the teachers was Johann Guts Muths, who went further in developing an educational philosophy around sports and gymnastics. He wrote *Gymnastics for Youth* (1792), *Games* (1796), and *The Art of Swimming* (1798) and wanted to recreate in his pupils the ancient German virtues of "bodily robustness, strength, courage, and virility" together with a culture of the heart.[5] At the same time, at first sight incongruously, another of the prime texts of this movement was Benjamin Franklin's *Autobiography*, and tables of improvement were kept, in imitation of Franklin's, to show the pupils' week-by-week progress in swimming, jumping, and running. The Enlightenment showed both these aspects: a physically exuberant love of adventure, and a rational drive to quantification. We find them together in *Robinson Crusoe* after all.

4. Described in R. D. Mandell, *Sport: A Cultural History*, 160.
5. See Peter McIntosh, *Fair Play*, 43–45.

The cult of adventurous sports and athletics was taken up, in connection with Germanness, by Ludwig Jahn in 1810, who wrote a book foreseeing the unification of Germany with a capital on the Elbe, to be called Teutonia. Jahn's work was part of the German nationalist reaction against Napoleon's conquests in Germany. The athletes who belonged to Jahn's *Turnen* (towers) went bareheaded and barehanded, wore special clothing of gray canvas, and claimed a lineage that went back to the German tribesmen who defeated the Roman general Varus.

Later, sport in the sense of rowing, rugby, and tennis did come to Germany and was associated with England. However, Jahn's disciples regarded this kind of sport as un-German, unpatriotic, and upper-class, and they also disapproved of the competition and specialization and record-keeping that went with it. But this was not simply a difference between national styles. Baden-Powell, for instance, claimed to have read Jahn, and there was a strain of feeling in the Anglo-Saxon Scout movement too, which was distinct from and in some ways hostile to the cult of spectator sports, including even school sports. It is expressed in Kipling's famous lines "The flanelled fool at the wicket, The muddied oaf at the goal." Schools offered a less adventurous kind of sport, though one still of some interest to us.

In England at the end of the nineteenth century, spectator sport (vicarious adventure) was a means by which the different classes came together, and typically in ways that endeared the aristocracy to the lower classes. The sporting peers owned the racehorses that even proletarian cockneys bet on, they owned the yachts that represented England in races, and so on. There were also, of course, sports that were exclusively proletarian, and others that varied in form with the class of the players. The football and cricket played on vacant lots in, say, Birmingham slums had often only a notional connection to the national games at Wembley and Lords. But still, Edwardian England was for many people, and not only the rich, the land of Twickenham (soccer), Lords (cricket), Wembley (rugby football), and Wimbledon (tennis).[6] And seen in a world (or Western world) perspective, the English were the people who had bred the racehorse and the sporting dog, had built yachts and sculls, had invented goalposts, boxing gloves, and stopwatches, and had come up with the concepts of finishing lines, fair play, records, odds, and the rules most widely observed for most games.[7]

6. Jennifer Hargreaves, *Sport, Culture, and Ideology*, 80.
7. Mandell, *Sport*, 132–33.

Betting, and gambling in its various forms, organized or not, was traditionally a social surround to this sort of sport, and gambling is another kind of adventure. Much of this detail seems pretty remote from narratives of adventure as we most often use the word, but if we think of the hostility toward work and the social contract as one of the forces that define the idea of adventure, we see how often that idea comes into view in different kinds of sports.

Adventurous sport has long been linked with athleticism, with the cult of the body, and with risk even to the participant's life—and therefore, by an indirect but recognizable logic, with right-wing (or fascist) politics. Marxist socialism, with its pedagogical and puritanical strain, has not such a strong sports-affinity, at least in its revolutionary or conspiratorial phases. (The sports displays put on by the socialist countries seem to have little to do with their Marxist ideology.)

John Hoberman says the issue that really divides the field of political ideas is aggression. For some ideologies, the fostering of aggressiveness is a prime concern and quite unabashed; for others, the use of aggressive force is legitimate only in the last resort.[8] Thus, Mussolini called punching a Fascist means of self-expression, and hunting was a protest against the enlightened bourgeois world the Nazis favored; and Göring was a great hunter who praised hunting and horse-racing as "the last remnants of a dead feudal world."[9] When we read about the hunting parties of Kremlin and East European leaders, we take it as a sign that they have become "fascist," whatever their professed ideology. The key question in cultural theory, Hoberman says, is not a political question but a historical one: "Which came first, work or play?" The Marxists say work, their opponents say play—those opponents including not merely fascists, but intellectuals like Ortega y Gasset, Johann Huizinga, Max Scheler, Josef Pieper, and Gaston Bachelard.[10]

Scheler attacked nineteenth-century utilitarianism, and the bourgeois mentality, in an essay entitled "Ressentiment" (1915). Following Nietzsche and preceding Laban, he says that in his day European culture neglects the body. The old civilizations had had "life-techniques," practices that served the body as well as the mind; these included games, tourneys, caste loyalties, all of them things independent of use. The key value was joy. Similarly, Gaston Blanchard says, "It is in joy not in

8. John M. Hoberman, *Sport and Political Ideology*, 18.
9. Ibid., 16, 19.
10. Ibid., 23.

sorrow that man discovered the intellect." This idea is connected, for post-Nietzscheans, to that of excess. The conquest of the superfluous is of more spiritual value than the conquest of the necessary. Scheler and Ortega y Gasset both opposed the mechanicism and utility-thinking of Enlightened culture; "We cannot breathe, confined to a realm of secondary and intermediate themes," Gasset says.[11] There is a kind of Nietzschean atavism in all this line of thought.

The athletic body—usually male—was an important emblem of this philosophy and politics. Marinetti and the Fascists tended to see the state as a living body. Indeed, Hegel had said, in *The Phenomenology of Mind*, that the well-built warrior was the incarnation of the state.[12] This is the idea that Leni Riefenstahl embodies in her films made in Hitler's Germany. In natural opposition, the leftward-leaning Frankfurt School of cultural theorists, and socialists in general, have disparaged the cult of the male body and the cult of adventure.

This is part of the mutual contradiction between two politics. Sontag says that all fascist politics tends toward theater, and all communist politics toward pedagogy. The latter is a highly moralized version of the civic contract. Marinetti accused the communists of wanting "a life without surprises, the earth as smooth as a billiard ball."[13] Of course, all political regimes call for healthy citizens; the difference is a matter of emphasis. Ernst Nolte, in *The Three Faces of Fascism*, writes: "That which for Marx and Lenin had been an obvious, unspecified element in the case—bravery and strength, courage and heroism, vitality and separateness—becomes for Mussolini independent and self-aware."[14]

Sport can naturally be given a cultural character in other than twentieth-century terms. Mark Twain saw baseball as a symbolic cult of the values of the entrepreneurial nineteenth century. He described a game of baseball played on the Sandwich Islands as absurdly incongruous: "Where life is one long, slumberless Sabbath, the climate one long, delicious summer day. . . . And these boys have played baseball there! — baseball, which is the very symbol, the outward and visible expression of the drive and push and rush and struggle of the raging, tearing, booming 19th century."[15] Here sport is seen under the aspect of its organization but still as deploying a disruptive "violence."

11. On Scheler, Bachelard, and Ortega y Gasset, see ibid., 39.
12. Ibid., 74.
13. Ibid., 94.
14. Quoted in ibid., 94.
15. Quoted in Allen Guttmann, *From Ritual to Record*, 15.

Some sociologists, on the other hand, tend to minimize the importance of adventure. They see sports not as a departure from the social contract but as a form of social organization, as a phenomenon cognate with Protestantism and science. Allen Guttmann quotes from Robert Merton's essays on puritanism, pietism, and science and from Hans Lerk, who says: "Achievement sport, that is, sport whose achievements are extended beyond the here and now through measured comparisons, is closely connected to the scientific-experimental attitudes of the modern West."[16] All this is true enough, though it needs to be balanced by acknowledging the adventure element.

On the whole, of course, it is conservative politics we expect to find linked to the praise of sports. We are not surprised that Michael Novak, writing in reaction against his earlier political radicalism, speaks up about the moral value of sports but anticipates left-wing disapproval. (Intellectuals, he says, believe that to love sports is to love the lowest common denominator, to be lower-class, to be patriotic in a corny way.) For himself, at the age of forty, he says that baseball was "deeper in my being than most of what I did, [and] spoke to me of beauty, excellence, imagination, and animal vitality—was *true* in a way few things in life are true."[17]

Novak declares, "Sports is part of my religion, like Christianity, or 'Western civilization,' or poetry, or politics" (p. xiv). He spells this out: "If war is the teacher men have turned to in order to learn teamwork, discipline, coolness under fire, respect for contingency and fate, football is my moral equivalent of war. Say, if you like, that men *ought* to be less primitive, less violent, less mesmerized by pain and injury," but if you accept men as they are, you must value sports. "Football makes conscious to me part of what I am. . . . Seeing myself reflected in the dance, the agony and the ritual of a heated contest, I am at peace" (p. xv). The opposite is "death by continuous committee meetings," the fate toward which progressivist civic virtue leads its devotees.

A particularly interesting case within sports is hunting, which J. M. MacKenzie discusses in *The Empire of Nature*. He deals explicitly with the history of the English in Africa and in India, and implicitly with the atavism of imperial peoples everywhere, their reversion from the technical, commercial, and industrial modernity they bring to other lands to a sentimental and archaic version of the hunting phase of social develop-

16. Ibid., 84.
17. Michael Novak, *The Joy of Sports,* xi.

ment. It is a way to make class and race divisions, and hierarchical rule, seem immemorial.

This happened among the Boers in Africa and among the Spanish emigrants to South America, colonists whose lifelines to their parent empires were cut, who became socially fossilized. But it happened also to the colonists of expanding imperial and industrial powers, such as England. "Thus hunting, the earliest phase of man's struggle for survival, had become the prerogative of the bearers of industrial civilization."[18]

The love of the hunt is always backward-looking. (Even in ancient Greece, according to John MacKenzie, Xenophon said hunting was necessary to give young men the virtues their ancestors had "by nature" [p. 11]). As we know, such atavism is always an important feature of the cult of adventure and of empire. Adventure makes it seem possible for people to go back to an earlier social condition and revive the best part of the past—or the fiercest and grandest parts—in more favorable conditions.

The Hunt in the grand sense distinguishes game from vermin and reserves the former for hunters. Game have fine moral qualities, which pass into the hunter who kills them. Vermin are the object of (lower-class) snaring, fowling, and poaching. Some such activities are outright dishonorable. It was and is considered dishonorable to shoot foxes in England or pigs in India. Sport then becomes a ritual, and hunting becomes The Hunt. In primitive societies, women hunt, to feed the family, but the Hunt was largely, though not entirely, sex-segregated (p. 21).

We have one example of that in the reversion of the Boers in South Africa to a patriarchal style of family and social life; another in the Indian Mogul princes' pig, tiger, and elephant hunts, in which the English joined; and another in the English and Irish county families' fox-hunting (in which women *did* take part). In Kipling's school-stories, *Stalky and Co.*, M'Turk denounces the shooting of a fox as murder in one episode, while the boys' killing of a cat in another episode is comedy. That dichotomy exemplifies hunt morality.

Spokespersons for the Enlightenment had tended to disapprove of hunting in the eighteenth century. Gibbon saw it as belonging to the distant past, and Blackstone saw the game laws as an example of "the Norman yoke" imposed on the Saxons in violation of their freedom (pp.

18. John M. MacKenzie, ed., *The Empire of Nature*, 164.

12–13). Indeed, the Normans did "reserve" whole forests and held large ceremonial hunts. The latter are often signs or institutions of an imperial culture. Perhaps the shift they mark from Saxon to Norman England was like that from republican to imperial Rome and that from Bronze Age to Classical Greece (p. 13).

In seventeenth-century England the Stuarts were, predictably, fervent hunters, but the activity lost prestige in Cromwell's Commonwealth. The ideology of hunting was not in sympathy with that of Puritanism, not even in the secularized form the latter took on in the eighteenth century. Hunting became the mark of the squirearchy. From 1671, the royal privilege was gradually modified to give "royal" advantages to the upper landed gentry. Blackstone said this put a little Nimrod into every manor house (p. 16). And this developed largely in the course of the nineteenth century; three million acres of Scotland were converted from pasture to moor. In *Stalky and Co.*, M'Turk's feelings about foxes derive from his being the son of an Irish landowner and "viceroy of four thousand naked acres."

The ancient hunt after lion and boar was, as MacKenzie says, in effect royal or imperial propaganda, showing a king/emperor/lord enjoying his privileges and increasing his prestige before a wide audience (p. 10). Both Persians and Greeks called deer parks "paradises" because they were an ultimate in privilege, delight, and reward. Thus, all this was alien to the official ideology of Enlightenment or Puritan societies.

And yet in the nineteenth century, the Hunt became part of the upper-class lifestyle even in England, perhaps because England was, after all, an empire. The paintings of Victoria and Albert and their family in Scotland by Landseer and Winterhalter included scenes of the men hunting. Prince Albert introduced the fashion for building hunting lodges of a German type; the architecture was usually Gothic, with dark wood, high ceilings, and large stone fireplaces inside. Trophies hung on the walls, and there were sometimes exhibitions of trophies and of native weapons. In country houses there were smoking rooms, gun rooms, saddle rooms. These were domestications of the Hunt—and so of adventure.

Taxidermy, stables, and also nature study were associated with the Hunt. Prince Albert asked Richard Owen, a hunter, to teach the royal family natural history. The Prince of Wales became trustee of the Natural History Museum. When Landseer died in 1873, the auction catalog of his property listed thirty pairs of stag heads, bull horns, ram heads, wild boar heads, bison and tiger skins, and a stuffed swan (p. 31). His three favorite subjects were dogs, stags, and lions; his picture of two stags fighting was entitled "None But the Brave Deserve the Fair"; and dying stags were emblems of nobility and romance.

This sensibility led naturally to a cult of royalty. Landseer's *Monarch of the Glen* was an allegorical image of royalty. Landseer also designed the lions that guard the national memorial, Nelson's column in Trafalgar Square. And the study of nature, especially of animals, was part of the adventure movement in other ways too, such as the Scout movement; Baden-Powell recommended natural history highly.

Hunting was naturally linked to other forms of adventure, such as travel and exploration, and it determined the patterns of travel. The country a traveler chose to visit, Dennis Lyall said, was usually the country that had the game he wanted. (We should note the rich ambiguities of "game," which are similar to those of "play"; game ranges from the tigers of India, via the Great Game of Anglo-Russian rivalry, to the games of cricket and football.) Hugh Gunn said in 1925 that the spirit of the chase had been greatly responsible for "the adventures and enterprise of . . . exploration and settlement in 'unknown and pagan lands.'"[19]

This meant that together with the pleasures of displaying skill and courage, and those of exploration, hunting also offered the subtler pleasures of historical perspective. Elspeth Huxley, in *Out in the Midday Sun*, says: "What is so interesting about Kenya's history is that events belonging by rights to a bygone century, to the era of covered wagons and the Oregon Trail, should have taken place . . . now."[20] This is to be compared with the geographical perspective we note in Kipling and Buchan. History and geography carried the message of imperialism subliminally.

It was as the land of hunting and sport—for European immigrants—that Elspeth Huxley's Kenya was so much the White Man's Country at the beginning of this century. (*White Man's Country* was her first book, published in 1953.) It was a land of literal adventure. The erotic kind of adventure is what recent books and movies have shown us (*White Mischief*, for instance), but the other kind was more important.

19. Quoted in ibid., 296.
20. Elspeth Huxley, *Out in the Midday Sun*, 25.

5

Education and Migration

I have defined adventure as a breaking of the social contract, and most of us think of adventures as appealing to the imagination and against moral reason, against prudence. But putting these ideas together makes a complex configuration that has contrary aspects. Adventure can get social—for instance, educational—endorsement, as we have seen in school sports and as the history of migration shows.

Some striking examples of the way adventure themes of a nationalist kind were allied to schoolwork in the early nineteenth century are found in Charlotte Brontë's posthumously published first novel, *The Professor*. The heroine, Frances Henri, is a lace-mender in Brussels who learns English from a strict schoolmaster who has his pupils write on themes of England's past and present; Frances writes an essay on King Alfred's burning of the cakes, and then another that is "an emigrant's letter to his friends at home."

Brontë's description of this second essay gives us a vivid picture of how the schools could fit stories of adventure and emigration into official value schemes. Frances begins with an adventure landscape:

> Some natural and graphic touches disclosed to the reader the scene of virgin forest and great, New World river—barren of sail

and flag—amidst which the epistle was supposed to be indited. The difficulties and dangers that attend a settler's life were hinted at; and in the few words said on that subject Mademoiselle Henri failed not to render audible the voice of resolve, patience, endeavour. The disasters which had driven him from his native country were alluded to; stainless honour, inflexible independence, indestructible self-respect there took the word. Past days were spoken of; . . . feeling, forcible and fine, breathed eloquent in every period. At the close, consolation was suggested; religious faith became here the speaker, and she spoke well.[1]

It is also interesting to see Brontë introduce the emotions of adventure into the form of education as well as the subject matter. Frances writes a poem about what a severe master she has and how she triumphs in finally winning a school prize:

> At last our school ranks took their ground,
> The hard-fought field I won;
> The prize, a laurel wreath, was bound
> My throbbing forehead on. . . .
> The strong pulse of Ambition struck
> In every vein I owned;
> At the same instant, bleeding broke
> A secret, inward wound. (pp. 189–90)

Brontë used many of these images and themes again in the more sophisticated *Villette,* where the strict teacher, this time a Frenchman, is actually presented as a Napoleon of the schoolroom. Values derived from the adventure tale, such as leadership, egotistic heroism, even fierceness, are domesticated—as they are in other, erotic aspects of the Brontës' stories, with heroes like Rochester and Heathcliff. But here it is schoolroom education that becomes—metaphorically and yet really—adventure.

Migration was one of the major institutionalized forms of adventure in the nineteenth century, for all Europeans. Edwin Guillet says: "History records three great migrations: the Barbarians who swept over Europe and captured Rome; the Mongols under Genghiz Khan; and the Atlantic Migration to the New World."[2] Between 1770 and 1890, eleven

1. Charlotte Brontë, *The Professor,* 130.
2. Edwin C. Guillet, *The Great Migration,* vii.

million people left the British Isles for North America, generally making the passage in vessels unsanitary, verminous, and unseaworthy (p. vii).

Howard Malchow puts it that "each year, some hundreds of thousands of Queen Victoria's subjects saw 'the Last of England' from the decks of over-age sailing ships and cheap steamers. . . . In the second half of the century the annual attrition of the most vigorous part of the nation reached a level quite comparable, in numbers at least, to that of the First World War."[3] The phrase "in numbers, at least" invites us to consider whether the migration was comparable to World War I in imaginative importance, despite the way it has been overlooked.

Britain, and other white countries to only a lesser degree, sent out emigrants every year with the purpose both of alleviating distress and disorder at home and of building an empire abroad. As early as 1584 Richard Hakluyt said England could solve its vagrancy problem, create colonial markets, and increase employment at home, all by settling paupers in America. In 1618 the city of London sent out a hundred homeless children only a few years after the first English settlements were established.

Many of these enterprises were officially sponsored, though most by churches and charitable groups. Fostering emigration was seen as socially responsible action. Malchow says: "This unprecedented exodus . . . was accompanied by a near-consensus of approval from contemporaries" (p. 1); Charlotte Brontë showed one way in which that approval was expressed. And some of the enterprises were governmental. After 1815, the Scots especially were solicited to emigrate to Canada and South Africa.

To take just one example, in 1819 the British government made a grant of £50,000 to help about a thousand families emigrate to the Cape Colony in South Africa. Out of those who applied, six parties were selected, each of which included at least ten workers over the age of eighteen. Most members were artisans and tradesmen—blacksmiths, chandlers, bookbinders, former soldiers—but there were also ministers, teachers, and merchants. They were not explicitly told of the military service that would be expected of them in the colony, but they were warned: "When you go to plough, never leave your guns at home."[4] The number of people who emigrated under these official auspices and in

---

3. Howard C. Malchow, *Population Pressures: Emigration and Government in Late Nineteenth-Century Britain*, 1.
4. See *The Illustrated History of South Africa*, 98.

this organized form was not so large as those who made their own way, and all such emigrants were the object of a great deal of interest, as symbolic heroes, as the theme Frances Henri is asked to write on suggests.

The literature of emigration is full of adventure language: epics and heroes, winning the land and reigning like kings. Guillet quotes an immigrant chant about mountains and kingdoms:

> Cheer up, brother, as we go
> Over the Mountains, westward ho!
> When we've wood and prairie land
> Won by our toil
> We'll reign like Kings in fairyland
> Lords of the soil.[5]

Guillet himself describes the immigrants' ascent of the St. Lawrence River as "an epic of navigation" and "avoided by the Indians on account of its rapids," requiring special boats (p. 164). He also quotes a contemporary description of the French Canadian crews who guided the immigrants: "[They] resembled a band of freebooters. Most of them were very athletic, and had the sharp physiognomy and sparkling eyes of a Canadian. The red glare of the fire communicated additional animation to the rude features; and their bushy black beards and discordant voices rendered them a rather formidable-looking set of people" (p. 204). The immigrants who were not afraid praised the experience in terms of adventure, like a certain Dr. Dunlop who found it "far from unpleasant, for there is something of romance and adventure in it" (p. 168).

Even where romantic rhetoric and literature are not in question, readers are reminded of *Robinson Crusoe* and its successors as they read the lists of tools, clothing, and equipment the emigrants took with them; everything is listed—one knife, one fork, two spoons, a metal plate and mug, and so on.[6] This flat factuality was charged with the excitement of adventure for all readers of, among others, Defoe.

The migration of unparented children, poignant and disturbing as it is to us, clearly played a part in associating emigration with youth and promise and a fresh start—that is, with adventure. Gillian Wagner's

5. Guillet, *Great Migration*, 204.
6. Ibid., 33.

Children of the Empire includes as frontispiece an 1882 advertisement from *The Christian,* complete with pictures of happy children breaking new soil abroad. The director of the London Samaritan Society, J. J. Jones, was appealing for subscriptions to make up £800 in order to take 120 children to Canada. Tens of thousands of children between the ages of five and seventeen, orphans or criminals or homeless, went overseas, unaccompanied by family, most often to become domestic servants or farm laborers in Canada, Australia, or South Africa. Between 1870 and 1930 there were as many as 3,000 to 4,000 a year. They were "called," by various social bodies, to a life of adventure.

The connection of child migration with empire and adventure is suggested by lines from "Veld Verse," written by one of the later organizers of this migration, the South African Kingsley Fairbridge:

> I looked, and beheld . . .
> The brown of the veld, the unending immensity,
> League after league of the houseless and homeless,
> The smokeless, the gardenless wealth of the desert,
> The river unfished and the valleys unhunted,
> An empire peopled with nothing—a country
> Abandoned to emptiness, yearning for people,
> A mother well fit for the birth of a nation.[7]

Fairbridge began with this vision of empty land in Africa, and only later did he see the East End of London children whom his farm schools could "save." Yet, according to Wagner, he was one of the best and most sympathetic organizers of juvenile emigration.

Fairbridge was born in South Africa in 1885, in a shack where jam tins were used as cups, and kipper tins as plates. As a boy, with his father's help, he built a hut for himself out of an old wagon with a tent pitched on top. He lived the Crusoe life himself, which he later taught to the boys at his farm schools. Having met Rhodes, he went to Oxford and began to solicit support for his scheme from various sources. He was first offered 50,000 acres in Newfoundland but was warned that only adults, and probably only Scotsmen, should be asked to survive there. Then he was given land in western Australia, and boys began to arrive there in 1913. Fairbridge taught them to box and read to them

---

7. Quoted in Gillian Wagner, *Children of the Empire,* 188.

out of the jingoistic *History of England* written by Kipling and Fletcher. The boys' cottages were named after a variety of British imperial heroes—"Shakespeare," "Raleigh," "Livingstone," and "Rhodes"—literature being thus assimilated to adventure and missions.

In the late nineteenth century the values of imperialism, and so those of adventure, began to be naturalized in English schools even at home. This development did not go unprotested. J. A. Hobson, in *Imperialism*, spoke about the atavism of these attempts to seize the school system for jingoism and to "cultivate the savage survivals of combativeness . . . to establish a 'geocentric' view of the moral universe in which the interests of humanity are subordinate to that of the 'country.' "[8]

Hobson held the clerical masters of the great public schools mainly responsible, as did Mark Starr in his later book of 1929, *Lies and Hate in Education*. The key figures in this imperialization of education were the headmasters: Warre of Eton, Welldon of Harrow, Almond of Loretto, Thring of Uppingham, Moss of Shrewsbury, Norwood of Marlborough, Rendall of Winchester. These schools, under the direction of these masters, created a semi-playful ethos of adventure outside but all around the classroom—on the playing field, on speech days, in the school magazine—a playfulness surely comparable to the kind of games we saw Jefferies, Beaumont, Lowell, and the Brontës playing in family settings. Moss, who was at Shrewsbury from 1872 to 1908, blamed England for its habitual antimilitarism.[9]

This ethos was serious as much as playful. After the Boer War, for instance, Moss's school was one of the first to set up a cadet corps to give the boys military training. Almond said in 1899 that schools like his should produce the "neo-imperial warrior: untroubled by doubt, firm in conviction, strong in mind and muscle."[10]

The school magazine of Fettes between 1878 and 1898 published old boys' letters from all over the empire and stories of military adventures and actions. A poem published there in 1899 entitled "The Adventurers" makes clear the connection between individual exploits and patriotism:

> For her we wandered, and for her we died,
> And to her feet we brought our trophies real. . . .

---

8. J. A. Hobson, *Imperialism*, 1st ed., 229.

9. J. A. Mangan, "The Grit of Our Forefathers," in John M. MacKenzie, ed., *Imperialism and Popular Culture*, 118.

10. Ibid., 120.

We brought her merchandise, we brought her gold.
Our chosen strength we sold to work her will. . . .
We are her power, hers to hold us in her hand;
So shall it be until the end of all.
With hand on sword we guard our native land,
And gladly die, if once we hear her call.[11]

We shall see later, in discussing Maurice Samuel's reminiscences of his boyhood, how far down the ladder of English education the influence of these ideas reached.

In our own day, adventure remains an ally of education in many schools and colleges, though at the college level favored more by administrators than by faculty; and it is associated now with such words as "survival" rather than words like "empire." In England the revival and reshaping of adventure values was the work of Kurt Hahn at Gordonstoun and the projects that developed from him, such as the College of the Atlantic and the Duke of Edinburgh's awards. In America the Kennedys and the Peace Corps had their equivalents, in Outward Bound schemes.

The style of this adventure teaching was forecast in some of Jules Verne's Robinson books. In *The Two Years Vacation,* for instance, Verne describes how a shipload of boys, who had been assembled to cruise in the South Seas for purposes of education and training, are wrecked on an island and must take the next steps toward survival and self-dependence by themselves. In *The School for Robinsons* he describes how an American millionaire arranges for his spoiled son to go through the Robinson experience (apparently alone on an island) by means of a gigantic hoax. A similar idea is implicit in Kipling's *Captains Courageous.* Thus, while we may properly distinguish adventure in the first half of the twentieth century from that in the second half, by identifying the former with organized troops like the Scouts, and the latter with individual experiments in survival, both activities were in fact operative as adventure ideas from 1900 and before.

Adventure as initiation was a form of education, in college fraternities and in books. Initiation (often making conscious allusion to tribal initiations) is what many of the famous adventure tales were about, and they were read in the public schools, as semi-official reading—for in-

11. Ibid., 124–25.

stance, read aloud by a master to the boys in his "house." And perhaps the finest intellectually of Kipling's treatments of the ethos of the empire's master-caste is his book of initiations: the school stories, *Stalky and Co.*

In his autobiography Kipling talked of his boyhood friends and fictional heroes, notably "Stalky" and "M'Turk," in aristo-military terms. Stalky was a soldier even as a boy. "For executive capacity, the organization of raids, reprisals, and retreats, we depended on Stalky, our Commander in Chief, and Chief of his own Staff."[12] While Kipling depicts his other schoolfriend, M'Turk, as an aristocrat, "in his holidays he was Viceroy of four thousand naked acres, only son of a three hundred year old house, lord of a crazy fishing boat, and idol of his father's shiftless peasantry."[13] But both the caste elements, combined in the aristo-military type, are only supplementary to the central theme of the book, which is adventure. And although these are school stories, it is adventure taken seriously, taken in relation to its historical function.

This book is both a more characteristic and a more significant Kipling success than *Kim*, because of the aggressive moral realism of the meaning and because of the corresponding intricacy of the artistic means. Here the reader is not indulged in such books' usual sense of the boys' physical beauty or the emotional pathos of their passing out of boyhood into manhood; here boyhood too is full of ugliness and stress, and the moral scheme is full of painful contradictions. When the boys are exhorted to be patriotic and are shown the flag, they are so deeply offended by this exploitation of symbols sacred to them that they withdraw from the cadet corps the school has just formed. That is a typical paradox. *Stalky and Co.* is an unpleasant and difficult book but a powerful study of discipline and authority. (Kipling said his original idea had been "tracts or parables on the education of the young."[14])

He distances the boys and the discourse about them from both Christian and Enlightenment moral measurements, by means of atavistic and would-be anthropological ideas. We are told in "An Unsavoury Interlude" that "outside his own immediate interests, the boy is as ignorant as the savage he so admires; but he has also the savage's resources." And this is a persistent theme; Stalky and Beetle (Kipling) and M'Turk "spun wildly on their heels, jodelling after the accepted

12. Rudyard Kipling, *Something of Myself,* 372.
13. Rudyard Kipling, *Stalky and Co.,* 25.
14. Kipling, *Something of Myself,* 449.

manner of a 'gloat,' which is not unremotely allied to Primitive Man's song of triumph."[15] Later they are initiated into the brotherhood of rulers, "learning, at the expense of a fellow-countryman, the lesson of their race, which is to put away all emotion and entrap the alien at the proper time" (p. 38). This they do by deceiving one of the masters, and the point is made by the specificity of Kipling's analogy, by the credibility of the schoolboys' behavior and the seriousness of the parallel Kipling draws between that and "Primitive Man."

They play on a West African war-drum, an adventure trophy, a gift from M'Turk's naval uncle, originally made to signal war, we are told, across estuaries and deltas. "A deep devastating drone filled the passages as M'Turk scientifically rubbed its top. Anon it turned to the blare of trumpets—savage pursuing trumpets. Then, as M'Turk slapped one side, smooth with the blood of ancient sacrifice, the roar broke into short, coughing howls such as the wounded gorilla throws in his native forest" (p. 60). And as Kipling evokes behind the boys this somewhat fantastic picture of the primeval jungle, he evokes ahead of them a somewhat more realistic picture of the people they will be ruling and fighting in their adult careers. Stalky is adopted by enthusiastic tribesmen as a worthy comrade and warrior, both as a Sikh and as a Pathan.

The book's central moral paradox, around which its other paradoxes are organized, is that of authority. One of the great lessons the boys learn at school is to obey at all costs (and that word "obey" is the climax to his poem "The Law of the Jungle"), and yet the heroes are rebels. This is a serious paradox, for obedience is of the essence of the boys' interactions. Beetle is obedient to Stalky, for instance, and yet Stalky is a serious rebel against those above him. Kipling described Stalky's real-life model as displaying "an unaffected contempt" for all the masters at their school.

The paradox is mediated through the figure of the headmaster. He represents true authority, such as the boys recognize, and he in effect legitimizes their rebellion against the untrue or partial authority of the other masters. He implements the paradox by imposing on them punishments that are categorically "unjust." Intellectually, this paradox gives irony a role within a system of piety, gives rebellion a role within a system of authority. Kipling builds a convincing model of how sincerity can be taught—or perhaps we should say authenticity—the kind of

15. Kipling, *Stalky and Co.*, 27.

sincerity appropriate to originality and leadership: how a model of aggression and resistance can be built into the teacher-student relationship and not destroy it but energize it.

In the boys' future stands the life of heroism-in-service, most typically in India, on the northwest frontier. It is represented by the old boys who return to the school and are just as devoted to the Head as they were as pupils, and by the later story in which we hear of Stalky's exploits there, where he has "become a Sikh" but where he behaves exactly as he did at school and is again in trouble with "the authorities." (In fact, the real-life Stalky's career, culminating when he became Major-General Dunsterville, did parallel the fiction. Long after *Stalky and Co.* was published, he, in the Great War, led an irregular force from India into Persia and camouflaged his cars to look like tanks, and so on. He was of the rogue-commander type Waugh portrayed as Ritchie-Hook in his war novels.) Thus, the picture Kipling draws is essentially a triptych—primitive man, the school, and the frontier—but with no panel from what literature usually calls mature life, or civilization. This is education as initiation, as the most radical theorists of adventure imagined it.

In the public schools, adventure and patriotism were only ideological themes that surrounded (and no doubt permeated) the educational work, but at the turn of the nineteenth century there were other public bodies that took it as their primary purpose to organize and institutionalize adventure for boys in the Anglo-Saxon countries. Besides the Boy Scouts, there were the Boys' Brigade, the Empire Youth Movement, the Navy League, the Legion of Frontiersmen, the National Service League, the Girls' Patriotic League, the League of Empire, the British Empire Union.

One leader in this broad tendency was Reginald Brabazon, the Earl of Meath (1841–1929), who worked through the Lads' Drill Association, the Duty and Discipline Movement, and the Empire Day Movement. Meath, who had been a diplomat in Germany, was alarmed by the threat to England's world position that Germany presented. His activities in the 1880s and 1890s were primarily philanthropic, but he turned to imperial causes in the new century. He was afraid of decadence, and in his *Essays on Duty and Discipline* he wrote about "The Grit of Our Forefathers."

His Empire Day Movement was founded in the early 1900s, with the first public meeting in 1904. The Labour party and the Irish nationalists opposed it, but by 1916 it was officially accepted. In South Africa, Gandhi welcomed it. By 1922 some 80,000 British schools were observing Empire Day, and the empire, the land of adventure, became a part of state education, as it had long been part of public school education. John Reith at the BBC took up the idea, along with other ideas that promoted national and imperial unity. John Buchan was a spokesperson for it, as well as a writer of adventures and also—at the end of his career—governor general of Canada, one of the great provinces of the empire.

One of the most interesting of these institutions was the Boys' Brigade, founded in Glasgow, a city of terrible slums, in the 1880s. The institutions of adventure were one way to solve the civic/moral problems the slums represented. And as we know, John Buchan, while living in his father's Glasgow manse, taught Sunday school classes of slum boys and told them adventure tales under the name of biblical stories.

The Boys' Brigade aimed to promote "all that tends towards true Christian Manliness."[16] What did *not* so tend, among religious institutions? The most popular answer, among Protestants, was Roman Catholicism, which was seen as introspective and effeminate (a celibate priesthood, a Latin liturgy, monks and nuns in their secret buildings). But even within Protestantism there were practices, such as Bible-reading, which came to be deprecated. Boys' Brigade values were significantly different. The founder, William Alexander Smith, who was addressed as "Captain Smith," said, "All a boy's aspirations are towards manliness. . . . We must show them the *manliness* of Christianity" (p. 55). The famous boys' adventure author G. A. Henty was vice-president of the Brigade, and it was Smith who suggested to Robert Baden-Powell that he should start a Scout movement for boys.

We today often associate the Boy Scout movement primarily with England and Robert Baden-Powell, but in fact it was begun by Ernest Thompson Seton in America, where it was originally rather different. (Seton's *Two Little Savages* is a still readable, and still much read, account of "savage" adventure.) However, the section on organization in the latter's *Boy Scouts of America* is taken from Baden-Powell. Organization was the strength of the British scouting movement, and this is one explanation for why the American leader lost the leadership as he did. But the American manual makes it clear that the two movements are to be considered as one. It includes a brief history of the flag that stresses the closeness of the two Anglo-Saxon nations despite their quarrels.

16. John Springhall, "Building Character in the British Boy," in J. A. Mangan and J. Walvin, eds., *Manliness and Morality*, 53.

The manual also makes some attempt to reconcile scouting values with those of traditional culture—for instance, church traditions. The manual prescribes that scouting on Sundays, in particular, should concentrate on nature study and on doing good turns. There is also a reconciliation of Thompson Seton's interest in Indian skills and tribal ways with Baden-Powell's more contemporary, paramilitary "Be Prepared" side of scouting. One test Second Class Scouts must pass is Kim's Game, the test of observation—obviously English in origin. On the other hand, the American Silver Wolf was a high Scout title, and Scouts were to draw their badges after their signatures, like the hieroglyphics of Indian script.

In England especially, perhaps, the concept and value of "character" (another name for the same idea as "grit," and with similar nationalist connotations) came to be associated especially with scouting, and with the comparable organizations. The Scouts leaders thought they could *produce* character, which they saw as a kind of opposite to personality and personal relations. After 1911, Baden-Powell spoke often of "our character factory."[17] In the complex of character, discipline was the most important virtue: " 'A dull lad who can obey orders is better than a sharp one who cannot.' For Baden-Powell, the self is a source of selfishness, nothing more" (p. 8). Hence the opposition between the Scouts ideology and those of modern readers and writers—taking Joyce and Lawrence as examples. The linking of character (and physique) to national and imperial safety was important. Both Baden-Powell and Prime Minister Lloyd George said: "You cannot maintain an A-1 Empire on C-3 men" (using the language by which army recruits were medically classified).[18] Training in adventure made A-1 men.

Baden-Powell made much reference to stories by Kipling (the great celebrant of discipline and adventure), Kim being a model of what valuable work a Boy Scout could do for his country. "The ability to disguise yourself to give the impression that you are someone other than yourself, and to carry it through successfully, is a gift that can be of infinite value for 'intelligence' purposes" (p. 19). And Baden-Powell's short paper in the April 1906 *Boys' Brigade Gazette* stressed powers of observation and reasoning. "The instructor should read to the would-be scouts a detective tale from Gaboriau or Conan Doyle (Sherlock Holmes)

17. See Michael Rosenthal, *The Character Factory*, 6.
18. Ibid., 3.

laying special stress on the clues to the crime, . . . noticing details and remembering them."[19]

Thus, both the inner city and the imperial frontier became dramatic locations in the boys' minds, and both were integrated with the institutions of boyhood. The forms of adventure were allied with other forces in the national life and reinforced with moral approval. This was done so insistently and pervasively that it produced a counteraction. The images of scouting (saluting, knot-tying, doing good deeds) became tainted with irony, at least in intellectual circles. But in other circles that was not true, even of scouting, and other of the ideas of adventure survive triumphant.

These are almost random examples of the institutionalized or semi-institutionalized forces of social play that oriented boys toward adventure in the late nineteenth and early twentieth century in Britain. They represent many other such forces in other countries and other periods, especially strong in the white nationalities, and they lead us on to other aspects of the history of adventure.

19. Ibid., 63.

6

Resistance and Revision

I have now offered several examples of the cult of adventure working in concealed ways to energize our social ethos, and we shall see several others. But my topic is more complex than a list of parallel forces all aligned in the same direction; it also includes interactions and oppositions between adventure and other ideas, interactions that between them weave much of our moral and imaginative life.

Even in the age of imperialism, such ideas as empire and (still more) violence were not always socially approved. And the related idea of adventure only seemed innocent sometimes—for instance, when it was set in the context of play and childhood. When action outside the law was taken at all seriously, or set in an adult context, it was most often disapproved, and the story of resistance to the adventure idea, when that resistance meant the idea was revised, is part of the history of adventure.

As an example, some of the sharpest attacks on the English schools' sponsorship of adventure were delivered by J. A. Hobson, apropos of the Boer War, as was suggested. He did as much as one man could do to re-moralize imperialism and to criticize adventure. Hobson's ideas are found both in his famous book, *Imperialism* (1902), which was so useful to Lenin when he wrote on the same topic later, and in his *Psychology of Jingoism* (1901).

Perhaps the latter is the more valuable to us, for its direct focus on the nation's Olympus or Valhalla of adventure heroes. Hobson described the Renaissance man of the Elizabethan age (who was often cited as an English paragon from which later ages had fallen away) as "a man of powerful, aggressive, self-willed personality, with violent passions, generous, brutal, laborious and domineering, with an undisguised contempt for the sixth, seventh, eighth, and tenth Commandments, and no deep concern for the other six."[1] (In Germany, Nietzsche had recently said similar things but had given them a different emotional color.)

This period thus saw a revival of that debate over violence and its prohibition which must often surround religion. (In this context, religion is the civic contract, raised to a high moral power and charged with faith.) Christian ethics, Hobson said, had never taken deep root in the British soul. "Just as we are not for peace 'at any price,' we are not for the Ten Commandments or the Sermon on the Mount 'at any price.' . . . In fact these teachings have never furnished us with vital, veritable ideals" (pp. 43, 44). The American imperialist Theodore Roosevelt had recently used the phrase "peace at any price" scornfully. He had attacked Tolstoy as a "peace at any price" thinker, when Tolstoy backed William Jennings Bryan as a candidate for the Presidency against Roosevelt, because of their respective stands on America's ventures in imperialism.

Hobson surveyed the manifold imperial propaganda of the time, which used adventure as its cover. He saw the importance of those jingoistic music-hall songs of the turn of the century that were ballads of adventure, and he quoted Fletcher of Saltoun: "Let me make the ballads of a people, and let who will make the laws." But Hobson seemed to allude to writers like Kipling and Stevenson when he added, "But this rude instrument of public opinion . . . does not stand alone. . . . [There are] other instruments of instruction more reputable in appearance, and often more insidious in their appeal" (pp. 2, 5).

During the Boer War, some of Hobson's friends brought out a collection of essays called *The Heart of the Empire*. In the long essay entitled "Imperialism," G. P. Gooch talked about the amoralism of contemporary imperialists, citing Nietzsche's "beyond good and evil" and a phrase he associates with Karl Pearson, "Blessed are the strong, for they shall prey upon the weak."[2] Indeed, even the immoralist slogan

---

1. J. A. Hobson, *The Psychology of Jingoism*, 46.
2. G. P. Gooch, "Imperialism," in C.F.G. Masterman, ed., *The Heart of the Empire*, 312.

"Might is right" was freely attributed to and more-or-less accepted by the jingoists. Gandhi, reporting on his discussions of Eastern versus Western civilization with General Smuts, declares that Smuts accepted that phrase as a mark of Western thought.

At the same time, Gandhi honored the English as adventurers, and Gooch himself begins a list of "our race's" good qualities with "its high spirit, its love of adventure."[3] Attacking jingoism, they still praised adventure. Perhaps it will be interesting, therefore, to look at some of these attempts, in the same period, to separate adventure from jingoism and to employ the glamour and dynamism of the former in the service of peace and reform and social work.

The Salvation Army, a revivalist Christian movement trying to redeem the poor and the slum-dwellers, made a striking attempt to use the current glamour of war and adventure images in the service of the opposite values. "Sally Army" members wore military-style uniforms and sang hymns and marched to military-style brass bands, and the officers had military titles, like commander and general—even though their key concepts were sin, penitence, and confession, and even though so many members were women. Their music came from drums and banjos; they had marches and campaigns; their buildings were citadels; their publication was *The War Cry*.

The Salvation Army movement used all the language of military activity and adventure. "General" Booth, the founder, inspired by an American evangelist called James Caughey, began by rebelling against Wesleyanism. Booth's book of 1890 was entitled *In Darkest England*, in allusion to Stanley's *In Darkest Africa*, a famous book of literal adventure that had come out a few months earlier. It is interesting to find that adventure writers, such as Kipling, Haggard, and Buchan, wrote on the side of Booth and his Army, while the secular socialists—and liberal men of letters—were often hostile, even when seriously concerned about social problems. The differences between the Army and the socialists were often explained by saying that the latter group were "scientific" in their approach to social problems, but it is probably just as significant that the former were "adventurous."

Like the Scouts, the Salvation Army was interested in detective work and had departments of investigation, all because it saw the inner city (and indeed much of modern society) as being a frontier like the literal

3. Ibid., 311.

frontier—that is, a place of adventure that needed to be "policed" by voluntary forces supplementary to the official police. But the larger category into which the Salvation Army fits is the Evangelical movement, and we find a number of connections between that movement and adventure. People who answer to the description of Evangelicals could be found among the Methodists, the Nonconformists, and the Church of England. In the early nineteenth century their offices were mostly near Exeter Hall. It was the Anglican Evangelicals who in the 1820s first published and distributed a huge body of popular literature with a religious interest, which included fiction from *Pilgrim's Progress* to *The Dairyman's Daughter,* and periodicals like *The Christian Observer* and *The Eclectic Review.*

Nineteenth-century Evangelicals were concerned with social reform and humanitarianism. They were suspicious of such entertainments as card games, dances, music, and the theater. They were "serious about life," which they saw in terms of moral issues. This means, in this book's language, that they held by the civic contract and were hostile to many ordinary departures from it. Seen in their relation to empire, however, they looked different; they were the early writers of boys' adventure stories, and promoters of Protestant missions. Geoffrey Best says they virtually invented modern missionary work. Their committees subscribed to missions, read about them, had lectures and sermons on them, took part in them;[4] they also took part in home missions.

As much as seemingly opposite groups, such as the military, these Evangelicals were agents of adventure; indeed, those categories were somewhat intertwined. About General Gordon ("Chinese Gordon" or "Gordon of Khartoum"), for instance, Best says: "General Gordon's life—his many charities, evangelical work, and self-imposed martyrdom—was quite characteristic of the Evangelical mind at its most highly developed" (p. 55). Thus, adventure and military heroism seemed to go together with evangelical religion. On the other hand, some radical pacifists had become suspicious of all adventurism, pagan or Christian. For instance, Tolstoy said (speaking of General Gordon) the expression "Christian soldier" was as self-contradictory as "hot ice."

The most characteristic Evangelical adventurers were the missionaries themselves, and in some ways significantly unlike most other adventurers.

4. See Geoffrey Best, "Evangelicalism and the Victorians," in A. Symondson, ed., *The Victorian Crisis of Faith,* 52.

They came, for instance, from a different part of British society from the military officers and governors. At least up to 1850, Victorian missionaries were drawn from the ranks of the "skilled mechanics," according to Max Warren.[5] By becoming missionaries, they were rising socially but holding onto their religion, and they were naturally viewed with some skeptical hostility. They were often mocked by intellectuals, such as Sydney Smith, and called "didactic artisans and delirious mechanics."

A famous example was John Williams, who died a martyr at Eromanga in the South Seas in 1839. He had begun life as a blacksmith but was converted and went out to the islands for the London Missionary Society and used his skills to build a ship on the islands. He promised commercial expansion as well as moral reform to his supporters at home. Williams was a hero and martyr to other Evangelicals, but not to most liberal humanists.

Joseph Doke, a Baptist minister in Johannesburg who befriended Gandhi, was another adventurous Evangelical with no formal intellectual training. He left England at the age of twenty-one having been turned down for missionary work because of his health—to seek regular ministerial work abroad. Doke served as a minister in Africa, New Zealand, and then Africa again. In 1913 he finally got permission to prospect for a mission in central Africa, but he died there before he could make his report.

Another martyr was Bishop Patteson of New Zealand, who was honored by the Anglican Society for the Propagation of Christian Knowledge. In 1871 four men rowed the bishop to Nukapu, a small island in the Santa Cruz group, at a time when the natives were angry because whites were kidnapping them in "labor vessels," something Patteson had himself protested. Canoes came out to meet the bishop's boat, and he went ashore in one of them while his boat waited near the reef. When a signal cry came from the land, poisoned arrows were fired at his four men, who fled. Upon returning, they found the bishop dead, his body wrapped in a mat in a canoe, floating in the lagoon, with five club-inflicted wounds and a palm branch with five knots (five being the number of natives recently kidnapped).[6] This was an adventure story— referred to by Thompson as a glory of the Melanesian mission—and clearly it was very like the more tragic episodes in the adventures of secular English heroes.

5. Max Warren, "The Church Militant Abroad," in ibid., 62.
6. H. P. Thompson, *Into All Lands*, 427.

As has been indicated, however, not all their contemporaries admired missionaries. Dickens and most of the Victorian novelists we now read were as suspicious of missions as Sydney Smith. And Sir Richard Burton represented many freethinkers when he said—apropos of Stanley's famous pursuit of Livingstone—that he thought it "rather infra dig. to discover a mish." On the other hand, the imperial administrator Frederick Lugard took Livingstone as his life-model.

Perhaps the most striking case of the use of adventure images and ideas by a resistance and reform movement is that of Gandhi's satyagraha campaigns in South Africa. Long before that, as a student in London in the years 1888–91, Gandhi had been ready to define Indians, or at least Hindus, as being weak and unadventurous, compared with the English. To use Hindu caste terms, he saw the English as a Kshatriya race, and the Indians as Banias. He was pointing primarily to physical strength and weakness, but he also saw the English as strong in certain moral and political ways.

He accepted the Nonconformist version of English history, according to which the Protestant English, more than other nations, had resisted the oppression of kings and aristocrats, adventurously by armed revolt and then rationally by Parliamentary debate. In the first decade of this century, the Nonconformists were rebelling against new education laws, and John Hampden, Oliver Cromwell, and John Bunyan were frequently cited among their heroes and those of Gandhi. And one aspect of Englishmen's political strength, according to Gandhi, was their character of being adventurers.

Joseph Doke wanted to entitle his biography of Gandhi "The Pioneer" or "The Jungle-Breaker" in order to bring out the adventurous aspect of his politics. And indeed, when he began his political activities in South Africa, Gandhi set out to arouse his compatriots to English-style virtue. This virtue took the form of political action—as, for instance, in the Natal Indian Congress—and then of military action, as when he raised an ambulance corps to work with the British army in the Anglo-Boer War. Adventure and imperial military action went together. When *Punch*, the famous London periodical, saluted the Indian effort with a poem, in which the refrain was "We are sons of the Empire, after all," Gandhi accepted the compliment in the spirit in which it was offered; he quotes the line in his *Satyagraha in South Africa*. He published short articles on British adventure heroes, such as Nelson—a hero of duty—as well as Indian heroes, who were more peaceable.

Most striking is that when Gandhi began his campaign of passive resistance and going to jail he continued to use the language of adventure—calling it an adventure to go to jail, in his newspaper *Indian Opinion,* and publishing poems in which such figures as Alexander the Great and Julius Caesar are saluted as adventurers the Indian satyagrahis are to emulate, with the important difference that the Indians are to be nonviolent adventurers.

The best example of Gandhi's propaganda is a 1906 poem (translated into very lame English) by the Gujarati poet Narmadashankar. He offers a list of world-historical figures rather like the list of Protestant heroes offered by the Nonconformists:

Forward ye all to battle, the bugles sound.
Raise the cry and take the plunge, for victory's around.
There are deeds that may not be tarried,
Doubts, fears ever abound, and courage is harried;
They waste the days saying the time is not yet—
No such excuse ever did bring profit.
By plunging in and savouring success is strength found.
Raise the cry and take the plunge, for victory's around.
Through adventure did Columbus to the New World make his trip;
Through adventure did Napoleon have enemies in his grip;
Through adventure Martin Luther did the Pope defy;
Through adventure did Scott his debts re-pay;
Through adventure did Alexander have his name resound.
Raise the cry and take the plunge, for victory's around.[7]

In the article that followed, Gandhi explained who those European heroes were and what they did, and interpreted their adventures for the Transvaal Indians, whom he was exhorting to engage in civil disobedience.

Later in his career, however, after his return to India, when his thinking became more religious and traditional, Gandhi warned Indians against adventure. On December 27, 1928, he wrote: "English books

7. M. K. Gandhi, *Collected Works,* 6:480.

have taught us to applaud as heroic, deeds of daring, even of free-booters, pirates and train-wreckers. . . . Some of us have successfully learned this art of applauding as heroic anything adventurous. . . . This cannot be regarded as anything but a bad omen."[8]

The interest here for us is in part that Gandhi was, like Hobson, one of the great enemies of jingoism, and that Gandhi, like Hobson, was to hold up the standards of the Sermon on the Mount to measure the British Empire against (both of them accused the European nations of having never taken the New Testament seriously). And yet Gandhi, during those years in South Africa, tried to use the ethos of adventure to energize satyagraha and to promote peace.

He was not the only person to do so. William James looked for a moral equivalent of war in 1910. He declared the martial virtues to be absolute and permanent human values for which a place must be found in the most peaceful of societies. Even in more recent times, after Gandhi's death, the Gandhians in India organized a Shantih Sena, a peace army, and the Kennedy administration in the United States orga-nized the Peace Corps, as a way to offer young people adventures in the name of peace. It is notable that we can here, in reference to these adventures, speak of young people, including women, just as Gandhi included both women and children in his forms of political action.

The involvement of women in their politics has been a mark of pacifist and anti-imperialist movements for centuries, from at least the time of the early Christians under Rome. Without using the language of adven-ture, the Quakers of seventeenth-century England made in practice a similar interpretation of Christian ethics. Between 1640 and 1660 the English Puritans reacted against various freedoms and initiatives, includ-ing such feminine ones as women's preaching, and emphasized the dignity of the man's role as head of household and source of authority.[9] The family was seen as "a little church and a little commonwealth." This was an understandable reaction against the wild immorality and irrationality of some of the seventeenth-century sects, but it made Puritanism gender-reactionary, compared with the practices of the Lol-lards and even with some of the convents of medieval times.

The Quakers were different. In 1656 George Fox, founder of the Society of Friends, published a pamphlet, "The Woman Learning in

8. Ibid., 38:275.
9. Margaret Hope Bacon, *The Mothers of Feminism*, 6.

Silence," that declared women could be prophets, but Margaret Fell published her "Woman Speaking" in 1666. The mother of eight, Fell was jailed for her convictions when she wrote it, and Fox, ten years her junior, married her in 1669. The relevance of this to our topic of adventure is seen most clearly in the fact that the first traveling Quaker ministers to go to America from England were women. In 1656 Mary Fisher and Ann Austin came to Boston, where they were immediately imprisoned and deported. Between that year and 1700, eighty-seven such "Public Friends," supported and encouraged by their Home Meetings, made the crossing, and twenty-nine were women (not counting those who went as wives). They usually traveled in pairs, to support each other. The Puritan revolution for order, and the stress on male authority, made most American settlements especially hostile to Quakers, and that is why William Penn began his "Holy Experiment" in Pennsylvania in 1681.

The feminist and anti-imperialist tradition persisted among the sect's members. One example of this is their work in the abolition of slavery movement, another is feminism itself—of the five women who planned the feminist convention at Seneca Falls in the early nineteenth century, four were Quakers. Putting these ideas into practice was eminently a matter of adventure. As Bacon says of the seventeenth-century Public Friends, we can imagine how, even later, "the stories of their adventures with the perils of sea and land were told again and again" and how "the re-telling increased the respect that members of their communities came to feel towards any female called to the ministry.[10] But this is not the kind of story that our culture on the whole has assimilated to the concept of adventure, just as, to use the terms of the 1980s, it is Oliver North and not Terry Waite who incarnates, or appropriates, the idea of adventure today. In particular, women have been taught that adventure is something that belongs to the other gender, despite the actual adventures they have engaged in. One important reason is undoubtedly that, at most, the Quaker women cunningly escaped violence while traditional adventure heroes inflict it.

This explains why a feminist movement is often an important source of opposition to adventure, or of efforts to reinterpret the idea to women's uses. A 1978 document can illustrate that for us. In that year, Judy Grahn published a collection of adventure stories for women with

10. Quoted in ibid., 41.

an interesting introduction. She says: "I began gathering these stories together in 1974, having asked myself the question, What *is* a woman's adventure story, and getting no answer whatsoever. . . . As a teenager in a small town during the 50s, I spent many afternoons reading my father's men's adventure magazines, tense dramas of men alone in the mountains with a lion, and only one long range rifle, six powerful shells, and a quart of Seagram Seven to knock him over with."[11] There was no story equivalent for women, no such way for them to energize themselves in their gender role by reading. As her self-education in literature proceeded, Grahn began to read, first, women's stories. "I turned then to 'true' romance stories, gripping sagas of drive-in movie seductions, long scenes of how a family came to terms with their pregnant, unmarried daughters or other transgressions of patriarchal sexual taboos." Naturally, this reading did not satisfy Grahn. "Finally, I tried literary magazine short stories taught in literature classes. And here, I found, the point of view was almost entirely upper class, the bias that of the few people who hire service workers. . . . I found them boring, condescending, and false to living as I know it" (p. 6).

In fact, the stories Judy Grahn finally chose for her anthology cannot be called adventures at all, as I understand the term; they are stories of lesbian relationships. But that does not diminish—perhaps it actually increases—the interest of her introductory remarks about women and adventure. It seems to show that the word "adventure" is attractive to feminists but that actual adventure stories are not, that the concept of adventure, at least as it has been embodied in the majority of historical cases, is gender-linked and repellent to women. Some of the most impressive feminists make this very point.

In *The Man-Made World* (1911) Charlotte Perkins Gilman, in a chapter entitled "Masculine Literature," makes interesting feminist comments on the issue. She says she rests her case against men on their handling of history and fiction. "History is, or should be, the story of our racial life. What have men made of it? The story of warfare and conquest. . . . 'I, Pharaoh, Kings of Kings!'" . . . war and conquest, over and over, with such boasting and triumph, such cock-crow and flapping of wings as show most unmistakably the natural source."[12] "As to what went on that was of real consequence," Gilman adds, men historians

---

11. Introduction to Judy Grahn, ed., *True-to-Life Adventure Stories*, 6.
12. Charlotte Perkins Gilman, *The Man-Made World*, 90, 91.

were *not* interested in the great slow steps of the working world, the discoveries and inventions, the real progress of humanity" (p. 92).

Turning then to fiction, she asks, "What then is the preferred subject-matter of fiction? There are two branches found everywhere, from the Romaunt of the Rose to the Purplish Magazine;—the Story of Adventure, and the Love Story. The Story of Adventure branch is not as thick as the other by any means, but it is a sturdy bough for all that Stevenson and Kipling have proved its immense popularity. . . . All these tales of adventure, of struggle and difficulty, of hunting and fishing and fighting, or robbing and murdering, catching and punishing, are distinctly and essentially masculine" (p. 92). The preferred subject-matter is, then, this "special field of predatory excitement so long the sole province of men" (p. 94).

According to Gilman, masculine literary art is always imperialist, if not topically then aesthetically, in the stress it lays on self-expression. "The artist, passionately conscious of how he feels, strives to make other people aware of those sensations. . . . If a man paints the sea, it is not to make you see and feel as a sight of that same ocean would, but to make you see and feel how he, personally, was affected by it" (p. 85). This is obviously a sweeping charge to make against art, and one that it is not easy to confine to men artists. On the other hand, we must acknowledge that historically it has often been the men writers of a period who have laid claim to art, while in, for instance, the nineteenth century in America, the women novelists were likely to make a lower claim for their work, as something to amuse, comfort, charm the reader. In this century, one could contrast the "egotistically" brilliant styles of Nabokov, Roth, Mailer, and Pynchon with the much simpler and less assuming prose of, say, Sylvia Plath or Flannery O'Connor or Muriel Spark. (Of course, even agreeing with Gilman completely on this would not mean denying that women too can be "imperialist" in any of a dozen ways. We have already given examples from the Brontë sisters.) Conscientious and reformist politics today, insofar as it is inspired by feminism—and that is to a large extent—is suspicious of adventure.

On campuses, at least, this reformist politics was a powerful force in the 1980s and looks as if it is an even more important one in the 1990s. Such politics is linked to college campuses because, coming next after women, intellectuals have been some of the most consistent opponents of adventure, in ways largely independent of their individual political convictions, provided they are (as is the majority case) in the Enlightenment tradition. Adventure is essentially narrative and active, a series of actions in dynamic sequence, so by the very nature of their work, intellectuals are likely to be antiadventure. For instance, in literary criticism intellectuals tend to reduce dynamic narrative to static patterns of theme or form, to reduce action to analysis, the three-dimensional to the two-dimensional. They also tend to be opponents of adventure because their calling is, at least, felt to be in opposition to the expression of physical and emotional enthusiasm, activism, and "movement."

Thus, intellectuals often interpret adventure and imperialism as psychological disorders. Mannoni in his famous interpretation of Prospero and Caliban as imperialist and native subject, says that no one becomes a real colonial who is not impelled by infantile complexes not properly resolved in adolescence.[13] One might argue, surely, that people with "complexes" are found everywhere on the political map, that the intellectuals' stubbornly consistent *opposition* to adventure is itself, by the same token, involuntary, inconsistent, and irrational. In India, for instance, the Indian intellectuals' hatred of British imperialism was not to be relied on to outweigh their opposition to adventure. Gandhi's least receptive listeners, as he declared, were the educated people of India. Most of them could not be induced to take part in his adventure, and alleged there were a thousand reasons to discredit it.

The white male groups that are most linked to adventure include some individuals who are partial heretics as far as ordinary masculinism goes. Partly as a result of the feminist movement, we have recently had a number of declarations by men who feel oppressed by the masculine ethos. Among the most interesting have been Mailer's *Prisoner of Sex* (among works of nonfiction) and Roth's *My Life as a Man* (among works of fiction). But perhaps the most direct is Paul Theroux, who wrote an essay entitled "Being a Man" (1983) in which he says, "I have always disliked being a man. The whole idea of manhood in America is pitiful, in my opinion. . . . Even the expression 'Be a man!' strikes me as insulting and abusive. It means: Be stupid, be unfeeling, obedient, soldierly and stop thinking. Man means 'manly'—how can one think about men without considering the terrible ambition of manliness?"[14] Theroux attributes the worst features of American culture as a whole to the cult of manliness:

13. Octave Mannoni, *Prospero and Caliban: The Psychology of Colonization.*
14. Paul Theroux, *Sunrise with Seamonsters,* 309.

Nothing is more unnatural or prison-like than a boys' camp, but
if it were not for them we would have no Elks Lodges, no pool
rooms, no boxing matches, no Marines. And perhaps no sports
as we know them. . . . I regard high school sports as a drug far
worse than marijuana. . . . The quest for manliness [is] essentially
right wing, puritanical, cowardly, neurotic and fueled largely by
a fear of women. It is also certainly philistine. There is no book-
hater like a Little League Coach. But indeed all the creative arts
are obnoxious to the manly idea. . . . For many years I found it
impossible to admit to myself that I wanted to be a writer. . . .
because being a writer was incompatible with being a man.
(p. 310)

Faced with this problem, American writers have tried to be unmistakably manly, Theroux says. Hemingway is an obvious example "too
tedious to go into" (p. 311). Journalism, carrying with it drunkenness
and wrestling and shooting animals, was the best version of literature or
alternative to it. It is still believed, Theroux concludes, that "to be a man
is somehow—even now in feminine-influenced America—a privilege. It
is on the contrary an unmerciful and punishing burden" (p. 311).
Because a good deal of Theroux's writing, fiction and nonfiction, is
adventure in one form or another, what we must see in his essay is a
vigorous effort to repudiate the masculinist elements in the adventure
ethos.

There is something comparable in the antimasculinism of French
poststructuralists: their program of "abolishing man." This idea had its
foreshadowings in such precursors as Sartre (in *Les mots*) and Lévi-
Strauss. "Manliness" was an important spiritual source of the energy
that sustained the workings of the civilization they hated. Lévi-Strauss
said: "I have little sympathy for the century in which we are living, for
the total ascendancy of man over nature, and of certain forms of
humanity over others. My temperament and tastes carry me towards
more modest periods."[15] This means also being carried toward more
modest genders and other human groups. In *Tristes tropiques* he seriously defended cannibalism, the horror of which had long been the
shibboleth of white culture.

But Lévi-Strauss has also written, in *Tristes tropiques,* one of the finest

15. Quoted in E. Nelson Hayes, *Claude Lévi-Strauss: The Anthropologist as Hero,* 10.

adventure books of our century. He describes anthropologists as the multilated men of their culture, in revolt against their own society, who must go back to before Socrates to seize mind before it becomes *our* mind. He begins *Tristes tropiques* by saying, "I hate travelling and explorers. Adventure has no place in the anthropologist's profession." But of course his book is an adventure tale, at least in its landscape and even in its view of man, which is strikingly like Kipling's.

A more personal but related protest against manliness is found in Michel Leiris's *L'âge d'homme* (1939). Leiris is an anthropologist, no doubt one of the multilated men Lévi-Strauss was thinking of, and a friend of Bataille, to whom his book is dedicated. He hates white male manliness: "The hostility I feel towards my own father derives in particular from his inelegant physical aspect, from his cheery vulgarity, and from his total absence of taste in all artistic matters."[16] This is clearly a dandy protest against men as husbands/fathers/masters.

Leiris attacks his culture's claims to say what is "natural" and therefore inevitable, immemorial: "It would be almost impossible for me to say at what moments, even when I was very young, I was really *natural*, at what moments I was playing a part" (p. 149). The idea of manhood was presented as "natural." Thus, again, "I always obscurely hated this elder brother, originally because of his strength, and today because of his vulgarity. To me he is the perfect example of the philistine" (p. 117). The black experience of jazz in the 1920s led the writer to ethnography and to Africa, obviously adventure-related interests. These were his means of escape from his own culture.

Nevertheless, despite their hostility to manliness, there is a tendency in the French structuralists and poststructuralists toward a kind of adventurism. One is tempted to call it metaphorical adventure, but at the level of abstraction at which their discourse operates, such a distinction may be misleading. These readers draw a great deal from Nietzsche, so much that they cannot be totally loyal sons of the Enlightenment (in the sense that Locke and Voltaire were). They are hostile to all bourgeois forms of adventure, but they lead their readers toward, for instance, violence in Bataille's sense.

Thus in *Madness and Civilization*, Foucault says his masters Nietzsche and Artaud, together with de Sade and Goya, are leading Western civilization toward unreason. They make thought no longer theoretical

16. Michel Leiris, *Manhood*, 89.

but a perilous action—an adventure, we might say. In "Hommage à Georges Bataille" he writes "A Preface to Transgression," and that concept of transgression is important to him. In *Language, Counter-Memory, Practice* he says countermemory gives us the history of our otherness, via transgression—violence, madness, sexuality, death. We might suggest that the counterhistory of which he speaks is preserved—in candied or sentimentalized form, admittedly—in the adventure tradition. It is only readers who have turned their backs on adventure who need to discover their culture's violence as a secret kept from them.

The parallel between these French thinkers and adventure is suggested by the attack on them by one of their main philosophic enemies, Jürgen Habermas, in chapters 9 and 10 of his *Der philosophische Diskurs der Moderne*. Habermas *is* a loyal son of the Enlightenment and an exponent of the civic contract, and denounces what he finds in these men's works: "The revelations of a de-centered subjectivity, emancipated from the imperatives of work and usefulness, and with this experience they step outside the modern world." Habermas represents that view of civil society which is the main support of what we call moral and political realism. He says that the poststructuralists "remove into the world of the far away and the archaic, the spontaneous powers of imagination, of self-experience, and of emotionality. To instrumental reason, they juxtapose in manichean fashion a principle only accessible through evocation, be it the will to power or sovereignty, Being or the Dionysian force of the poetical. In France this line leads from Bataille via Foucault to Derrida."[17] In other words, they lead us into the idea realm of potestas—the will to power or sovereignty.

I have said before, and shall return to the idea, that there has always been a link between the ideas of adventure, imperialism, and aestheticism. That is why it has always been the writers of adventure, in fiction or philosophy, who have seen and favored an opposition between instrumental reason and the will to power or the Dionysian force. It is a long way from Habermas's stern rebuking of the poststructuralists to Gandhi's attempt to take over the adventure dynamics of British imperialists. But both, and all the other groups mentioned between them, are attempts to resist or redirect the intoxicating powers of adventure.

17. Jürgen Habermas, quoted in D. C. Hoy, ed., *Foucault: A Critical Reader*, 9–10.

7

The Case of the Jews

The modern history of the Jews provides a case of particular interest
for our discussion. For centuries the Jews of the Diaspora had no state
identity and no military. They therefore developed no tradition of virile
adventure—or at least no tradition that was dominant in their culture—
such as the Western nations (following the English and the Dutch)
developed in their imperial careers. There are plenty of rogues in the
world of Sholem Aleichem, evaders of the civic contract, but not figures
like Raleigh or Drake. The Western cult of adventure was a way the
forces of imperialism expressed themselves—the adventure tale was the
literary form of the expression of those values, and without them it did
not develop.

The Jews were traditionally victims, a suffering people, richly gifted
but in this sense passive. In the nineteenth century, as they emerged from
the ghettos, particularly in Germany, they became heroes of high culture,
like Moses Mendelssohn and then Felix Mendelssohn. Later they became
heroes of modernism—the architects of new systems of knowledge,
speculation, and art—such as Marx and Freud, Einstein and Proust. But
in the central areas of each national culture, they still remained the
denizens of a series of enclaves, only half-engaged in the national "life"—
that is, in the adventurous expansion of national borders, nationalist

feeling, and the white empire. Theirs was a social history without adventure in any of its triumphant forms.

But all this was changed by the development of Zionism, and then the establishment of Israel after 1945 and the new nation's military conflicts with Arab neighbors. The idea of leaving Russia, Romania, or wherever and establishing agricultural colonies in Palestine was clearly adventurous. From early in the century even the most idealistic kibbutz had to establish a defense force, a Hashomer. Later that force had to engage in aggression. After the establishment of Israel came the Six Days War and the raid on Entebbe. In many ways, this was a late example (by the timetable of Western history) of the widespread development into nationhood, which always relied on the energies of adventure.

These developments affected the Jews' sense of themselves, in their own eyes and in the eyes of other people, quite independently of settlements in Palestine and patriotic wars, and we can find evidence of both before and after the change, and of the change itself, in Jewish writers. An example of the change from Soviet Russia in the 1920s is Isaac Babel's series of stories (called, collectively, *Red Cavalry*) about a Jew who (like Babel himself) is attached to a Cossack regiment in the 1917 revolution. He wants to become like the Cossacks and not like his own people, to cease to be a passive sufferer and become an adventurer. Most of the stories have to do with the Polish campaign of 1920–21, and there are three groups of characters, Poles, Cossacks, and Jews, and three ideologies, communism, Judaism, and the Cossack cult of wildness, or adventure. The last is the one Babel explores, one his protagonist strives in vain to join.

One story, "After the Battle," tells how the narrator fails as a soldier and is scolded by a Cossack friend because in the battle he failed to fire at the Poles. It ends with him "imploring fate to grant me the simplest of proficiencies—the ability to kill my fellow-men."[1] The symbols of these incompatible options, Jewish and Russian, are juxtaposed. In "The Rabbi's Son" "his things were strewn about pell-mell—mandates of the propagandist and memorandum books of the Jewish poet; the portraits of Lenin and Maimonides lay side by side: the knotted iron of Lenin's skull beside the dull silk of the portraits of Maimonides. . . . pages of the Song of Songs and those revolver cartridges" (p. 212). The old Jewish

---

1. Isaac Babel, *Red Cavalry*, 204.

values are defeated. "He—the last of the princes—died amid his poetry, phylacteries and coarse linen leggings" (p. 213).

In his essay on Babel in *Beyond Culture* (1965), the American man of letters Lionel Trilling describes how much these stories meant to him as a young Jew, and Trilling's eminence as a critic (criticism being a branch of literature we expect to be largely immune to the subversive seductions of adventure) makes what he says doubly interesting. Babel, he saw, "was captivated by the vision of two ways of being, the way of violence and the way of peace, and he was torn between them."[2] Trilling invites us to see that he too felt the same fascination and that he is reflecting on his own fate in these same terms. Traditionally, he says, "the Jew conceived his own ideal character to consist in his being intellectual, pacific, humane. The Cossack was physical, violent, without mind or manners . . . animal violence, [of] aimless destructiveness . . . the enemy of . . . all men who thought of freedom" (p. 110).

We might recall that, in *Ulysses,* James Joyce conceives of the Jewish-Irish contrast in similar terms, contrasting the humane, nonviolent Bloom with the Irish nationalist, "the Citizen." However, it is easiest to read Joyce's intention as a simple, nondialectical endorsement of Bloom and a condemnation of violence. While Trilling's terms for the Cossacks are not so simply condemnatory, neither Babel nor his commentator intends them thus. The Cossack, Trilling says, stands for something we have unhappily surrendered: "the truth of the body, the truth of full sexuality, the truth of open aggressiveness" (p. 111). We might, for our purposes here, call those the adventurer's truths. Only in the liminal areas on society's frontiers can one live by those truths.

Talking about Babel as a person as well as a writer, Trilling says he had an intellectual's face, the face every Jew used to aspire to have or hoped his sons would have. (It will be obvious that Trilling and Babel use "Jew" to mean one cultural tradition among many that could be called Jewish—let us calls theirs the rabbinic tradition—but that does not invalidate what they say.) Babel wanted, ambivalently, something different, something opposite. He spoke with bitterness of the severe disciplines of Jewish education—for instance, of the Torah. The Torah was a prison shutting [Babel] off from all desirable life.[3]

Most striking of all is Trilling's quoting from a Babel story in which

2. Lionel Trilling, *Beyond Culture,* 107.
3. Ibid., 114.

the narrator saw his father kneeling in humiliation, his manhood lost, before a Cossack captain who wore lemon-colored chamois gloves and "looked ahead with the gaze of one who rides through a mountain pass" (p. 112). The manhood the narrator wants to inherit is in the keeping of his racial enemy. The narrator is a Jew like his father, with spectacles on his nose and autumn in his heart. He does not find the roles of manliness easy; he cannot even simply aspire to them—but even less can he renounce them. He loves the man who teaches him to swim, "with the love that only a boy suffering from hysteria and headaches can feel for a real man" (p. 115).

American goy literature of the nineteenth century was full of treatments of this theme—the boy's aspiration to a manhood that only the adventure *rite de passage* can win him. Two classic cases are Dana's *Two Years before the Mast* and Parkman's *Oregon Trail*. (In both cases the writer's literal father was a man of letters, from whom the son turned away toward an opposite image of masculinity.) In the twentieth century, we see, the theme returned enriched from Russia and the ghetto.

Trilling points out the likeness between Babel and Crane and Hemingway: though what is required of the Americans is ostensibly courage, for the Russian it is openly the willingness to kill. (But that was a general twentieth-century change. As we have seen, Hemingway had made that change too, and Blaise Cendrars's essay about World War I was called *J'ai tué*.) Babel was recognizably a member of the modernist movement; there is, for instance, a grotesquerie and a blatant sexual excitement to his cruelty and violence. In "My First Goose" (the Jew wins his place among the Cossacks by killing—a goose) the long legs of his adored leader, Savitsky, are said to be like girls, sheathed to the necks in his riding boots.[4]

The Jew has to change his nature and cease to be intellectual. "Violence," says Trilling, "is of course the contradiction of the intellectual's characteristic enterprise of rationality" (p. 120). But intellectuals can be seen as men chained to the wall of the cave, like Plato's cave, turned away from its mouth, and when they hear reality outside they must struggle, *with violence*, to turn and look. To Babel, as a Jew, that news came late, in the form of the violence of the Russian Revolution.

The Gentleman and the Jew by Maurice Samuel, (1950), a volume of autobiography and political reflection, shows us some of the same

4. Ibid., 119.

themes of Jewish consciousness from a different angle. Samuel was brought to England from Romania in about 1900 at the age of six (the imperial England of Rhodes and Chamberlain) and attended a state school in Manchester. In school, and even more in the English boys' magazines he read, he met a culture that seemed to him the opposite of his parents'. The English ideology of playful adventure and potestas, of mutual challenge and fair play in lighthearted conflict, seemed so remote from Jewish suffering and resignation that he assumed Anglican church services taught the very reverse of synagogue religion. When he attended a church service, he was amazed to find that the liturgy and sermon proclaimed the same moral message as the synagogue, one that English culture denied in practice. But writing as he did in 1950, Samuel sees Jews in Israel developing an aggressive "English" ideology for themselves.

Something comparable seems to have been true of the development of Isaac Deutscher, who grew up as a Hassidic child prodigy in Chrzanow, Poland, immersed by his family in the Talmud and the Torah. His parents were Orthodox, though his father was torn between Judaism and German literature. Isaac became a rabbi at the age of thirteen but found all that he was taught to be pseudo-knowledge. The only thing he learned at "cheder" that seemed of any real value to him was the adventure of the Flight of the Jews from Egypt, because one teacher was able to recreate this piece of history as an adventure story. Deutscher was sent to a Polish gymnasium, where the ethos was highly patriotic and religious, Polish and Catholic, romantic and adventurous. His father set him to study his own literary heroes, Goethe, Lessing, Spinoza, Heine, figures of German intellect, but Isaac preferred Mickiewicz and Slowacki, the romantic Polish patriots, figures of adventure.

Both men turned away from traditional Judaism. Samuel's best-known book was *The World of Sholem Aleichem,* and Deutscher also chose "the fantasy of the Yiddish folklore [and Jewish humor] as opposed to the rigidity of the orthodox religion."[5] Deutscher turned for a time to communism, a move Samuel did not make. But the struggle between adventurous and nonadventurous morality is the same in both, and Deutscher, like Samuel, came to dislike the nationalist mysticism that Israel as a nation-state took over from the Western nations.

Samuel introduces his book by saying he believes "an understanding

5. Isaac Deutscher, *The Non-Jewish Jew,* 9.

of the Jewish episode in civilization is the key to the Western world's intellectual and spiritual difficulties."[6] The story begins for him with his family and with the community of Jews to which they belonged in Manchester, all feeling intense admiration, respect, gratitude, and affection for England (p. 10). They preferred it to all other Western countries, because there the fierce energies of capitalism and industrialism and imperialism were tamed and restrained. The Jews admired England's material achievements, such as cars and trams and electricity, but also "the spiritual achievements of this extraordinary English race, whose name had been a portent and a beacon even in the wilds of Rumania" (p. 11). But what his elders admired or named as the primary English moral qualities were politeness, order, and quiet, while the boy Samuel and his coevals saw those as secondary. The boys admired instead the opposite aggressive English qualities: pluck, gallantry, and spontaneous energy. These latter were of course the strengths of the briar, onto which the civilized rose was grafted and without which the latter would not bloom.

Thus, Samuel's parents' values were pacific: "Jews did not come to blows, in public or in private" (p. 12). They acknowledged the difference between themselves and the English, and they sent their sons to the English school in order to learn Englishness, but they also sent them to "cheder" (an elementary Jewish school) for two to three hours, six evenings a week, to preserve their Jewishness. The two educations implied opposite values.

For a long time Maurice Samuel assumed that Jews *had* to be poor, as a part of their religion. He was sure, for instance, that the well-to-do Anglicized Jews long settled in Manchester must be less Jewish than his parents (p. 17). But he himself, if still Jewish by his poverty, was in another way Anglicized, made English by his adventurousness. So his elders' homage to England, sincere though it was, seemed to him self-deceiving, and it was certainly pale beside *his* blazing loyalty (p. 19). He and his old friends were quickly integrated into English culture by their attendance at school, and much more by what he calls the Union Jack boys' magazine literature they read, which included *Magnet* and *Gem*, for Samuel is discussing exactly what George Orwell discussed in his famous essay "Boys' Weeklies."

This literature was, both authors say, a powerful influence in the

6. Maurice Samuel, *The Gentleman and the Jew*, 4.

maintaining of England's moral tradition, one that deserves much more serious study than it has received. Lord Northcliffe and the other proprietors of those magazines had a mission. The values inculcated in those stories were profoundly English: fair play, pluck, cheerfulness, loyalty. To quote Samuel, "They were Kipling brought down to semi-slum levels, as Kipling was Shakespeare's *Henry V* brought down to Victorian levels" (p. 21). And the gulf between the Jewish parents and their magazine-reading sons widened as the latter entered ever deeper into the fake "public school" traditions of Greyfriars and St. Jim's (the fictional schools in which those boys' stories were set). One might say that the parents had chosen Victorian-Liberal England to move to, but the boy grew up in jingo-imperialist England, where Kipling had replaced Gladstone.

The parents could never understand that "playing the game" was a morality—*the* English morality (p. 24). This was partly because they did not understand games. Samuel has a long section on the difference between the Jewish attitude to games—so unenthusiastic—and the Greek or Roman or Anglo-Saxon attitude. By the same token, it was also because of the Jews' slighter esteem for youth and for adventure. "They had a more sombre attitude towards youth than did their Christian neighbours" (p. 24). They could not believe, as the English believed, the noisy exuberance of adolescents to be a moral value, something fit to be compared with Mosiac law. The same was true of sports. Samuel describes how his father puzzled over the long articles the English newspapers ran on the famous cricketers of the day, such as W. G. Grace.

From age six to age thirteen the young Maurice Samuel spent his days in school and his evenings in the "cheder," welcoming the first education, resisting the second. Not until he reached twenty, as a student at Manchester University, did he take Jewish culture seriously. The best part of the "cheder" was the Saturday study of the "Ethics of the Fathers," from the Mishnah, where he was taught to love his neighbor as himself, and such propositions as "By three things the world is sustained: by truth, by judgment, and by peace" (p. 28).

The "Ethics of the Fathers" represents an aspect of Jewish culture that Trilling also discusses, calling it pedagogical and antiheroic, in his essay "Wordsworth Among the Rabbis." For him the contrary force (comparable to the English boys' stories) was perhaps embodied in *Huckleberry Finn*. At least that is hinted in his novel *The Middle of the Journey,* where the Trilling representative must defend himself against a delayed-adolescent rogue-figure called Duck Caldwell. Duck seems to be an allusion to "Huck," a hint to us to see the story's conflict as being between Trilling and American populism. Duck's equivalent in the world of English boys' stories might be Tom Merry or Kipling's Stalky. But in *Stalky and Co.* the writer as boy (Kipling portrays himself in the story) morally succumbs to the rogue, becomes his follower, while in Trilling's novel he fights against Duck/Huck and defeats him. The Jewish rabbinical heritage no doubt counted for something in this difference.

According to Samuel, the basis for this sad, wise pacifism is the humble doctrine of humanity taught by Jewish religion: "Thou comest from a stinking drop, thou goest to a place of dust, worms, and maggots" (p. 28). This is the negation of the pride of life implicit in adventure. It is, in fact, negativism itself.

All this Samuel found to be profoundly un-English. "Where, in the cheder code, was the cheerfulness, gaiety, and magnanimity of life at St. Jim's? Where was the gallantry and where were the affirmations? . . . There was no hurraying in the Mishnah, no feeling of loyalty, attachment, camaraderie" (p. 29). In short, there was no atmosphere of adventure. Samuel went on: "English history was adorned with poems like 'The Charge of the Light Brigade' and 'The Revenge, a Ballad of the Fleet.' There was nothing like this in the bits of Jewish history and legend that we got on Saturdays. . . . Jewish wars were gloomy things; Jewish heroes, though impressive in their way, were without form and style; Jewish songs of triumph were too furiously triumphant. Where in Jewish history was a Hereward the Wake or a Black Prince?" (p. 30). These were the heroes constructed by the adventure writers for the boys of England. The warrior-caste qualities of fire and form, which even the women novelists of England gave to their heroes, seemed to be non-Jewish. (The Jewish Daniel Deronda in George Eliot's novel is not a successful hero, compared with Ladislaw or Lydgate.)

Samuel's parents' religion treated the prohibition against killing as an absolute. "How could one convey to them [his elders] the spirit in which an Englishman did his killing? It was almost not killing. . . . Where, within ["The Ethics of the Fathers"] could you find room for the dashing buccaneer type, who could make his prisoners walk the plank," and yet remain a gentleman? (p. 31). For the English, the great prohibitions were morally negotiable and the social contract had many exemptions.

Thus, Samuel was for a long time "deeply convinced that in the churches of the Christians there were wonderful prayers and rituals which expounded and expressed the code of St. Jim's" and celebrated an "apotheosized Tom Merry" (p. 31). (Tom Merry and Bob Cherry were two heroes of the boys' magazine stories.) At the age of twelve he sneaked into a church service—he had seen the curate of that parish playing cricket, so he knew he must be a Tom Merry type. There he was utterly confounded by the sermon he heard, which "had nothing what-soever to do, in spirit or in substance, with that gay, magnanimous, adventurous and gamesome world which I had come to hear glorified." In fact, the sermon "rehearsed what I had been learning in cheder" (p. 35). It taught that you did not respond laughingly with a straight left when someone hit you, that you meekly turned the other cheek.

By this reminiscent analysis, Samuel is preparing us to see that England, as a sovereign state and empire, lived by values opposite those it officially professed, and that Israel too, in 1950, as a newly sovereign state, was beginning to show the same split between its moral tradition and its national future. Samuel had spent more than twenty years writing and speaking for the Zionist cause. He lived in Palestine from 1929 to 1939 and was a friend of Chaim Weizmann, but he is now full of doubts.

He follows the analysis of English popular culture with what amounts to literary criticism and literary history. Tennyson and Kipling "took him by storm" in his thirteenth year and stayed with him until he was sixteen or seventeen. Of the two, Kipling affected him more deeply. A little later, Shakespeare's royal heroes, a "supreme formulation of Eng-land's Ideal Man," came into his life (p. 39). But now, in 1950, Samuel sees the Elizabethan Henry V as a grown-up Tom Merry: the fighting gentleman, the courtly and winning adventurer, the laughing, demo-cratic, and fearless prince (p. 40). Henry's motto is "But if it be a sin to covet honour, I am the most offending soul alive." The sympathetic reader or audience rushes to reassure the speaker that this is no offense, Samuel says, but *he* now knows that love of honor *is* a sin, and the father of other sins, "the deep wound in our natures out of which have flowed the blood and decency of countless generations" (p. 43). He extends this diagnosis of the deleterious effects of "honour" to cover more of Europe by going back to Castiglione and Machiavelli and the Italian Renais-sance, and he brings it up to the present by discussing Olivier's film *Henry V*. His argument reaches its climax with "The gentleman, the lover of honor, is essentially a killer!" (p. 45).

Thus, for Samuel, the noncombative, noncompetitive Jewish tradition developed in the enclave is divided by a tremendous gulf from the morality of the leading states of the Western world (p. 96). Up to "now," Judaism had rejected the competitive or power principle, as embodied in the nation and in the individual (p. 317). Samuel implicitly defines this will to power as belonging to the warrior caste; he gives examples from the European aristocracy and from the will to slavery in the southern states of America (p. 323). The opposite, the biblical tradition of prophecy—the moral denunciation of kings in their pride—had constituted the peculiarly or uniquely Jewish identity. The great question for Jews in our time is: Will they hold to that identity? And if not, won't Israel become a nation like any other, while in a parallel development the Jews of the Diaspora assimilate to England, France, and America?

Like Samuel, the early settlers of the kibbutzim believed in that exceptional identity and national destiny. And Martin Buber gave a philosophical voice to that hope, which was still to be heard as Samuel was writing. Buber and his friends wanted a bi-national state in Palestine, and he took Gandhi as one of his heroes. But they were a minority, and Israel became a militarily powerful state.

By the time another quarter-century had passed, Samuel's first question, we may say, had also been answered in the negative. In 1987 we had a novel, Philip Roth's *Counterlife*, which deals in part with the same questions of Israel and the Jewish identity. In the second part, "Judea," Nathan, an American writer who represents Roth, goes to visit his brother Henry, who has decided to make his life in Israel. The latter puts pressure on the writer to do the same himself, to find his true self as a Jew, but he refuses, saying he was born an American: "My sacred text wasn't the Bible but novels translated from Russian, German, and French. . . . Not the semantic range of classical Hebrew but the jumpy beat of American English was what excited me."[7] To use Samuel's terms, Nathan chooses to assimilate while his brother chooses to help make Israel a fighting nation. The third option, Buber's and Samuel's idea, has faded from view.

The choice is between the life of adventurous, nationalist action in Israel (seen by Henry as patriotism, not violence) and unadventurous, humane writing in America. (The central character writes "the books Jews love to hate"—like those Roth himself writes.) Babel's and Trilling's motifs sound again. Their father, Nathan admits, would have loved to

7. Philip Roth, *The Counterlife*, 53.

see that "Jewish helplessness in the face of violence is a thing of the
past. . . . The American Jews get a big thrill from the guns [in Israel].
They see Jews walking around with guns and they think they're in
Paradise" (p. 75). Brother Henry has joined a settlement, Ago, where
everyone is puritanically patriotic. His friends see the assimilated American Jews, who, like Nathan, chose the easy option and "live the life of
Riley" (including a widely extended erotic freedom) as the great betray-
ers, especially the writers. Why, asks Henry, is Norman Mailer so
interested in murder, criminals, and killing and yet does not go to Israel?
(p. 126). But the fact that the killing in Israel, like the sex, is politically
innocent—in effect nonviolent—which makes it so attractive to Henry,
makes it unattractive (uninteresting, inauthentic) to Mailer and Roth.

Henry has fallen in love with Israel just because it is ugly, is not an
aesthetic phenomenon but a political one. All the superficial charm has
been stripped away from life; it is real, which is better than beautiful.
He looks around him and sees "not a colour, a flower, a leaf . . . nothing
bright or attractive anywhere, nothing trying to please you in any way.
Everything superficial has been cleared away . . . big ugly underwear
having nothing to do with sex, underwear from a hundred years ago. . . .
I looked for a pretty woman and I couldn't find *one*" (pp. 60–61).

That is Henry's paradoxically positive assertion. Negatively, his main
charge is that the only world that exists for his brother is the world of
psychology, of sex and personal relations (p. 105). Nathan replies that
their life began in that world, in the parental kitchen. Henry replies
indignantly, " 'What matters is not Momma and Poppa and the kitchen
table, it isn't *any* of the crap you write about—it's who runs Judea,' "
or, again, " 'Here Judea counts—not *me*' " (p. 139). He accuses his
brother of retreating—from a crucial moral challenge. But Nathan says
the only real retreat is turning back, away from that which you know,
that which is your reality. In other words, retreat is choosing Henry's
form of adventurous action. Thus, we see again the conflict between
adventure (linked to nationalism and Puritan virtue) and literature
(linked to domestic life and complex consciousness).

Even more directly than Roth, Norman Mailer too has tackled the
themes of violence and its attraction for the modern Jewish writer. He
for a long time planned a series of novels built around a character called
Sergius O'Shaughnessy, a bullfighting Hemingway-style adventurer who
is shown, in a story in *Advertisements for Myself,* as originating as a
fantasy in the mind of a mild, middle-age, middle-class Jew. Mailer's

own development as artist and citizen follows that pattern. In his public persona and in reflections on that persona and politics, such as *Armies of the Night,* Mailer has insisted on acting the adventurer, in an O'Shaughnessy style.

However, *Why Are We in Vietnam?* (1967) is somewhat *less* direct than *Counterlife* in the way it dramatizes the dilemma of American Jewish urban writers. Mailer here keeps silent about his Jewish identity and makes central strategic use of the literary adventure tradition that (associated with the WASP ruling caste and the preurban landscape as it was) had before seemed so alien to the Jews. His book makes a parodic yet affirmative response to the challenge of that kind of Americanism. One finds something like Mailer's use of adventure in Saul Bellow's *Henderson the Rain King* and in Bernard Malamud's *New Life,* but Mailer's treatment is both the most parodic and the most committed to its own version of the same values.

It was also Mailer's generation of writers who introduced the Jew into war novels and into peacetime-army novels like James Jones's *From Here to Eternity.* Before 1945, Jews stood opposite the American imagination, of adventure and armies, but in many novels about World War II a Jewish soldier was a central figure, and a great many of those novels were written by Jewish writers, such as Mailer himself, Herman Wouk, and Irwin Shaw. According to Alfred Kazin, 1945 was the pivotal year for Jewish-American writers. They began to write about adventures and about themselves as adventure heroes, although with a note of irony or self-parody that seemed especially Jewish.

Like other adventure writers, Mailer has always taken a political interest in *Machtpolitik* and a sexual interest in sexism. His answer to the feminists' charges against him was entitled *The Prisoner of Sex,* and the words sum up or suggest all one might say about him, with a touch of the grotesque as well as its confessional truth. (One might compare him in this way with Kipling as well as with Hemingway.) Mailer can see beyond the obvious limits of his male persona, but he "cannot" step beyond them. It is his fate (his chosen but immutable fate) to stay within them, to describe the prison yard rather than any landscape beyond. He is the prisoner of adventure too, and both those ideas are subdivisions of a larger one: the prisoner of manliness. It is a value that he, as American but also as Jew, cannot jeopardize.

It is worth noting, also, that when the film *Gandhi* came out and controversy surrounded Gandhi's name it was the Jewish journal *Com-*

mentary that launched the most bitter attack on the apostle of nonviolence. Thus, the Jewish writers, challenged by the contemporary history of their people, have been thinking about the questions of violence and adventure in quite interesting ways.

8

The Case of the Scots

The case of the Scots is quite different from that of the Jews, partly because adventure was as present in Scottish history, for hundreds of years, as it was absent from Jewish history, and partly because the function of adventure tales within an imperial literature, and the way this function parallels that of adventure deeds within an empire, is evident in the case of the Scots. The latter had waged "adventurous" wars (rebellions, skirmishes, guerrilla tactics) against England, their richer, stronger neighbor, for a long time, and then, after 1707 Scotland was absorbed first into Great Britain and then into Greater Britain, and fought for it. Then in the nineteenth century, when England needed adventure literature, Scotland supplied it. Scott, Ballantyne, Stevenson, Buchan—these are the great names of a hundred years of adventure writing in English, and they are all Scottish.

The history of Scotland simply *was* more tragic than that of England (and a lot of what we call "adventure" is really tragedy with a high-spirited name), so it is not surprising that Scotland developed a richer treasury of legends than England. However, one can find all the elements of tragedy and legend in Irish and Welsh history, too. Why then was it Scotland which produced the adventure literature? Something must be allowed for the individuality of that brilliant talent Walter Scott, but, that aside, the explanation is surely the way that Scotland—and not Ireland and Wales—became a full partner with England in the empire. The Scots transformed their bitter memories of oppression by their richer partner into romantic legends involving both.

John Buchan's own autobiography and that of his sister tell us how Scotland's adventurous history appeared to young Scots at the end of the nineteenth century. A book of Scottish history that Anna Buchan alludes to more than once as embodying that history is Jean Lang's *Land of Romance*. The first five chapters deal with the remote past of Scotland (the Romans, King Arthur, the saints, the wizards, and the monks), which appears more as myth than as legend and scarcely at all as history. But with chapter 6, "The War of Independence," fought by Scotland against England, the author begins to tell a history that was quite meaningful to the Buchans as they grew up, however fanciful and romantic the writers' way of naming it.

Let's look at a few of the events of that history. Edward I of England installed a puppet king in Scotland in 1292, and when Scotland rebelled he punished the Scots with a massacre at Berwick in 1296. The Scots then ravaged Tyneland until Edward defeated them in a pitched battle at Dunbar, killing more than ten thousand men and pursuing the rest to the Forest of Ettrick. (These places and the legends attached to them were all familiar to the Buchans from their earliest days.) Edward drew up a pledge of allegiance to himself on the Ragman Roll and persuaded two thousand Scottish landowners to sign it. One of these was Robert the Bruce, then still a loyal Anglo-Norman noble who fought for and with Edward. But Scottish rebels soon gathered again around William Wallace, who became an outlaw in Ettrick Forest for killing an English sheriff. In 1297 Wallace besieged Dundee, defeated an English army, and invaded England. Defeated at Falkirk, Wallace went into hiding, but was betrayed and executed in 1305, still only thirty-five years old, and his head was stuck on a spike on London Bridge. The following year the Bruce denounced English rule and raised the rebel standard in Scotland with only forty followers at first and later with the comradeship of the Black Douglas. At Bannockburn, in 1314, they defeated Edward and chased him as far as Berwick.

The Buchan children heard that tragic but adventurous history as stories, read it in books, recited it as verse, and acted it out in plays and outdoor games, *being* Wallace and Bruce. Their imaginative life was all adventure. And the succession of battles, charges, and pursuits was

interspersed with splendid and pathetic personal gestures, like Wallace
kissing the dead face of Sir John Graham and calling him "My best
brother" before turning to flee for his life at Falkirk, or Douglas sailing
for the Holy Land after the Bruce died in 1330, carrying his dead king's
heart in a casket around his neck. These legends too Scots children acted
out.

The effect of these stories on Scots readers was to enhance their pride
in being Scots, of course, and even to enhance their sense of being
different from the English. But it also enhanced their pride in being
British, and co-rulers of the British Empire. The legends were "of the
past." Their bearing on the present was to ennoble the bonds that *now*
hold the English and the Scots together.

Anna Buchan tells how, when she was a young girl, the family received
a visit from an English cousin. Because of the Scottish history the
children had learned, "We stood and glowered, [we were] laying at this
innocent's door all the ill-done deeds of her country—the head of
Wallace on a spike, the ring of dead nobles round their king at Flodden,
not to speak of the cruel, lonely death of the loveliest queen in history."[1]
When their father understood why they were behaving like that, he
explained to them: "England and Scotland are one, have been for
hundreds of years. Our interests are the same; we work together, play
together, and, if need be, fight together" (p. 15). For Anna Buchan this
"goes without saying" for adults, but it is a significant turn of thought.

It was Scotland's fate for a thousand years to be overshadowed and
recurrently conquered by England. Their neighbors knew only snatches
of that tragic history, in lurid stories like that of Macbeth. Malcolm slew
the historical Macbeth in 1057, and the dynasty he founded (the House
of Canmore) forged a feudal state out of a Celtic kingdom. But this
could not compare with its southern neighbor in military might. Malcolm as king tried to imitate his Norman English enemies, with their
mounted knights, their stone castles, and their cannon, the heavy military
technology of the time. But his followers could not emulate that style in
war. Knights were too expensive for Scotland's village economy to
maintain; a knight needed chainmail armor to wear and huge chargers
to ride, and lived off, consumed, the work of a number of peasants.
Malcolm's subjects, in fact, still lived by barter and booty and dwelled
in branch-thatched, turf-walled hovels protected by palisades. The clans-

---

1. Anna Buchan, *Unforgettable,Unforgotten*, 14.

men warriors wore no armor; the claymore they wielded was a two-handed weapon, so they had to do without even the protection of a shield.

Scotland thus became, and long remained, at home largely a country of impoverished and backward peasants and of emigrants—adventurers—abroad. Rotterdam had a Scots colony one thousand strong in the Middle Ages, but such emigration did not build up a national expansion; Scots abroad served other foreign masters. Scotland had no equivalent for the frontier America later had. Scots soldiers served French kings in the Middle Ages, and later Louis XIV and Napoleon, but they also went farther abroad. By 1600 Scots traders were familiar with the Baltic, and Scots regiments became part of the Dutch army. James I planted Scots colonies in Ireland and in 1621 encouraged emigration to North America.

After 1688, Catholic Scots (and Irish) served in the French, Prussian, Spanish, and Russian armies. They were much prized as soldiers, as adventurers usually are. More "civilized" countries (and social classes) always rely on the less privileged to supply the fighting men they need, their own way of life tending to discourage the military virtues. The Highlands, and Highlanders, were images of fierce romance, for instance, to eighteenth-century Englishmen, such as Defoe.

This emigration was not all military in character. In later centuries, Scotland sent out missionaries and engineers to the British Empire as much as soldiers, and even the military adventurers of Scotland were likely to be pious. Thus, the religious history of Scotland is also important in understanding Scottish adventure. The Presbyterianism that established itself there after the Reformation contained some strains of moral extremism that allied themselves with the political rebelliousness of a much-conquered country. In this case (as also with the Israelis, in Roth's account), religious piety and devotion to work did *not* express themselves in social meekness (the bloodthirsty man of religion is a familiar paradox).

The two kinds of rebelliousness expressed themselves variously, in civil conflict and in emigration and empire adventures. In terms of storytelling, the two sides each had their own stories. Andrew Bullock and James Drummond point out that the country's national mythology has seven features, of which four owe their great power to the Presbyterian religion—John Knox and the Covenanters, and so on—and three that belong to a romantic counterlegend: Mary Queen of Scots, Bonnie

Prince Charlie, and Robert Burns.[2] These began in conflict with each other, but they gradually grew to be intertwined, as the Scottish heritage.

That intertwining was the work of Walter Scott more than any other individual. Edwin Muir, in his influential *Scott and Scotland* (1936), sees all Scottish culture and literature, as well as its political and military history, as determined by Scott's retelling of adventure tales of the Border Country between England and Scotland, a part of the country that for centuries was rarely quiet and ordered, and most often in a state of war. From Muir's point of view, this linking of Scotland to adventure was unfortunate. The Border Country was certainly the Scotland about which Scott, and later Stevenson and Buchan, wrote.

This history helped generate a rich store of legend and romance in Scotland, coloring Scottish history. Such legends had a stronger charge of pathos and splendor than their equivalent in England, no doubt because in prosperous England there were more stories of prudence rewarded. Such adventure tales served both the opposed sides in Scottish politics. Both kinds gave Scotsmen a sense of identity.

A somewhat opposite phenomenon—looking toward the future instead of the past—was economic development, with its promises of progress, civilization, peace. The secrets of development were something England promised to teach Scotland. In 1707, the year of the union with England, Scotland probably counted only a million inhabitants; England had five million, and a much higher standard of living. The promise was to be kept, as much as such promises ever are.

In the immediate future, however, the pressures for Scots to emigrate—to engage in adventure—were strong. "Scotland in 1707 was what would be described today as an underdeveloped country. Its economy rested on a stagnant agrarian base, initiative was fettered by prescriptive rights and outworn traditions, its trade was declining as mercantilism restricted its old European markets, and its few industries—principally coal, linen, and wool—were rudimentary, undercapitalized, and backward."[3] Even the Union, which was to be Scotland's economic salvation, had initial effects that depressed certain Scottish trades—the woolen cloth industry died, for instance. Agricultural reform came slowly, especially in the Highlands. Thus, there were still strong pressures to emigrate to the lands of imperial adventure. And in Scotland itself the clansmen of the

2. Andrew L. Bulloch and James Drummond, *The Church in Victorian Scotland*, 8.

3. William Ferguson, "That Part of the United Kingdom Known as Scotland," in M. Stokstad, H. L. Snyder, H. Orel, eds., *The Scottish World*, 149.

Highlands were still Jacobite, loyal to the Stuart kings and hostile to much of modern civilization.

But the linen trade developed, especially in the West with the American colonies, and by 1771 Glasgow was exporting two million yards a year. The Scots were heading toward prosperity. The Presbyterians, especially those who were by then prospering in trade under English auspices, bitterly opposed the eighteenth-century Jacobite risings, which they saw as foolish and reckless adventures, dangerous in every sense. The two parties were seen, and to some degree saw themselves, as espousing (to use anachronistic terms) the Reality Principle in the one case and the Pleasure Principle in the other. Prince Charles Edward Stuart was a hero of romance and was even referred to as "The Adventurer." The Low-landers preferred the stability and prosperity of British rule. Adventure was a historical option and a topic of dispute.

Intellectually, Scotland was split between those who accepted Enlight-enment secularism or moderatism in religion (carrying its gifts of peace and prosperity) and those who distrusted that option. The Union, which created the United Kingdom and took the first step toward building the English Empire, was (in Scotland) the work of the religious Moderates. That is one reason why part of Scotland—a small and separate part—developed intellectually to such a great degree, surpassing even England and doing as much as any country to develop the new ideas in social and civic theory. An example is Adam Ferguson's *History of Civil Society* (1767), a book that propounded the ideology of peace and prosperity, the escape from civil violence and adventure. This ideology was the equivalent of moderatism in religion, a justification of the new society.

But most of Scotland was very different. Hume and his friends were amazed at their group's success as exemplars of European civility when their country had so recently been redeemed from barbarity,[4] and T. C. Smout says that by 1775 all Scots knew they were advancing toward riches.[5] "During the prolonged period of Anglo-Scots imperialist expan-sion, the Scottish ruling order found that it had given up statehood for a hugely profitable junior partnership in the New Rome" (p. 129).

The governing or managing of Scotland that followed the Union, usually described as corrupt but efficient, was henceforth done for England's benefit by a "Lord Advocate." This felt like a betrayal of the

4. Tom Nairn, *The Break-Up of Britain,* 139.
5. T. C. Smout, *The History of the Scottish People,* 113.

romantic past, but Scott endorsed that partnership in the New Rome and draped it in so much tartan—in the form of his adventure tales—that it seemed no treachery to the past.

Thus, gradually, the love of romance and adventure became a partner to the seemingly opposite progressivism. Moreover, this adventurism was not just a nostalgia for the past. Paradoxically, this partnership in empire, while allied to Enlightenment values, again assigned adventure to the Scots. The Enlightenment was the ideology of an expanding society, moving from Europe out to exploit the other continents. Empires grow by the exploits and energies of adventurers, and the Scots acted as if they were the younger sons of the United Kingdom family, the ones who had to go out and make their own fortunes abroad, while the English were the older sons, who inherited and lived on the family estates.

By 1799 it was clear to ambitious Scots that for them the road to empire lay through making the English Empire British.[6] The East India Company and the Hudson's Bay Company both had especially close relations with Scotland and regularly recruited Scotsmen. This was another organized adventure, rough enough but less brutal at least than transportation. In 1707 the Scots had been given freedom of trade and shipping throughout the empire. And in their different ways, India and Canada were lands of romance, where Scots adventurers made their fortunes.

Despite the Romantic surface of his work, Scott was essentially a son of the Enlightenment (a period usually reckoned to run from the 1730s to 1820, in Scotland). He combined both sides of the Scottish dialectic. Ian Finley spoke in 1957 of the "bogus baronialism which began with Abbotsford."[7] But Marilyn Stokstad says that, before Scott, the Adams brothers had built castles in Scotland that stood in the same relationship to the Middle Ages as Scott's poems did.[8] In their buildings as in his novels, a surface medievalism lay over a classical core.

Scott was a genius of cultural politics who put the Scottish legends into a "modern" literary form and enabled them to do for England-and-Scotland (and many other countries) what they had done for the Scots. They reconciled bitterly opposed classes, and the contrary claims of a

---

6. George Shepperson, "The Scot Around the World," in Stokstad et al., *The Scottish World*, 236.

7. Quoted in Harold Orel, "Scottish Stereotypes," in ibid., 13.

8. Marilyn Stokstad, "Art During the Enlightenment," in ibid., 221.

rational future and a romantic past, by dramatizing the virtues and problems of the defeated and by responding to all of them imaginatively. He made Scotland a reservoir of adventure and romance images for English as well as Scots readers.

But his success occurred in the realm of art. In economic terms, the nineteenth century brought in still more poverty and consequently more migration. The Highlanders emigrated massively, especially after the potato famine of 1846–47. The glens were said to empty themselves into Canada and Australasia. (Already in 1776 one-seventh of the white population of America had been of Scots blood, and one-third of Pennsylvanians.) Under these circumstances, the myth of adventure reimposed itself on Scottish culture as a necessary imaginative pabulum. In the books it was historical adventure in Scotland that was exciting; in nineteenth-century fact, in the lives of the readers, it was adventure abroad.

Between 1861 and 1939 the net out-migration was 1,775,000, or 54 percent of the natural increase. Many emigrants returned, but between 1900 and 1971 two million people left Scotland.[9] George Shepperson says it was not a diaspora so much as a *Völkerwanderung*,[10] and John Hermes McCullough says the history of the Scotts is "largely a history of Scotsmen who have emigrated from the land of their birth."[11] There is an epic dimension, which like all epics contains its share of tragedy, to the dispersal of Scots abroad. That was reflected in the adventure writers' work, for which the migrants were an important audience, though also the entire middle-class reading public, in England as well as Scotland.

Indeed, already from 1760, English potters had produced teapots with Highlanders depicted on them.[12] Kilts and tartans and Scottish scenery became fashionable. Defeated enemies are a common source of sentiment and decoration, and humor, for an empire; *Punch* was full of Scots jokes—two of the twenty-five volumes in its Library of Humour were full of Scots material. Scott's achievement was to give dignity to this artistic colonialism.

What was bought with Scotland's suffering and with this cultural compromise was the Empire, including its first and essential component, the United Kingdom. Tom Nairn says, "England's pattern of foreign

9. Orel, "Scottish Stereotypes," 20.
10. Shepperson, "The Scot Around the World," 230.
11. Quoted in ibid., 230.
12. Orel, "Scottish Stereotypes," 15.

exploitation and dependency has lasted from the 16th century to the present, uninterruptedly."[13] That is why the adventure tale has been an English (and then Anglo-American) literary phenomenon.

As told by Scott, but also by Stevenson and Buchan, that form breathed a nationalist ideology, but in Scotland itself that nationalism had an anomalous timetable of development. The period 1800–1920 was when nationalism developed in Europe as a whole, and it is ironic that a powerful literary stimulus to that development was the fiction of the Scots but that nothing parallel happened in Scotland.[14] Scott saw and presented Scotland's nationalism as entirely a thing of the past.[15] As John and Anna Buchan showed us, in their own present time at the end of the nineteenth century England was no longer the enemy or rival, but the protector and sponsor. Scottish and anti-English nationalism developed later—together with the anticolonialism and nationalism of the Third World—and in *opposition* to Scott.

Nairn sees a popular militarism as historically a part of Scottish culture; it is a militarism more strident than anything found in comparable levels of culture in England.[16] He rejects the romantic populist tendency to treat Scotland as a peaceful peasant people on whom the English forced war. On the other hand, he does not ascribe much power or meaning to the images of Scottish adventurism devised by Scott, Stevenson, and Buchan. Adventure literature is difficult for intellectuals to take seriously, as we know.

But while agreeing with most of what Nairn says, it is surely possible to believe that a large part of Scottish history—as distinct from the industrial history and all that other part the Kailyard school of literature represents—*was* a history of adventure, and that the part that took place abroad was a continuation in spirit of the Borderland struggles Scott described.

That, at least, is the way Robert Louis Stevenson saw Scottish culture in his essay "The Foreigner at Home": "A Scottish child hears much of shipwreck, outlying iron skerries, pitiless breakers, and great sea lights; much of heathery mountains, wild clans, and hunted Covenanters. Breaths come to him in song of the distant Cheviots and the ring of foraying hoofs. He glories in his hard-fisted forefathers, of the iron girdle

13. Nairn, *Break-Up of Britain*, 21.
14. Ibid., 94.
15. Ibid., 144.
16. Ibid., 165, 166.

and the handful of oatmeal, who rode so swiftly and lived so sparely on their raids. . . . The heart of young Scotland will be always touched more nearly by paucity of number and Spartan poverty of life."[17] This sense of Scotland is just what we get from Scott at the beginning of the nineteenth century, and from Buchan in the twentieth century. (The last sentence quoted, for instance, explains a Scots characteristic Buchan often calls "Calvinist," though it clearly has nothing to do with theology.) This is the source of the adventure feeling that permeated Scottish culture and that played an important part in English life too, through literature.

If we compare the Scots with the American Jews, we might say that writers like Mailer have recently been claiming the heritage of adventure that came naturally to John Buchan fifty years earlier. (There are, in fact, some interesting parallels between Buchan's last novel, *Sick Heart Country,* and Mailer's *Why Are We in Vietnam?* Both are adventure novels about the Arctic Circle, and both treat the spirit of the North mystically.) Meanwhile, the strongest drive in Scottish writing today seems to be away from adventure.

17. R. L. Stevenson, *Memories and Portraits,* 19, 20.

Part

3

THE IDEAS OF ADVENTURE

THIS SECOND HALF of the book describes adventure ideas that are important as ideas in themselves or as parts of systems of thought, rather than being important as ideas embodied in institutions or social organisms. Although the two groups are not as mutually exclusive as one might wish, at least the principle should be clear. In this case too I present the ideas as the object of cultic devotion, as being made potent in people's lives by the means of such devotion, cultivation, or worship. It is easy to see the likeness between the cult of national adventure and a religious cult. A nation's identity—its past and its future—is celebrated, like a religion, on official occasions, with special images and music, and by "priests." And that identity is often rooted in remembering adventurous events, such as England's defeat of the Spanish Armada, or the South African Boers' Great Trek, which have much in common with the stories of the Bible or the Qur'an.

But I also sometimes omit the adjective "national," and then, because adventure, when unspecified, can take many forms (not only large historical events), the result is to make the resemblance to religious cults less specific and vivid. It becomes more abstract and general. However, it does not lose all meaning. To go back to the religious comparison, the spirit of adventure is an entity no *more* protean than the spirit of religion itself. (As I pointed out when comparing potestas with eros, ideas of this kind are essentially manifold). Religion and adventure can each be embodied in many forms that are unlike each other without their multiplicity canceling an important identity at the core of them all.

In *Seven Types of Adventure Tale* (1991) I uncovered nationalist or imperialist messages beneath the surface of *all* the adventure-tale types, though they are quite different from one another. And even in cases where the link to *politics* is oblique or tenuous, the *moral* virtues of the adventure hero—and the power of adventure thinking, and the thrills of an adventure situation—are still the objects of what one can call a cult.

9

Philosophy and Metaphysics

When we look for adventure in philosophy, Nietzsche is the most important philosopher to examine. This is partly because of his critical attitude toward "the Christian virtues"—pity, humility, meekness—the moral antidotes to adventure. The latter qualities had nearly always been accorded the greatest reverence when European moralists discussed values, however little these virtues were practiced in European culture, but Nietzsche refused to take them on their own terms.

This development in the history of philosophy is important to us because, from our present point of view, those virtues are the expression of what I call the social or civic contract. Going "beyond good and evil," Nietzsche constructed an ethos very different from those values, one that could be called an ethos of adventure, which is familiar to us in popular stories.

Thus, Antonio Gramsci says we should always ask about, for instance, superman ideas, now called Nietzschean, whether they really derive from Nietzsche or just from adventure novels. "And was Nietzsche himself entirely uninfluenced by French serial novels? . . . This literature . . . was once very popular among intellectuals, at least until 1870, as the so-called 'thriller' is today. In any case, it seems that one can claim that much of the would-be Nietzschean 'supermanism' has its source and doctrinal model not in *Zarathustra* but merely in Alexandre Dumas's *Count of Monte Cristo*." (From our point of view, of course, "merely" is inappropriate, and the status distinction between the two men is meaningless. Both Nietzsche and Dumas are giving voice to the idea of adventure.) From such reading, Gramsci says, comes the popularity of such sayings as "It is better to live one day as a lion than a hundred years as a sheep."[1]

However, Nietzsche's more essential contribution to the philosophy of adventure is his declaration that God is dead and that the ideas derived from God's authority—the moral substantives with which Christendom, including its philosophers, had built its ethical structures—are all hollow. This is the starting point for Derrida, Bataille, and many of the other thinkers I have mentioned.

It is more than a mere coincidence that Nietzsche lived in the second half of the nineteenth century, the era when Germany and Italy became sovereign states and began to acquire overseas possessions, when England and France became conscious of *their* possessions as empires, and when artists began to claim a new freedom by asserting aesthetic values against moral ones. The adoption of the adventure material and the imperial themes by such ambitious writers as Stevenson and Kipling—a development that is still bearing fruit today—ties these three things together. (The anti-imperialist declarations of some of the later writers in this mode are in a sense self-deceptive.) And Nietzsche suggested the philosophy of these changes.

In *On the Genealogy of Morals* (1886) the concepts of adventure, conquest, and danger, and the imagery of laughter, triumph, and the keen air of the mountain heights, often appear. Nietzsche says that today we suffer from "man," that is, we suffer when we think of ourselves as men—because "man" is sickly, weary, ill-bred, and exhausted.[2] Nietzsche's "man" is civic man, to use the terms of this book. Bad conscience is a disease man was bound to contract when he found himself closed within society and peace (that is, when he gave up adventure) (p. 84).

Nietzsche associates the limines of society with past periods, thus disguising contemporary limines or changing space for time, as many thinkers have done. He says we instinctively yearn for a past we do not

1. Antonio Gramsci, *Selections from Cultural Writings,* ed. D. Forgacs and G. Nowell-Smith, 355.

2. Friedrich Nietzsche, *On the Genealogy of Morals,* 43.

know, a past with a different ethos, of which the traces are clear in our vocabulary when we examine it. "The knightly-aristocratic value judgments presupposed a powerful physicality, a flourishing, abundant, even overflowing health, together with that which seeks to preserve it: war, adventure, hunting, dancing, war games, and in general all that involves vigorous, free, joyful activity" (p. 33). He contrasts this adventurous type with "the priestly and the Jewish forms" of humankind (the Jews are a priestly people, Nietzsche says) which we have espoused and from which we suffer (here he alternates caste-difference with period-difference). The slave revolt began among the Jews when ressentiment gave birth to humble, nonnoble, values. (p. 34).

The knightly caste in history, moreover, has its origin in primitive or tribal man. Primitive man, the blond beast, is at the bottom of all the noble classes, Nietzsche tells us (pp. 40–41). He depicts Judea as having defeated Rome, in terms of moral and political influence on modern life, and Nietzsche, defying orthodoxy, sees in that a tragic defeat for modernity. Again he praises Napoleon the adventurer as against the liberty/equality/fraternity philosophy of the French Revolution that Napoleon was usually held to have betrayed (pp. 52–54).

We roughly denominate these ideas as Nietzsche's anti-Christianism. As for his antideism, we can focus on that at the epistemological level if we treat Derrida (according to his own desire) as Nietzsche's disciple. Derrida makes war against his composite enemy of "phallogocentrism"—the identification of the phallus with the logos, and the condominium of the two over the mind—by following Nietzsche in his work of emptying out the substance of moral and metaphysical terms. The false substantiality of those terms is the source of innumerable ills.

According to Derrida, the source of all meaning is not substance but difference. Each element of language—which is to say, each element of meaning—relates to something other but (1) retains the mark of a past element and (2) is hollowed out by the mark of a relationship to a future element. The interval that separates it from the other also divides the present in itself. Hence, the seeming substance to our words or thoughts is no substance, and because metaphysics was the ghost of theology the two are mutually dependent and God and Man are slain together.

Derrida connects traditional metaphysics' false claim to substance with the false supremacy of men over the human scene, and in making that connection he of course diverges from Nietzsche. Derrida has his own scheme and draws on more than one source. For instance, he aligns

Nietzsche's critique of metaphysics with Freud's critique of self-presence and Heidegger's critique of onto-theology. But what he makes from this convergence is still highly relevant to the discussion of adventure, violence, and power.

Philosophy is not really a diagram of values, he says, but the twilight of forces in conflict. Absolute chance is the "seminal adventure of the trace," and although "adventure" there is essentially metaphorical from our point of view, it is toward a serious meaning of adventure, or uncertainty or indecidability (to use one of Derrida's terms), that Derrida is leading philosophy. Poststructuralism is the equivalent in theory of magic realism in art, and the two endorse and influence each other.

Nietzsche's direct influence is widespread in the arts too. In Margot Norris's *Beasts of the Modern Imagination* he is paired with D. H. Lawrence. (Norris also discusses Kakfa, Max Ernst, and other artists who do not concern us here.) Her key idea is that biocentric artists like Lawrence, and philosophers like Nietzsche, implicitly criticize our anthropocentrism by their cult of animal gestures or acts of fatality. In their work the human is seen as lacking something in comparison with animals. And this dichotomy corresponds roughly to the cutting of the city man off from the adventurer and the cutting of the city off from its liminal areas.

We might add to Norris's examples the cases of the animals apotheosized in American adventure tales, fictional and nonfictional. In those books of the nineteenth and twentieth centuries we find a series of large and powerful animals (nearly always old and male) who confront the protagonist and challenge him in some climactic way. Perhaps the most familiar cases will be the near-contemporary ones, such as Faulkner's bear (in *The Bear*), Mailer's bear and wolf (in *Why Are We in Vietnam?*) and Hemingway's lion (in "The Short Happy Life of Francis Macomber") and shark (in *The Old Man and the Sea*). Some of the earlier examples, such as Melville's whale (in *Moby Dick*) and Parkman's buffalo (in *The Oregon Trail*), are just as remarkable. In all these cases the animal has an integrity of being, an authenticity, that puts the human being to shame.

Up to the time of Hegel, Norris says, westerners at least had seen animals as lacking something by comparison with humans. But Lawrence and Nietzsche taught, to the contrary, that animals had a more present, direct, original, spontaneous experience than humans. (This we might call the ethical myth of adventure—the promise of an escape from the contingencies of civility, the promise of an experience without traces.) The aggression of animals is a pure discharge of vitality and power, and the best humans are those who most nearly approach that condition, such as Cesare Borgia for Nietzsche. Lawrence's short novel "St. Mawr" uses the horse of that name as a standard by which to measure the humans, in exactly that way.[3] In Socrates, by contrast, we find no such discharge of vitality and power. Socrates, himself ugly and of low birth, was full of ressentiment, and so is all modern ethics that derives from him (p. 58).

An artist primarily in another field who shows the same parallel to Nietzsche is the master of modern dance, Rudolf Laban. His autobiography, *Ein Leben für den Tanz,* contains some remarkable evocations of landscape and animal life that exclude ordinary human consciousness and transcend it by a downward or Dionysian transcendence, and that experience is what his dance offered to share.

These ideas, like that of the death of man, are among those that inspire several of the contemporary French thinkers, and poststructuralism is clearly a philosophy of adventure, of violence, of power, in more than one way. Like Derrida, Foucault says that what we encounter after we accept that man is difference, is a world of power. Our will to power, which we mask from ourselves by calling it a love of the truth, is a will to wander, to trangress limits, a will that will not be overcome. Another of the same group of thinkers, Gilles Deleuze, also says that Nietzsche teaches us to think philosophy as force, and thus, if we let him criticize all transcendent values for us, Nietzsche can save us from Kant, the false philosopher of transcendence. Insofar as transcendent value, pure and absolute value, is the mark of the values that arise in the city and from the social contract, these new ideas are an attack on that contract and work in the service of adventure.

Standing between Nietzsche and the modern French thinkers, in terms of time, are other groups to take into account, though the word "adventure" is again somewhat hidden in their vocabulary. In the history of ideas another concept related to our topic that often points us toward adventure is "action" or "activism." Lewis Wurgaft wrote in 1977 that

3. Margot Norris, *Beasts of the Modern Imagination,* 4.

activism has been a marked trend in radical political thought in the twentieth century, that right-wing radicalism is *usually* associated with it, and the left is sometimes too.[4]

The idea of action derived from Nietzsche, though ultimately in part also from Fichte's idealism. Fichte and Hegel bequeathed Germany two complementary ideas: a spiritual idea of politics, and an aesthetic idea of self-development—in, for instance, political action. Activism is a form of that self-development somewhat detached from the consequences the action has for other people.

Wurgaft linked this idea to German literary expressionism. But he also saw Italian Futurism as a parallel and contemporary attempt to apply Nietzsche's ideas (and those of Georges Sorel) in art. In fact, the Futurists offer us the more striking examples and slogans expressing these ideas. In their manifesto of 1909, Marinetti and the other Futurists were clearly influenced by Nietzsche. That manifesto is an outright exaltation of adventure, beginning, as it does, "(1) We want to sing the love of danger, the habit of energy and rashness. (2) The essential elements of our poetry will be courage, audacity, and revolt. (3) Literature has up to now magnified passive immobility, ecstasy and slumber. We want to exalt movements of aggression, feverish sleeplessness, the double march [march at the double], the perilous leap, the slap and the blow with the fist. . . ."[5] Among the later points are "(7) Beauty exists only in struggle. . . . (8) We are on the extreme promontory of the centuries! What is the use of looking behind at the moment when we must open the mysterious shutters of the impossible? Time and Space died yesterday. We are already living in the absolute, since we have already created eternal, omnipresent speed" (p. 8). The ninth point was propaganda for imperialism and militarism, and the tenth was a call to demolish libraries, museums—and feminism.

This manifesto was published in Paris, where the leading writer-activist, Gabriele D'Annunzio, was then living. It was to him that Marinetti dedicated his second book of poems, *Destruction*. Destruction, conquest, violence—clearly these are the ideas of adventure. Marinetti's epic *La conquête des étoiles* (1902) had vigorous battle scenes. Alfred Jarry, a friend of the Futurists, also believed in violence, destruction, hatred of the past, and love of the future and machines. Their

4. Lewis D. Wurgaft, *The Activists*, 5.
5. The Futurist Manifesto, in ibid., 8.

politically minded sponsors associated these ideas with national status and international competitiveness. Thus, Giovanni Papini said in 1913 that Futurism would be absurd in Russia or America but that it was necessary in Italy; Italy needed to win respect from other nations, which meant it must become a great power with an aggressive foreign policy.[6]

In March 1909 Marinetti said, "In politics we are as far removed from international and antipatriotic socialism—that ignoble exaltation of the rights of the belly—as we are from timid clerical conservatism symbolized by the bedroom slippers and the hot water bottle. . . . We sing of war, the only cure for the world, a superb blaze of enthusiasm and generosity."[7] Thus, Futurism was an extreme endorsement of adventure, and a repudiation of the civic or social contract.

In February 1911, speaking in the name of the group, Marinetti, addressed England: "What we like in you is your indomitable and bellicose patriotism; we like your intelligent and generous individualism which allows you to open your arms to the individualists of all countries, libertarians and anarchists. . . . You have kept an unbridled passion for fighting in all its forms, from boxing—simple, brutal, and swift—to the roar from the monstrous throats of the guns crouched in their revolving caves of steel on the decks of your Dreadnoughts."[8] This is rather like Santayana's—and Kipling's—point of view on England: very unlike the view the Victorian humanists had of England, but logically consequent both on imperialism and on late nineteenth-century aestheticism.

Some of this political morality had a long history in modern culture (beginning way before the nineteenth century), though it always had a diabolistic sulfur-taint, from the traditional point of view. Chapter 8 of Michael Nerlich's *Ideology of Adventure* is entitled "From the Glorification of Adventure to the Bellum Omnium Contra Omnes"—in other words, the connection between adventure and Thomas Hobbes's political philosophy. Nerlich connects Hobbes and Bacon as the two primary spokespersons for modern ideology and agrees with Marx about their importance. He makes his point by quoting Marx on Bacon in *The Holy Family:* "According to [Bacon's] teaching the senses are infallible and are the source of all knowledge. Science is experimental and consists in applying a *rational method* to the data supplied by the senses."[9] This

6. James Joll, *Three Intellectuals in Politics,* 141.
7. Quoted in ibid., 141.
8. Ibid., 151–52.
9. Michael Nerlich, *The Ideology of Adventure,* 188.

sounds innocent enough, but this empiricism in knowledge turns out to be married naturally to a driving ambition in action, in a battle against theoretical or abstract scholasticism. Thus, Bacon said: "The human understanding is unquiet; it cannot stop or rest. . . . We cannot perceive of any end or limit to the world."[10] There is no point in our aiming at quietude, as Saint Augustine and the other Christian saints would have us do. We instinctively feel that the worst of all things is "a narrow and meager knowledge" of either time or place (p. 189). Discovery is our heaven, and the great modern discoveries Bacon celebrated were, geographically, the Americas and, technically, printing, gunpowder, and the magnet—in other words, the beginnings of the modern world.

Nerlich sees a significantly new amoralism in this philosophy: "Bacon already shows a tendency towards what becomes systematic in Hobbes: the justification of social relations by an imputed biological law" (p. 191). Thus, civil war is described as like a fever, but a foreign war is like the heat of exercise and "serveth to keep the body in health" (p. 192). And this amoralism is important because modern political philosophy finds its first systematic form in Hobbes.

Hobbes saw violence as man's natural element. In the famous chapter 18 of the *Leviathan,* entitled "Of the Natural Condition of Mankind as Concerning Their Felicity and Misery," the philosopher says that when men see no power over them to keep them in awe they live in that condition called war. "Whatsoever therefore is consequent to a time of war, where every man is enemy to every man; the same is consequent to the time, wherein men live without other security, than what their own strength, and their own invention shall furnish them withal." He goes on to describe that "state of nature" in terms of its miseries but (as "their own strength and their own invention" already suggested) as with a stern, dark splendor and as a place where only adventurers would survive. "In such conditions, there is no place for industry; because the fruit thereof is uncertain; and consequently no culture of the earth; no navigation, nor use of the commodities that may be imported by sea; no commodious building; no instruments of moving, and removing, such things as require much force; no knowledge of the face of the earth; no account of time; no arts, no letters; no society; and which is worst of all, continual fear, and danger of violent death; and the life of man, solitary, poor, nasty, brutish, and short."[11] Life therefore cannot be profoundly understood using the terms of morality and order.

10. Quoted in ibid., 189.
11. *Leviathan,* ed. John Plamenatz, 143.

This dark vision of life as something rooted in violence and ever-ready to revert to violence is implicit in adventure, at least when written by a truthful writer. Thus, though many adventure tales speak only in the language of gay optimism and we smile at the idea of it, this happens only by virtue of quite artificial literary conventions.

The connection between Hobbes and adventure, or at least the contradiction between him and the opposite, rational enlightenment philosophy, is implied in the comment of his recent editor, John Plamenatz, in introducing the *Leviathan:* "It was in the seventeenth century that the English laid the foundations of the political system which, more than any other, has served as a model to the world, and it was then also that the masterpiece of English political literature was produced. In the masterpiece there is to be found no hint of the model."[12] The former introduces us to the world of adventure, the latter introduces us to the world of reason, of the social contract.

There is the same contradiction in the work, and indeed in the life, of the French philosopher of violence, Georges Sorel. He was born in 1847 and trained as an engineer, but he retired in 1892 and discovered Marxism the following year. Later he joined L'Action Française, and then turned in preference to Bolshevism. Sorel wanted to see a proletarian revolution, but his understanding of the proletarian movement was different from Marx's. He worked out the idea of social myth as a major tool for analyzing political behavior.

Richard Humphrey says Sorel's theory of myth accounts for the expressions of will, as opposed to reason, that give a dynamic force to the manifestations of great social beliefs. One of those myths is the idea of a general strike. Such an action is an adventure even in thought, an invention, to be "justified" only afterward if at all. "When we act, it is because we have created an entirely artificial world, placed in advance of the present, formed of movements that depend on ourselves."[13]

Sorel's ideas are therefore irrationalist. Rational social philosophy, according to him, must proceed by means of a "diremption"—an examining of parts, independent of the whole, pushing them to independence in order to understand their type—after which, philosophy cannot reconstitute the whole.[14] Sorel therefore calls for action, as symbolic thinking, because symbolism fills its concepts with life—which is the

---

12. John Plamenatz, in Introduction to ibid., 6.
13. Richard D. Humphrey, *Georges Sorel,* 10.
14. Ibid., 97.

real cause of the importance thoughtful people accord to memorable actions. The popularization of science, and the glamour attached to scientific models of knowledge, are bourgeois doctrines.[15]

Rationalism annuls, enfeebles, contracts the mind, according to Sorel. Art, religion, and philosophy can flourish only when in contact with overflowing vitality.[16] Philosophers (for instance, Descartes) have often believed that a system deserves trust only if it looks like Euclidean geometry. "Societies, however, do not offer data that one is able to incorporate in such an arrangement; that is why the men of the seventeenth and eighteenth centuries looked on history as a lowly form of knowledge."[17] Citing Henri Bergson, Sorel says socialism must be conceived in a purely dynamic sense, not as a geometrical diagram but as an entity of uninterrupted flow. The passage from capitalism to socialism is not a logical development, but a catastrophe whose course escapes analytic description.

According to Jack Roth, Sorel wanted to see a return to "les temps héroiques," which suggests the parallel between him and contemporary adventure writers.[18] Though he found Rousseau too abstract, Sorel saw virtue as residing in a regime of peasant soldiers and was therefore predictably hostile to the rational Socrates and admiring of the anarchist Proudhon's peasant-style morality and its stress on property and the patriarchal family. Sorel and Proudhon were moralists whose social commentaries avoided the traps of moral abstraction and kept value and fact united.

A key word for Sorel, as for Hobbes and Bataille, was violence. He made a distinction in value—indeed, an opposition—between state force and proletarian violence. We must distrust the former but expect— welcome—the latter.

John Stanley has discussed Sorel's version of socialism, saying that it differed from Marx's in that Sorel wanted the socialist movement to be more concerned with the virtue of its members and less with the distribution of goods in society.[19] He wanted socialists to be concerned more with dangerous proletarian action and less with a well-drilled obedience to a class of intellectuals and political professionals, and to be concerned with the productive process itself and with the class

15. Ibid., 100.
16. Ibid., 98.
17. Ibid., 100.
18. J. J. Roth, *The Cult of Violence*, 4.
19. J. Stanley, ed., *From Georges Sorel*, 30.

struggle itself, rather than with their respective final outcomes. Marx believed the epic belonged to the past, but Sorel believed in myth and epic.[20] By that token, he therefore also believed in adventure. So too did Nietzsche, who rejected the contemplative idea of truth as something static. Nietzsche saw truth as that to which the individual won his way by means of struggle, which would end when he saw it. For him, as for Gandhi, truth was a form of action and was therefore enmeshed in risk and inconsistency and dependent on courage and force of will.

There was much of this in Sartrian existentialism too. In *The Second Sex,* Simone de Beauvoir says existentialists reject the idea that those at rest (i.e., those who are stagnant) are happy. "Every subject plays his part as such specifically through exploits or projects that serve as a mode of transcendence; he achieves liberty only through a continual reaching out towards other liberties. There is no justification for present existence other than its expansion into an indefinitely open future."[21] We see here too the similarity to Gandhi's idea of truth in action, though the asceticism and piety of Gandhi's moral philosophy alters the meaning of these ideas.

In *Saint Genet,* Sartre writes, "The decent man . . . will define himself narrowly by traditions, by obedience . . . and will give the name *temptation* to the live, vague swarming which is still himself, but a himself which is wild, free, outside the limits he has marked out for himself."[22] This attack on the decent man can be seen as a contradiction of what Nerlich calls the tradition of the "honnête homme," beginning with Montaigne; the *honnête homme* hates all excess and impropriety, preferring the golden mean always—an idea that is hostile to adventure.

The existentialists are themselves contradicted by later feminists and structuralists, as when Josephine Donovan says, "It seems that de Beauvoir and Sartre have succeeded in simply endorsing the Western, Faustian model of active transformation of the world as a proper means to fulfilment or redemption. We now know that this dynamic of Becoming, of perpetual consumption of the resources of one's environment, a perpetual attempt to stamp the materials of reality as one's own, . . . [has] led to ecological disaster."[23] This is the voice of antiadventure thinking.

So the idea of adventure runs through many kinds of philosophy,

20. Ibid.
21. Simone de Beauvoir, *The Second Sex,* xxiii–xxiv.
22. Jean-Paul Sartre, *Saint Genet: Actor and Martyr,* 35.
23. Josephine Donovan, *Feminist Theory,* 125.

without often being named as such. If we removed all traces of adventure thinking from Western thought, what was left would be quite different from what we have now. Perhaps we can agree that it would be much tamer—postponing the next stage of the discussion, over the definition and the value of tameness.

10

Science and Social Science

In the history of science, we can look for adventure among the silent partners to the comparatively notorious concept of masculinism. The idea that the mind is used in a specifically masculine way in modern or western science is one that has been studied a good deal recently. Feminist scholars, such as Evelyn Fox Keller and Sandra Harding, have shown us how closely that modern science was tied to a masculinist vocabulary from the beginning, so that the development of that science— a development fraught with great consequences for our civilization's sense of itself, and indeed for our white culture's dominance over others and perhaps for our planet's self-poisoning as well—was also a matter of the male gender dominating over the other forms of human life— women and children and the sick, aged, and infirm, not to mention males who failed to measure up to the standards of masculinism. So much, then, has been argued a good deal recently. Few scholars, however, have yet made the connection between masculism and adventure, but it is a logical next step.

In *Reflections on Science and Gender* Keller speaks about "the historic conjunction of science and masculinity, and the equally historical disjunction between science and femininity."[1] She declares: "For the found-

---

1. Evelyn Fox Keller, *Reflections on Science and Gender*, 4.

ing fathers of modern science, the reliance on the language of gender was explicit; they sought a philosophy that deserved to be called 'masculine,' that could be distinguished from its ineffective predecessors by its 'virile' power, its capacity to bind Nature to man's service and make her his slave (Bacon)" (p. 7). In the Royal Society (the generally acknowledged place of origin of modern science) the mechanical philosophy overcame the hermetic, and masculine and feminine were polarized in a new way that became central to industrial capitalism. Capitalism required an opposition between work and home, between men and women. In the hermetic tradition, matter was suffused with spirit; in the mechanical philosophy, spirit and matter were divorced, as head and mind were divorced from the heart (p. 47).

Benjamin Farrington says that according to Bacon, the "older science represented only a female off-spring, passive, weak, expectant, but now a son was born, active, virile, generative."[2] Bacon's most important essay from this point of view was "Temporis Partus Masculus" (The Masculine Birth of Time, 1602–3), this masculine birth being an image that contrasts with the alchemists' key image of coition. In terms of sexual symbolism, Bacon's followers wanted chastity—that is, a limitedly masculine and heterosexual desire full of limits and constraints (p. 47). This was part of a general "military" discipline.

The ideas of Aristotle and, even more, those of Plato must also be driven out, and the mind laid open to truth alone. The members of the Royal Society, developing modern scientific method and philosophy, were hostile to Plato because the latter had restricted knowledge to the realm of theory (not practice), and nature to the realm of form (not matter). Bacon's idea of knowledge was both more realistic and more aggressive than Plato's. He equated knowledge and power, and Nature was to be laid low in being known.[3] In matters of theory, Bacon rejected all traditions and made it the moral responsibility of every man to assume and exercise power.[4]

As a result, most modern scientists have assumed that control and domination are basic to the scientific impulse. Bacon spoke of three kinds of ambition—personal, patriotic, and universal (power over the universe)—all of which require both knowledge and skill to be fulfilled.

2. Benjamin Farrington, *Centaurus*, 1:194.
3. Ibid., 31.
4. Ibid., 33.

Ambition, aggression, and masculinity—these are all ideas that come together in potestas, and therefore in adventure.

In *The Death of Nature*, Carolyn Merchant points out how the social and technical development of Renaissance Europe corroborated Bacon's ideas visually and experientially: "As European cities grew and forested areas became more remote, as fens were drained and geometric patterns of channels imposed on the landscape, as large powerful waterwheels, furnaces, forges, cranes, and treadmills began increasingly to dominate the work environment, more and more people began to experience nature as altered and manipulated by machine technology."[5] These mechanical enterprises were triumphant parts of civilization, and achievements. Mining, for instance, was rescued from the disapproval in which it had traditionally been held as an antiorganic and antimaternal activity.

Bacon's ideas were rooted in an emerging market economy that widened the class gap and brought wealth to merchants, clothiers, entrepreneurial adventurers, and yeomen farmers through their exploitation of nature.[6] Nature *needed* to be subdued and developed: "The image of nature that became important in the early modern period was that of a disorderly and chaotic realm to be subdued and controlled."[7] This image of femaleness was connected with the idea of witches (those enemies of modern science), people who raised storms, killed infants, caused illness, destroyed crops, and obstructed generation. Bernard Fontenelle and others saw the great Copernican revolution in cosmology as a matter of the masculine Sun displacing the female Earth.[8]

Science became essentially a matter of power. "The Baconian method achieved power over nature through manual manipulation, technology, and experiment."[9] People were taught that abstract notions would not help us achieve this power, that what we needed were the instruments of the mind and the hand that could squeeze and mold nature.[10] The most useful arts are those that alter the material nature of things, such as agriculture, chemistry, and glassmaking.[11]

5. Carolyn Merchant, *The Death of Nature*, 68.
6. Ibid., 80.
7. Ibid., 127.
8. Ibid., 128.
9. Ibid., 216.
10. Ibid., 171.
11. Ibid., 172.

The connection between these ideas and adventure is established most easily by pointing to the archetypal adventure tale *Robinson Crusoe*. That story clearly answers to the ideas of Baconian and Royal Society science, including the emphasis on experimentation. "Experiment," Merchant says, "expresses the spirit of action, of a 'doing' devoted to 'finding out' " (p. 37). Defoe's hero is a great experimenter, always doing something, making something, finding something out. And it is not surprising that there are no women on Crusoe's island. His only significant relationship, as far as human beings go, is with Friday, a disciple and an admiring audience for Crusoe's skills and achievements.

Evelyn Keller also sees the history of thought in feminist terms. She says modern science gave men a new and plausible basis for celebrating their manhood and virility.[12] This cult of science was another way in which women were ejected from the vocal and active roles they had played in the prophetic and radical sects of the seventeenth century— either they were ejected or those roles were narrowed and diminished. The Enlightenment wanted order at any cost, and by means that included the allocation and enforcement of social roles along gender lines that denied women the option of most kinds of work. It has been said that fishwife, alewife, oysterwife and so on, were all replaced by "housewife" as the seventeenth century turned into the eighteenth.

We can also find in the character of social science some equivalents to this masculinism. At least in his *Myth of Masculinity* Joseph Pleck says the social sciences were dominated, from the 1930s until the rise of feminism, by the "male sex role identity" paradigm, which made masculinity the most important of values and of explanatory principles. It assumed, for instance, that sex-role insecurity must lie at the root of homosexuality. The arguments derived from this paradigm made much use of male "insecurity" and "inadequacy," saw the man's relation to his mother as at the root of his problems, and saw homosexuality as a man's worst fate.[13]

But perhaps to detect this masculinism of method is less interesting this time than looking at a social scientist addressing our problem, the problem of adventure, from his professional point of view—for instance, Lionel Tiger in his *Men in Groups*. Tiger's book describes the activities of men as men—activities that include war and adventure, notably—and

12. Keller, *Reflections on Science and Gender*, 64.
13. Joseph Pleck, *The Myth of Masculinity*.

their roots in male bonding. He also discusses the likelihood that such bonding would be a biological propensity and thus one of the least variable parts of social systems.[14] All-male groups, of primates as well as humans, go hunting together, and in both populations this activity is linked to the achievement of dominance and the rules emanating from territoriality.

Whether biologically or socially derived, Tiger argues, male-male bonds are as important for defense, food-gathering, and the maintaining of social order as the male-female bond is for reproduction (p. 55). Thus, he draws the same parallels between eros and potestas, as Bataille does, but Tiger takes a different philosophical vantage point: He is concerned with both powers of thought insofar as they are incorporated *into* the social contract and so are seen as forms of order, not as freedoms or disorders. For instance, potestas or political power is typically associated with men, and politics is a male group phenomenon (p. xv).

Thus, Tiger says, Seymour Lipset's *Political Man* naturally deals with men and not with women. (It is hardly necessary to say that feminists and pacifists deal with such phenomena in quite different ways and that, even from a common-sense point of view, reform politics constitutes an exception to these generalizations.) In fact, Tiger says, armies, sports, secret societies, training patterns, and economic and religious power-structures all offer data to prove the importance of this male bonding (p. 72). These activities are linked to each other by the importance of that kind of bonding in all of them. For instance, the basis of most sports is a preparation for or rehearsal of war (p. 148). The same is more obviously true of hunting. Initiation ceremonies, with their pains and humiliations, separate the initiate from home and family and generate strong new bonds that enable adventurers (p. 73)—for we hardly need to point out that all these are forms of adventure.

We see behavioral evidence of this in school playgrounds, in college fraternities, among criminals, and among political revolutionaries. Paralleling our comparison of eros with potestas, Tiger suggests that we could call secret political societies the demi-monde of politics (p. 101). The two things—the demi-monde and the secret societies—are both partial withdrawals from the light of social day and are often felt by women (the guardians of that daylight) as inimical. As literary reflections

14. Lionel Tiger, *Men in Groups*, xvi.

of these truths, contemporary when he was writing, Tiger discusses William Golding's novel, *Lord of the Flies* and the Broadway musical *West Side Story*. As a parallel to tribal life in contemporary capitalism, he points out that wealthy business companies and corporations often maintain hunting and fishing lodges for their executives (p. 98). (Norman Mailer had dramatized this line of thought and shown its connections to war and politics just before Tiger's book, in his novel *Why Are We in Vietnam?*)

There is plenty of evidence that dangerous and adventurous masculine vocations, such as coal-mining and ocean fishing, produce strong gender bonding. But there are also more "civilized" activities that are adventurous in a different sense, like card-playing and gambling, which are in certain societies exclusively male and can generate similar feelings. In relation to such bonding, women are offered a number of roles, different from each other but all marked by being quite different from the men's roles, and most of them responsive to the latter.

This male bonding is often taken entirely for granted, Tiger says, and not thought about analytically. When it is thought about, it is often seen as merely primitive and residual, or vestigial (p. 177). But in fact, he argues, it is the spinal cord of human communities, that which gives them their structure, coherence, and continuity (p. 78). It is especially strong in its effects on war and aggression. Human aggression in its social-organization sense is a propensity of males and is released by their association with other males (p. 204).

Peter Stearns's *Be a Man!* also takes man-in-society as its focus and takes into account a decade of feminist scholarship after Tiger; it analyzes masculinism in a more skeptical and indeed hostile way. But Stearns's analysis, as is the case with other scholars, therewith averts any direct gaze from adventure. (This is a good example of the way our best habits inhibit response to the challenge of this topic.) More exactly, seeing the concept of Western manhood as rooted in war and aggression, Stearns examines primarily the contradiction between that illusory "manhood" and the actual life of man in society.

The mythical history of our kind of manhood, Stearns says, begins with the German invaders of Rome, whose descendants became the knights of the Middle Ages[15] (this is what nineteenth-century adventure writers, such as Kingsley and Haggard, taught). Medieval Europe's

15. Peter N. Stearns, *Be A Man!* 25.

maleness was therefore class-based or caste-based and was associated mainly with war and hunting. Military values were embodied in the aristocracy and penetrated the rest of society to varying degrees. (There is indeed an obvious sense in which maleness is associated with the warrior caste, at least for the members of that caste, even in Hindu culture.) And even in novels written by women and centered on women, like those of nineteenth-century England, the soldier or squire is peculiarly acceptable as the man the heroine shall marry.

"Western culture has carefully preserved a selective memory of hunting traits to support a belligerent upper class, a fighting aristocracy," Stearns continues (p. 13), but other cultures—for instance, among Asians—developed gentler men (p. 14). "Soft" men were not favored in nineteenth-century Western society, for example. "The male heroes were the unflinching captains of industry, the warriors, the frontiersmen, or even the two-fisted missionaries" (p. 51). These were the men who at least seemed to be adventurers.

As Western society was modernized, men and women became more different from each other. Men first learned to live by clock time and intensive labor, and began to die younger than women (p. 52). The two sexes spent more time apart from each other, except that young boys spent more time with their mothers and away from their fathers and so had a hard struggle to leave the former (p. 54). The tests that separated the men from the boys, the adventure rites of initiation, became more dramatic.

All this bears on our topic, but it is frustrating that scholars such as Stearns so often avert their attention from adventure itself as a present reality. However, the German historian of ideas Michael Nerlich has recently written at length on the adventure concept, which he sees as one of the most important and most neglected concepts in the history of thought. In his essay "The Unknown History of Our Modernity" he sees the cult of adventure as a part of modernity. He emphasizes the elements of innovation and the unknown in adventure, and he sees these elements as characterizing modern culture. "What distinguishes our modern culture (art, literature, music, and so on) from all other cultural systems, including the Greek, is the absolute priority given to innovation and the increasing taboo on repetition, the loss of fear of the horizon, the desire for the unknown, and the integration of the other."[16] All these criteria

16. Michael Nerlich, "The Unknown History of Our Modernity," 13.

can be seen as aspects of adventure and even of particular adventure tales—taken literally—as episodes or themes of stories in which the hero is the inventor and explorer par excellence.

The shift from the older cultural systems to our own, according to Nerlich, began to occur between the tenth century and the thirteenth century, when the knightly class in France brought to the center of consciousness "la queste de l'aventure." European consciousness began to base itself on two systems: one ascetic and static (the Christian religion) and the other dynamic and earthly (adventure ideology and the calculations of chance). From Chrétien de Troyes on, art and literature cease to be religious (p. 17). Thus, modernity starts with the adventure tale.

Nerlich's thought is not primarily gender-oriented, but he does see the connection between his theme of adventure and the social dominance of men. Nowadays, he says, women have begun a revision of the male preemption of adventure privileges, and "writing in the feminine" is one of the greatest and most exciting aesthetic enterprises humanity has ever undertaken (p. 19). Whether or not one sees all the writing of the past as "in the masculine," there can be no denying that adventure has been "written in the masculine." And a great deal that extends beyond literature in the ordinary sense, including science and social science, has also been written in that gender.

11

Nationalism and History

Scholars of nationalism usually see it as something broader than the kind of politics that claims that title. They see it as a cultural and psychological phenomenon that includes—among other things, especially in the case of the Anglo-Saxon countries—the spirit of adventure. "Thus nationalism," says John Plamenatz, "is primarily a cultural phenomenon, though it can, and often does, take a political form."[1] Gerald Newman, who quotes Plamenatz approvingly, sees English nationalism as developing in the eighteenth century, beginning in the age of Defoe and taking pride in England's primacy in what we now call development.

It was, almost by definition, aggressively xenophobic and populist, having from the first a marked anti-French and antiaristocratic bias. Henry Fielding wrote "The Roast Beef of Old England," and Hogarth used that phrase in a popular print of 1749. The national anthems "Rule Britannia" and "God Save the King" appeared in the 1740s, and, Newman says, by the 1750s were firmly established. But these were the traditional and "historical" faces of a phenomenon that was also mer-

1. John Plamenatz, "Two Types of Nationalism," quoted in Gerald Newman, *The Rise of English Nationalism*, 56.

cantile and adventurous. Defoe's *Tour of the Whole Island of Great Britain* exults in the modernization it finds everywhere at work.

The national heroes England chose for itself included many adventurers, such as the Elizabethan sailors Francis Drake and Walter Raleigh, and others of the eighteenth century, such as Captain Cook and later Admiral Nelson, as well as famous soldiers like Clive and Wellington and explorers and martyrs. (The boys' cottages at Kingsley Fairbridge's farm school in Australia were named mostly after such heroes.)

Robinson Crusoe does not seem to have been associated with English nationalism by the English themselves, but he certainly was by people of other nations. (The sense in which Crusoe was the effective international emblem of England is discussed in my earlier books, *The Robinson Crusoe Story* and *Seven Types of Adventure Tale*.) Defoe's character represented the innovative entrepreneurial class of Englishman, while John Bull and "Roast Beef" represented the conservative squirearchy and peasantry.

In *Nations and Nationalism*, Ernest Gellner and others say that nationalism is the inseparable ideological counterpart of modernization and that in Germany and France it was the spearhead of an attack on feudalism. (We saw this relationship between nationalism and modernization in the history of Scotland.) Adventure, as one of the energizing myths of the modern world system, was therefore a partner to nationalism, and Robinson Crusoe belongs in the English gallery of notables as much as d'Artagnan does in the French gallery, or Natty Bumppo belongs in the American.

It is above all in the work of historians that we see the idea of adventure directing adult intellectual activity. The most striking examples are the nineteenth-century American historians, from Prescott to Bancroft. Herbert Butterfield has remarked how many of the Whig interpreters of history were Americans who saw frontiersmen as epic heroes. These historians gave America the feeling of nationhood in the nineteenth century.

The connection of their work with adventure reading is clear. In the middle and second half of the nineteenth century the historians of America, like other readers, read James Fenimore Cooper intensively in their boyhood. Allan Nevins, writing as late as 1954, seems still close to that experience. He says, "Men do not easily forget an early devotion to Scott, Dumas, Maryatt, and Lytton" (we might emend that to read that when men do forget that devotion it still continues to mold their minds) and calls Cooper's Leatherstocking tales "the nearest approach yet made to the American epic" because they deal with "our rude heroic age, our Homeric period of national life."[2] Even in more recent times, such historians as Bernard de Voto, Samuel Eliot, and W. P. Webb have kept up the same interest.

The four nineteenth-century American historians David Levin deals with in *History as Romantic Art* are William Prescott (1796–1859), George Bancroft (1800–1891), John Lothrop Motley (1814–77), and Francis Parkman (1823–93). Some of the relevant titles are Prescott's *Conquest of Mexico* (1843) and *Conquest of Peru* (1847), Motley's *Rise of the Dutch Republic* (1856), Bancroft's *History of the United States* (1859–76), and Parkman's *Discovery of the Great West* (1869). All four celebrated the development of the United States, telling that story as a triumphant political adventure. All four disliked Hume, Locke, Voltaire, and the irony, skepticism, and materialism of the eighteenth-century Whigs, which seemed to act as a check on the expansive imaginations of the next generation—on their adventure ideology.

As the titles of their books indicate, those four historians tell the story, celebrate the epic, of the development of the modern world system both inside and outside America. In their hands that development becomes an adventure tale, for epics are the most prestigious species of the adventure genus. Prescott's Spain, Motley's Holland, Parkman's England, and Bancroft's America were core states of the modern world system, and each in its turn became a leading power. The true hero of history, they said, was the People, but in their narratives they focused their feelings on individuals they called Representative Men. Such were, for instance, Isabella of Spain, William the Silent, the older Pitt, and George Washington. Representative men were "natural"; they wore simple, austere dress and had deep-lying passions, warmth, *nature*. In American heroes in particular, naturalness was associated with Nature herself, and with adventure. Bancroft said Washington went into the wilderness as a surveyor for three years and "Nature revealed to him her obedience to serene and silent laws. . . . From her he acquired a divine and animating virtue."[3]

Of the four, Parkman was the most temperamentally assertive, and he was determined to keep up the spirit of adventure, in order to keep the

<hr>

2. Allan Nevins, "Introduction," in J. Fenimore Cooper, *The Saga of Leatherstocking*, ed. Allan Nevins, 3, 5.

3. David Levin, *History as Romantic Art*, 53.

political power, and the reins of progress, in his own people's hands. He once said, "An uncommon vigor, joined to the hardy virtues of a *masculine* race, marked the New England type. . . . The staple of character was a sturdy conscientiousness; an undespairing courage, patriotism, public spirit, sagacity, and a strong good sense."[4]

That expresses the late nineteenth-century version of the Whig interpretation of history, which is somewhat different from that of the eighteenth century, for there was a marked transition from moralism to racism in the course of time. That went naturally with the rising power of nationalism and racism. The story of the Teutonic race became a world-history adventure tale. Bancroft and Motley were keen readers of primitive epic and saga, as were Kingsley and his friends in England. Stubbs and Freeman not only traced the history of England's political and legal institutions but also refurbished Anglo-Saxon art and taste and made Beowulf and Caedmon great poets again.

The taste of these men in the writing of their own time was what one might expect. In an essay in the January 1852 *North American Review,* Parkman said Cooper and Scott were both "practical men, able and willing to grapple with the hard realities of the world. [He contrasts them with such writers as Nathaniel Hawthorne.] Either might have learned with ease to lead a regiment, or command a line of battle ship. [Cooper's] readers are not persons of sedentary and studious habits but of a more active turn, military officers and the like, whose taste has not been trained into fastidiousness."[5] Cooper dealt with realities, whereas Hawthorne dealt with conceptions.

The single narrative that best reflects this American triumphalism and its accompanying anxiety (Were the men of the educated class strong enough, American enough, to rule this powerful nation?) is Parkman's *Oregon Trail,* which shows also the heroic therapy by which that anxiety was cured. In that book we see the old traditions of American philosophy, the tradition of New England Christian piety, summarily dismissed in favor of an almost opposite tendency toward militarism and *Machtpolitik.*

The contrast is sharp because Parkman's father was a Unitarian minister and a pupil and associate of William Ellery Channing, the great saint and hero of the Boston Unitarians and of all America's peace-

---

4. Quoted in ibid., 35.
5. See George Dekker and J. P. McWilliams, eds., *Fenimore Cooper: The Critical Heritage,* 262.

lovers. The father was himself a notable preacher, and we read that his voice was praised as being of a "sweet, mild, unctuous smoothness." But such a voice must have been a liability with many—think what such a phrase would mean to any reader of Dickens. And the young Parkman was one of those who counted it a liability. "For his high-mettled son, in turn, the ministerial calling, the 'decorum of the cloth,' and much else his father personified were to be lifelong irritants and subjects of incisive sallies."[6]

Happily quartered aboard a British troopship on holiday, the young Parkman wrote: "A becoming horror of dissenters, especially Unitarians, prevails everywhere. No one cants here of temperance reform, or of systems of diet—eat, drink, and be merry is the motto everywhere, and a stronger and hardier race of men never laughed at the doctors. Above all, there is no canting of peace. A wholesome spirit of coercion is manifest in all directions."[7] Coercion is the enemy of freedom as well as of peace, and one of the faces of potestas. And indeed the most striking thing about Parkman's Oregon Trail, considered as a New England document, is its overt enthusiasm for war, especially for a war between Indian tribes.

This did not stop with the nineteenth century. If Parkman saw white history as the adventure of the Anglo-Saxon race, H. G. Wells saw world history as the adventure of the human race, and Jawaharlal Nehru saw revolution as the grown-up continuation of adventure. In his letters to his daughter, later herself the prime minister of India, he sounds just like Parkman as he speaks of "the exciting adventure of Man" and asks her to imagine the Aryans invading India: "Can you not see them trekking down the mountain passes into the unknown land below? Brave and full of the spirit of adventure, they dared to go ahead without fear of the consequences. If death came, they did not mind, they met it laughing. But they loved life, and knew that the only way to enjoy life was to be fearless."[8] This is the rhetoric of adventure at its most familiar.

Nehru's historical sensibility was, however, also determined by his enthusiasm for revolutions—the French and the Russian—and by figures of masterful rebellion, like Napoleon and Lenin. In the chapter "Napoleon" in Glimpses of World History, he says: "A strange wild beauty had France then. A French poet, Barbier, has compared her to a wild

6. Howard Doughty, Francis Parkman, 4, 5.
7. Parkman's journal, quoted in ibid., 69, 70.
8. Jawaharlal Nehru, Glimpses of World History, 13.

animal, a proud and free mare, with head high and shining skin; a beautiful vagabond, fiercely intolerant of saddle and harness and rein, stamping on the ground" (p. 380). This is the feeling the American historians had about their country.

Indeed, Nehru's enthusiasm for Lenin, in the same book, was more ideological and discipular, less sentimental and whimsical, than his affection for Gandhi. Lenin was a mastermind and a genius in revolution, Nehru said. "There was no doubt or vagueness in Lenin's mind. His were the penetrating eyes which detected the moods of the masses; the clear head which could apply and adapt well-thought-out principles to changing situations; the inflexible will which held on to the course he had mapped out, regardless of immediate consequences. . . . So, calmly but inexorably, like some agent of an inevitable fate, this lump of ice covering a blazing fire within went ahead to its appointed goal" (pp. 643, 645).

We find much the same enthusiasms in the life and work of Jack London, for whom the Oakland Public Library was a university where he majored in adventure. "I read everything, but principally history and adventure, and all the old travels and voyages."[9] (His first authors were Washington Irving, Horatio Alger, Ouida, and Paul du Chaillu, the scholar first of the great apes and then of the Vikings.) But if one of London's titles is *Adventure,* another is *Revolution,* and in a 1905 essay with that title he talks of the million people in the United States alone, then, dedicated to making a revolution, and the six million more worldwide—it is the greatest revolution ever known, already happening. Clearly he feels it as a glorious adventure.

And no doubt everywhere revolution (and its minor forms and tributaries, such as marches, protests, building occupations, strikes) has fed on the love of adventure. But in the work of Marx himself, and in some orthodox Marxists, we meet a frame of mind that is the reverse of, the enemy of, adventure. It believes in the civic contract and develops from that Enlightenment thought which is everywhere the adversary of adventure. In its cutting edge we might label this criticism, analysis, logic, aiming at an impersonal and ruthless will and scorning "temperament." Intellectually, it derives from the same kind of *work* as Mill and Spencer. Lenin made a hero of Chernyshevsky, and a Bible of his novel, while the

---

9. Jack London, quoted in Richard O'Connor, *Jack London,* 37.

young Tolstoy, in love with adventure, scorned both in the name of "temperament."

We see the international spread of adventure ideas most clearly in the way they were adapted by other countries—Russia, for example—from the Anglo-Saxon models in which they were first developed. In the middle of the nineteenth century, for instance, the novelist Ivan Goncharov was invited to accompany Admiral Putyatin, as official observer and recorder, on a journey around the world in a three-masted schooner, beginning in 1852. Russia, like America, wanted to begin trade with Japan, and Putyatin was in fact in rivalry with the American Admiral Perry on this voyage.

Goncharov's book about the voyage is written in the form of letters home, ostensibly addressed to the man of letters V. G. Benediktov. The author acknowledges the Anglo-Saxon model immediately; everyone, he says, knows about the sea from reading Cooper and Marryat.[10] Goncharov had long enjoyed such reading but always felt it deprived his imagination of something. When, as a boy, he had "passed from maps and teacher's guidance to read of the exploits and adventures of Cook, and Vancouver" he "became sad: to what did the exploits of Ajax, Achilles, or even Hercules, amount, compared to them? Works of children" (p. 5). The Anglo-Saxons were making legends out of reality, and thereby enfeebling all merely literary legends.

But this voyage was more exhilarating than depressing, on the whole. He had been, Goncharov said, a timid country boy all these years, but now, "I want to go to Brazil, to India, to places where the sun squeezes life out of a stone, . . . where man, like our first ancestor, garners fruit that he didn't plant, where the lion roars, where the snake slithers, where eternal summer reigns—to the shining places of God on earth, where nature, like a temple dancer, breathes voluptuousness, . . . where the unbridled imagination becomes drunk before the reality, where the eyes gaze ceaselessly, where the heart beats" (p. 5). This is the landscape of adventure, clearly.

Goncharov's is partly a sensual and imaginative enthusiasm, but it is partly also the triumph of reason and science he is celebrating, as Defoe and Verne celebrate it in their fiction. Both are part of the triumph of Renaissance man. In the past, people gave childish explanations for the earth's secrets, Goncharov says. "But then came a man, a wise one and

10. Ivan Goncharov, *The Frigate Pallada*, 4.

a poet, and he threw light into the secret recesses. He went with a directional compass, a spade, a drawing compass, a measuring line" (p. 5). This is the representative of modern Western knowledge, from Crusoe to Rider Haggard's heroes.

Goncharov exults in the prospect of all he will see. "I shall be in China, in India, I shall swim over the oceans, my foot will step on to those islands where in primeval simplicity the savage walks. I shall gaze at all these wonders—and my life will cease being a row of shallow, annoying details" (p. 6). It is a personal liberation that he will inherit by grace of the cultural change.

Preparing to set off, Goncharov felt his world, his identity, split in two, the one Russian and clerical, the other English and adventurous. "In one of them I—a modest official, dressed in a formal frock coat, cringing before the eyes of my superiors, afraid of catching cold, a prisoner in my four walls, in the company of tens of persons all looking the same, with the same uniforms. In the other world I—a new argonaut, with a straw hat, in a white linen jacket, maybe even with a plug of chewing tobacco in my mouth. . . . Here I was an editor of reports, relations and regulations; there, I was a bard, an appointed chronicler of the voyage" (p. 7). The word "bard" reminds us of Kipling, to whom it was so often applied; in Russia as in England, the writer about adventure is seen to be more like Homer or Virgil than like Tennyson or Wordsworth.

On the voyage, Goncharov in effect becomes an Englishman or an American, an embodiment of freedom. "How wonderful is life, especially because a man is able to travel" (p. 73). And in his famous novel *Oblomov* the hero is a satire on "the Russian temperament," and Goncharov depicts an opposite character, Stoltz, who has all the Robinson Crusoe or entrepreneurial characteristics. Despite his German name, Stoltz has in effect an English temperament. He is the friend of the hero and defines him by the contrast he makes.

Goncharov's description of Stoltz's heritage and development reflects the adventure idea in various ways. In part 2 we are told of Stoltz's boyhood and how, "when his lessons were over he went bird-nesting with the village boys . . . [and came home] without his boots, his clothes torn, and his nose bleeding—or the nose of some other boy."[11] When he disappeared for a week and came home with a gun and a pound of

11. Ivan Goncharov, *Oblomov*, 153.

powder, his father simply kicked him in punishment and told him to go away and come back with two chapters of Cornelius Nepos translated and a part in a French comedy learned by heart. But the boy's lessons were not merely literary. They were primarily practical, and they prepared him for the modern world. "Ever since he was a boy of eight, he had sat with his father over maps, spelt out the verses of Herder, Wieland, and the Bible, cast up the badly written accounts of the peasants, artisans, and factory hands" (p. 153). These are German and English ideas of boys' education, from Defoe and Campe through Marryat to *Tom Brown's Schooldays*.

Stoltz's father, we are told, was an agronomist, a technologist, and a teacher, who had himself wandered adventurously through Switzerland and Austria for four years before he came to Russia. There was no sentiment between him and his wife, though much honest feeling. From his mother, a Russian, Stoltz learned delicacy and understanding. She "disliked the coarseness, independence, and self-conceit with which the German masses everywhere asserted the civic rights they had acquired in the course of centuries" (p. 155). She taught her son the claims of elegance and aristocracy, as Scott understood those—a necessary addition, though only a grace added to a virtue. Mr. Stoltz is the adventurous male; Mrs. Stoltz represents the other and secondary side of the English tradition.

In the present time of the novel, Stoltz as a young man is "on the board of some company trading with foreign countries. He was continually on the move: if his company had to send an agent to Belgium or England, they sent him; if some new scheme had to be drafted or a new idea put into practise, he was chosen to do it. . . . He was made of bone, muscle, and nerve, like an English race-horse. He was spare: he had practically no cheeks, that is to say, there was bone and muscle but no sign of fat; his complexion was clear, darkish, and without a sign of red in it; his eyes were expressive, though slightly green" (p. 161). This is the way nineteenth-century novelists and illustrators depicted the Crusoe figure.

Goncharov thus gives us a vivid picture of the English mixture of adventure, practicality, and nationalism from outside. An interesting case of the same things seen more from the inside can be found in Sir William Butler and his wife Elizabeth. This is interesting partly because it is slightly oblique as a linking of nationalism and adventure to art in England. At the end of the nineteenth century, Lady Butler was the most eminent painter of imperial military history, and yet—by more than gender—she was alien to that history. Born in 1850 as Elizabeth Thompson, she was the sister of the well-known poet Alice Meynell. In 1877 she married Lieutenant General Butler, who commanded the boats on the expedition that arrived too late to relieve Gordon in the Sudan—one of the tragic adventures of history, from the point of view of British imperialism.

Both husband and wife were in some ways outside the WASP orthodoxy of Britain. For instance, both were Catholics, and he was Irish by birth, one of the large family of a small landowner in County Tipperary. Butler had risen in the army by attaching himself to Garnet Wolseley, one of the great Victorian soldiers, but he was on the side of radicals and rebels and read, for instance, Wilfred Scawen Blunt's attack on the English in India with agreement. His was the aristo-military adventurous temperament. He dismissed most colonial campaigns as "sutlers' wars" fought to line the pockets of the unworthy, and he saw the British intervention in Egypt in 1882 as a result of financiers controlling politicians.[12] He opposed the Boer War and was described as "an intuitive sympathizer with rebel nationalists all over the Empire" (p. 62).

Lady Butler had been brought up outside England, by a dilettante father, and in some ways outside English culture. Her approach to her subject-matter seems to have been "aesthetic," in the sense that she detached it from its political and moral challenges. She declared, "Thank God I never painted for the glory of war, but to portray its pathos and heroism. If I had seen even a corner of a real battlefield, I could never have painted another picture" (p. 66). This is, of course, an evasion of the moral problem, since the glory of war was always—at least in the liberal democracies—depicted in terms of its pathos and heroism. Her paintings *were* "for the glory of war." It is significant that General Butler was not at ease with his wife's subjects.

Lady Butler's 1874 painting *Roll Call*, depicting Crimean War soldiers, caused a sensation at the Royal Academy because it brought military subject-matter into the realm of art. Another famous painting was *Floreat Etona* (1881), celebrating the martyrdom of graduates from the famous Eton College and depicting the battle of Laing's Neck in

12. John Springhall, "Up Guards and At Them!": British Imperialism and Popular Art," in John M. MacKenzie, ed., *Imperialism and Popular Culture*, 63.

South Africa in the campaign of 1881. Lady Butler was quite popular and made thousands of pounds just from engravings of her work by the Fine Art Society. During the Great War, however, her popularity waned, as did Kipling's, and that of most of those who celebrated militarism in the arts, and in 1924 the painting she submitted to the Royal Academy Exhibition was rejected. For the fifty years of conscious imperialism, though, her pictures hung in schools, clubs, officers' messes (especially in the Empire), and upper-class homes. Then she fell victim to the national (indeed, international) revulsion against imperialism, and so against adventure.

A modern expression of very self-conscious adventure-and-national-ism is the American space program of the National Aeronautics and Space Agency (NASA). Adventure is at the heart of the official propaganda for the program. Chris Bonington includes the moon rocket among the adventures of his *Quest for Adventure* (1982). He indicates, however, that the elaborate organization of the program contradicts the individualism of adventure, and one suspects he believes the direct link to government has the same effect. Thus Bonington contrasts the astronaut Neil Armstrong, who has always worked within organizations and who is not physically adventurous, Bonington says, with the mountaineer Reinhold Messner, whose ascent of Everest had the opposite imaginative character, Messner being an outspoken individualist, dreamer, and philosopher.

Norman Mailer's *Of a Fire on the Moon* drew the same contrast between the spacemen and the political and cultural radicals of 1968, asking who were the true adventurers and implying that the former group were not. But these contradictions and redefinitions are part of a continuing dialectic. Wherever men seek out danger, the question of adventurous heroism must be in the air, and if sometimes, to some groups, the accolade is denied, at other times it is accorded. Thus, Tom Wolfe restored the setting and the ethos of adventure to the spacemen in *The Right Stuff.*

Inevitably, adventure and nationalism and history-writing are bound up together, and have been from the very beginning of national feeling. It is impossible to account for national competition and national identity as forces without the idea of adventure.

12

Politics and Economics

We have already sufficiently considered the connection between adventure and imperialism, associating the latter with conservative nationalist politics. But often—and, for instance, in America—the enthusiasm for adventure and masculinism are a part of the heritage of radical politics too. After all, the master myth of American politics is the revolution of brave, unprivileged, poorly armed colonists, primarily men, against the redcoats and the king and the British Empire. Radical movements, as well as conservative ones, have to seem to be the true heirs of those colonists.

Therefore the Wobbly movement (the Industrial Workers of the World, or IWW) around the turn of the nineteenth century was particularly attractive to Americans (including artists and intellectuals) because its propaganda and self-image was rooted in the myth of adventure. It began among the miners of the western states, but when it reached the East Coast (notably in the Lawrence strike of 1912) it carried the magic of American adventure with it for the mill workers, even though many of them were immigrants and women. The Wobbly phenomenon was probably what Jack London was primarily thinking of when he wrote enthusiastically about "the current revolution" in his 1905 essay "Revolution." Charles Ashleigh, an English-born Wobbly, wrote:

The striking feature of the Pacific country is that it is a man's country. . . . Conditions render it impossible for the worker to marry . . . [and] . . . the arduous physical toil in the open air does not have the same deteriorating effect as does the mechanical, confined work of the Eastern slave, . . . the wandering proletariat of the West. In health and in physical courage he is undoubtedly the superior of his Eastern brother. . . . A mighty wave of fertility sweeps up through the various states into British Columbia, drawing in its wake the legions of harvest workers.[1]

This way of spreading a political enthusiasm picks up the nonpolitical Americanism of Twain's passage on the young men of California in *Roughing It*. "It was a driving, vigorous, restless population in those days. . . . For observe, it was an assemblage of two hundred thousand *young* men—not simpering, dainty, kid-gloved weaklings, but stalwart, muscular, dauntless young braves, brimful of push and energy, and royally endowed with every attribute that goes to make up a peerless and magnificent manhood—the very pick and choice of the world's glorious ones."[2] This adventurous male imagery was part of the American national religion, and the Wobblies claimed it as especially their heritage.

This tradition was particularly strong and public in America because, as I have said, America was the land of adventure for the rest of the world and for its own citizens. Every one of the many meanings we have descried in adventure in the course of this discussion—geographical, historical, psychological, political—has a place in the myth of America, masked though it may be by other words: the West, the Frontier, Crossing the Delaware, Rough Riders, log cabins, covered wagons, migrant workers, immigrants, or freedom.

But what is most evident in America is nevertheless detectable in other countries. The American Revolution, the French Revolution, the Russian Revolution—all the revolutionary traditions are adventurous, and what country is without one such tradition? The Civil War in Spain, the Resistance in France, the Minutemen in New England—all the militia traditions are adventurous, and most of them are ostensibly left-wing. In countries like England, it is or was the Socialist or Labor party that was

1. Charles Ashleigh article in Joyce Kornbluh, ed., *Rebel Voices: An IWW Anthology*, 82.
2. Mark Twain, *Roughing It*, 309.

likely to march or to camp, to hike or to cycle, and to sleep out on the way to meetings.

In an autobiographical novel, Ashleigh again described the attraction the Wobblies had for young men like his hero, Joe. "They fascinated Joe. . . . There was an atmosphere of recklessness and daring about these fellows, who strolled along the streets in their blue overalls, or khaki trousers, with gray or blue shirts, open at the throats, and their black slouch hats. They knew the Western states from British Columbia to the Mexican border, from Chicago to Portland, Oregon. In all the vast territory where great railroads are still being built, or giant reservoirs . . . forests . . . [they] travel illegally, hiding upon freight or passenger trains."[3] They beat up or literally threw off the train anyone they found using a Wobbly card without being a Wobbly. Joe finally becomes "a hobo and a Wobbly, one of the reckless rambling boys who despised the soft security and comfort of a dull-paced city existence" (p. 103).

Adventure and physical bravery were part of the glamour of the Kennedy brothers. We associated Robert Kennedy with mountain-climbing, and Jack with sailing and swimming and with his heroic saving of men under his command during the war. In general, all politicians can add to their political attractiveness by having a good war record or some other of the insignia of adventure.

And if the attraction of adventure is a deep-rooted truth about our politics, something comparable can be said about our economics. Taking a lateral leap, we may say that the idea of adventure also played a part in the history of capitalism. The whole idea of the joint stock company, and the Stock Exchange, on which so much else of our economic system rests, is based on adventure. The history of the word shows that. An adventure in medieval times could mean a share in a trading voyage (or a ticket in a lottery). This is not the primary meaning for *our* word "adventure," but there are connections; the idea of risk was there already, and so was the idea of travel and of passing beyond the limits of the known and secure, literally and metaphorically.

This was closely connected to the mathematical and statistical basis of insurance and banking. In the eighteenth century, J. H. Le Blanc said of the English, "The probability of life, and the return of ships, are the objects of their arithmetic. The same spirit of calculating they extend to games, wagers, and everything in which there is any hazard."[4] From the

3. Charles Ashleigh, *The Rambling Kid*, 92.
4. Quoted in Guttmann, ed., *From Ritual to Record*, 59, 60.

eagerness to risk and wager came the need to measure time and space. The captain's ledgers are close kin to the scorecard. We know things, as we do things, speculatively, risking our investment on our guesses about the future.

This is the part of the capitalist heritage that Michael Nerlich, in his *Kritik der Abenteuer Ideologie,* makes a great deal of: "I plead for the recognition of chaos, anarchy, movement, disorder, as an inalienable quality of reality."[5] Nerlich agrees that England after 1640 was a good place for economics to develop, because of a harmony there between theory and practice, between methodology and world-view—the harmony demonstrated in the quotation from Le Blanc—as well as because of a coincidence of thinker and profit-hunter. What Bacon and Hobbes offered as natural law, Munn, Child, Davenant, and Petty turned into economic equations. The revolutionary phase of bourgeois politics was over by then, but only because adventure had become institutionalized in capitalism (p. 249).

Marx put it that Locke drove out Habbakuk, that Cromwell's revolution had dressed itself in Old Testament righteousness, but then Locke (and Defoe) substituted rational language for Old Testament prophecy.[6] Locke was, as Engels said in 1890, a perfect son of the 1688 class compromise, in his teachings about both religion and politics.[7] By replacing the cynical idea of booty with the righteous idea of work, as the key economic fact, he saved his disciples from having to follow Hobbes into amoralism. He gave dignity to the trading classes and made them national heroes. His allies on the weekly journals, such as Addison and Steele, were, like Defoe, ironical about the claims of England's country squires to represent national virtue, and they insisted that a trader was as much the English gentleman as they.

Respectability was therefore an essential if hidden part of the *Weltan-schauung* of the trader, but so was adventurism. This was, in its beginnings, a revolutionary bourgeoisie fighting for all mankind's freedom, from Marx's point of view.[8] It was not bourgeois simply in the familiar nineteenth-century literary sense. Nerlich gives the topic a much broader historical scope. The three parts of his book deal with, first, the development of the knightly adventurer in France, then with the idea of the

5. Michael Nerlich, *Kritik der Abenteuer Ideologie,* vii.
6. See ibid., 260.
7. Ibid., 250.
8. Ibid., 14.

bourgeois adventurer in England, and then with the later history of the bourgeois adventurer in France.

Nerlich usefully traces the history of the word. "Adventure" had juristic and economic meanings from early on, but before the year 1200 these references were made in Latin (p. 82). By the fifteenth century, however, we find many references in many languages. Thus, in England, the "Adventurers of the Mercery" were formed in 1443–44. The word meant alternatively "soldier/bandit" or "merchant," with the ambiguity typical of all really crucial concepts. But in both cases it connoted travel and risk. The development of money-changing in the eleventh and twelfth centuries had made commerce mobile (p. 88).

Economically, Nerlich says, "adventure" really means not just the investment of capital but also the acceptance of change, risk, chance, the unknown.[9] This acceptance goes deep below consciousness. As Engels said, the merchant was a revolutionary element in medieval society, but in his social function, and by his activity, not by his consciousness.

It is obvious that the adventurer usually cooperated with certain other merchants,[10] but he was also a destroyer of human bonds—for instance, what might have been bonds with his competitors. As Marx said, trade more and more subjects production to exchange value and dissolves old relationships. Thus, the fully developed capitalist competes against all his fellows. Indeed, when it is dominant, commercial capitalism is a system of plunder, bound up with piracy, slavery, and the subjugation of colonies.[11] Historically, the process of developing capitalism was quite violent, involving the expropriation of the peasants, the latter's uprisings in protest, the revolts of the nobles, the wars of religion, the slave trade, and genocide.

Nevertheless, the process felt virtuous to those engaged in developing capitalism. Credit, even with interest, seemed to the seventeenth-century merchant quite different from usury, mostly because it seemed to be the friend of energy, work, and virtue—of risk and adventure.[12] Bacon stressed the way trade combined the youthful spirit of enterprise with the expertise of age. But the growth of trade had its enemies, especially among the traditional moralists. Luther, for instance, being a religious

9. Michael Nerlich, *The Ideology of Adventure*, xxi.
10. Ibid., 76.
11. Ibid., 89.
12. Ibid., 113.

moralist, predicted a global conflagration if an end was not put to large-scale commerce and trading companies.

The capital-derived explosion of cultural energy named its most glamorous aspect the Renaissance and associated adventure with great artistic and intellectual achievements. Even Communists like Engels shared the enthusiasm of the bourgeoisie for the Renaissance myth and used one of the languages allied to adventure to praise it. (We have seen that there was a family of styles in which the values of masculinism and imperialism was expressed.) "It was the greatest progressive revolution that mankind has so far experienced, a time which called for giants—giants in power of thought, passion, and character. . . . The adventurous character of the times inspired them." Such men, Engels said, traveled extensively, spoke four or five languages, shone in a number of fields. "Fullness and force of character made complete men."[13] These are Renaissance heroes like Leonardo da Vinci, Dürer, and Machiavelli.

But after them came their shadow, the bourgeois, which is "fanatically bent on the valorization of value" and consequently, "ruthlessly forces the human race to produce for production's sake."[14] The bourgeois narrowed down the range of interests and energies opened up by the Renaissance. Adventure became suspect. "Only as a personification of capital is the capitalist respectable."[15] But before the blighting influence of capital was felt, Nerlich concludes, "the magic word in which the interests of the different classes and strata seemed to converge was adventure" (p. 113).

All this could have been said (in only slightly different terms) by Kipling. And indeed Jack London wrote, in appreciation of Kipling, that to show the triumphant world career of the revolutionary bourgeoisie, to sing its triumphant paean of commercialism and imperialism, was precisely the Englishman's achievement. Kipling was the Homer of that class.[16]

Under its aspect of "let's pretend," capitalism has a lot in common with all kinds of fiction. (Issue shares that say they are worth ten million dollars, and people will buy them by exchanging real money for them.) Adventure narratives, whether fictional or nonfictional, live by the excitement they engender and by their promise of fantastic rewards. And

13. Quoted in ibid., 108.
14. Ibid., 111.
15. Ibid.
16. Jack London, "These Bones Shall Rise Again," in *Revolution*, 224–25.

venture capitalists and adventurer heroes both invite us to "leave behind what we know." Both are kinds of explorer/inventor/magician. Thus, the idea or ideas of adventure work deep in our understanding of politics and economics, art and spirituality, without often coming to consciousness as adventure. It is a master idea of our culture, whose activity is to be traced under the surface. Without it, our thinking would be different in many ways.

13

Religion and Therapy

There have always been religious adventures, some of them in the quite unregenerate and even military senses of the word. To take examples only from the history of Christianity, the Crusades were great adventures under the sign of the Cross. The Catholic missions of the Counter-Reformation, the Protestant missions slightly later, and the nonviolent sects, such as the Quakers and the Moravians, also engaged in adventures, which involved going into unknown lands and learning new languages and cultures.

Such adventurers knew they risked everything, in a matter of life and death. The Jesuit order founded by Ignatius of Loyola was military both in its discipline and in many of its members. Saint Teresa of Avila left home as a child, setting out to convert the Moors, and some of her brothers went out to America as conquistadores. There were also regenerate or antimilitary religious missions that deserve the name of adventures, as the name of the Spanish Dominican Bartolomeo de las Casas, will remind us.

Bartolomeo crossed the Atlantic, probably with Columbus in 1504, and took part, as Dominican priest but also as conquistador, in the conquest of Cuba in 1512. Like the other adventurers, he was given land as a reward, but by 1514 Bartolomeo was convinced that his countrymen's treatment of the Indians was tyrannical. In 1517 he proposed that black slaves be imported from Africa to do the work that was so uncongenial to the Indians. However, he soon repented of that idea too, and in 1520 he set up a community of Spanish pioneers at Cumaná, where the white men did their own work. The people of this community were massacred by Indians, and Bartolomeo retired to a monastery in Santo Domingo for eight years. He gradually made it his life work to be the voice of conscience to the Spanish people concerning the Indians and their fate—as, for instance, when he was seventy-six years old and speaking in the negative at the Council in Valladolid in 1550, which discussed the question "Is it lawful for the King of Spain to wage war on the Indians before preaching the faith to them?"[1]

Bartolomeo's work in South America was continued by the Jesuits. In 1596, five missionaries, one of them English, set to work in Paraguay and received royal support in 1607 and 1609. They set up a theocracy among the Indians there, using the skills and forces of this world in the service of otherworldly values, and for more than 150 years they were successful. The people they worked with, the Guarani, were "primitive"; they went naked, or nearly so, the number words in their language counted only up to four, and they were cannibals on occasion. They recognized the cultural superiority of the whites. Although they had already taken to agriculture, they were ready to be guided and instructed by the Jesuits. (I am relaying Jack Beeching's account, favorable to the Jesuits.)

When the latter were driven from their posts by the secular power of Spain, the Guarani petitioned the governor of Buenos Aires for the return of their protectors, declaring, "We desire to say that the Spanish custom is not to our liking, for everyone to take care of himself, instead of helping one another in their daily toil."[2] The Spaniards, then, were seen as being entrepreneurs, and the Jesuits as not being Spanish because they weren't entrepreneurs. We are used to seeing the Anglo-Saxons treated as supremely the individualists amongst the Western peoples, the Spaniards having an opposite social psychology; but in their encounters with native populations, all the white nations took on the aspect of entrepreneurs.

By 1614 some 119 Jesuits were at work in Paraguay, and by 1630

1. See Jack Beeching, *An Open Path*, 17.
2. Ibid., 15.

they were directing settlements in which 40,000 Indians lived, on the banks of rivers there. But they were persecuted by slave raiders from Brazil, called mamelucos and armed with guns and lances, who in 1630 killed or enslaved 30,000 of the Guarani. The conflict presented itself in ethical or religious terms of good versus evil; the mamelucos sometimes disguised themselves as Jesuits and attacked the settlements on Sundays, when the Guarani came together to attend church services. The Jesuit defence was nonviolent. When the mamelucos drove away a column of 15,000 Guarani in chains to São Paulo, Fathers Maceta and Mansilla followed, carrying the chains of the weakest, persisting, despite threats to their lives.

To avoid another such raid, in 1631 the Jesuits led the remaining 12,000 Guarani farther into the largely unknown interior on seven hundred boats and rafts. (The mamelucos immediately moved into the abandoned villages, burning the churches and turning the priests' quarters into a brothel.) Father Montoya, the Jesuits' leader, went ahead of the migration disguised as an Indian and found built near an impassable waterfall a Spanish fort waiting to destroy them. So he led them on a long detour overland, and they cleared a track with machetes as they went.

This is clearly an adventure story. The Jesuits marched at the head of the enormous column, wearing black habits and looped hats and carrying their altar plate and an image of the Virgin. Reaching another Jesuit "reduction" (their word for the large villages they organized), they bought new cattle for their people and started to build two new reductions of their own. After five years of prosperity, however, they were again threatened by slave raiders; so, having first built themselves a defensible site between two rivers, Father Montoya went to Madrid and there got permission for the Jesuits to take up arms in self-defense. The religious adventure became even more like the secular kind. (The paradoxes of the nonviolent man helping his violent comrades have been presented in English-language adventures, especially those about the Quakers; see, for instance, William the Quaker in Defoe's *Captain Singleton*.)

The Paraguay Jesuits included several old soldiers,[3] from whom the Guaranis learned how to be horsemen, leaping into the saddle and using their lance as a vaulting pole. They were armed with bolas and lassos,

3. Ibid., 28.

iron tipped arrows, and some guns, and they made their own gunpowder. In each village there was one technical enterprise—a tile kiln, a
stamping mill, a blast furnace—and everyone did agricultural work. In
each reduction there were two Jesuits, one acting as priest, the other as
administrator, and the Order included men of different nationalities.
They led their people into battle but carried no arms themselves, and
once the fighting began, they offered succor to all the wounded, no
matter which side they were on.

In the reductions, property was held in common, and the economy
was based on barter; money was used almost exclusively by the Jesuits,
who had to have dealings with the outside world. These anticapitalist
arrangements (together with their ecclesiastical affiliation) provoked the
hostility of such Enlightenment intellectuals as Voltaire, and the climate
of world opinion was unfavorable to the Jesuits. In 1742 the Spanish
authorities told them to move again, but this time the Guarani rebelled,
though ineffectually, and in 1753 were subdued by Spanish troops. The
struggle dragged on for decades. The crucial attack on the reductions
came in 1773, after which seventy-eight Jesuits were marched to Buenos
Aires in manacles.

In Canada as well, from 1630 on, the Jesuits were the most prominent
missionaries. They decided to concentrate their efforts on the Huron
Indians, who were agriculturists and therefore more "advanced" than,
for instance, the still-nomadic Algonquins. Father de Brébeuf, a Norman
noble by birth, led a group of priests nine hundred miles from Quebec
to a Huron settlement. But the Hurons culture was less gentle than the
Guarani's. Jack Beeching says the two groups had some cultural traits in
common, however; both the Hurons and the Jesuits despised the body
and made a cult of pain (p. 52).

Like secular adventure heroes, the Jesuits also carried the products of
Western technology—a clock, a magnet, a magnifying glass—and were
able to defeat their religious rival, the Huron sorcerer, by using Western
science: they accurately predicted a lunar eclipse. (Eclipse predictions
are part of many adventure tales, factual and fictional.) By 1649,
eighteen Jesuits were serving a flock of twenty thousand Indians. When
the Iroquois attacked, the Jesuits helped their people find shelter on an
island and build twelve-foot-high stone walls. Six thousand Hurons took
refuge there, and after a long siege, and despite being near starvation,
the Jesuits finally led the survivors out of their refuge and past their
enemy and back to Quebec. But Father Brébeuf, was captured, savagely

tortured, and killed. These North American and South American stories are both kinds of religious adventure.

The Evangelical movement in the Protestant churches seems to have been more closely connected with nationalist ideology. In the nineteenth century, Gerald Newman says, "it was the Low Church zealots of the Church of England, the Methodists and Evangelicals, who now sprang forward to become the chief standard bearers of the nationalist movement."[4] He is referring to the period 1789–1830. Even though ostentatiously loyal in politics, they were, he says, revolutionaries in social and moral matters because they created English nationalism. Their supporters included divines, barristers, bankers, entrepreneurs, missionaries, and colonists (p. 235). Reading that list of occupations, we note how many could be, on occasion, "adventurous," in one sense or another. We realize it is no coincidence that these people produced and consumed the adventure tale. Their influence was great throughout the nineteenth century.

The Salvation Army, founded in 1865, has a special claim on our attention, at the end of the century. We have already discussed the Army as an example of the use of military and adventure imagery, which must necessarily evoke adventure thought and feeling to some degree, in the service of peace and reform. But now, in order to consider the Protestant missions as a religious branch of adventurous imperialism, we must return to that topic. Spiritually, the Army was a movement of repentance and self-castigation, inward-turning. Its members believed in Christ as Savior, and in the gospel of suffering and the eternity of Hell. They had no sacraments and little theology, but the conversion experience was of great emotional importance to them. Members had to repent, renounce the world, obey. Confessions of former sins, made in public at the Penitent Form, were a dramatic feature of services. But this inward-turning was allied to fervent social action, at first at home, in the slums, and later abroad.

At the end of the century the Salvation Army engaged in projects of social reclamation by means of the three kinds of colonies: City, Farm, and Over Sea colonies. People reclaimed from vice and crime in the slums lived first in a City Colony, and then passed to a Farm, and then Over Seas, if they proved able. The Army was thus adventurous in taking men out to the edge of society, and it is not surprising that adventure-

4. Gerald Newman, *The Rise of English Nationalism*, 234.

writer H. Rider Haggard was hired to inspect their colonies and report on them. In February 1905 he was funded by the Cecil Rhodes trustees and appointed commissioner by the Secretary for the Colonies, to inspect three such settlements in the United States, in California, Colorado, and Ohio. He reported that he had been encouraged in his efforts by such eminent Americans as President Theodore Roosevelt and by Secretaries Wilson and Hay. They too saw the founding of colonies as a means of salvation for the American poor.

Canada had offered the Army 360 square miles, to make ten townships, for similar projects. Haggard consulted Wilfred Laurier and Lord Grey in Canada, and the Mormons in Salt Lake City. In the home country, the Salvation Army had made a great success of a three-thousand-acre colony and model farm at Hadleigh, near Southend, bought in 1891. But in England the Church Army (the Church of England's answer to the Salvation Army) was also competing in the setting up of such colonies, so they turned their eyes abroad.

According to Haggard, 123,000 people emigrated from the United Kingdom to the United States in 1903, and 100,000 in 1904. He himself saw emigration as the salvation of poor people from the evil conditions of parts of the big cities, where their health was ruined from birth. The return to nature and the experience of adventure would save them. He wanted people who would have to struggle and "make themselves" and he declared that a man without money made a better colonist than one with money. The whole scheme was seen as an adventure. Many people of British blood and fathers of families, Haggard said, wanted to "attempt the adventure of a different life in new homes upon the land."[5]

In Africa, Haggard recommended particularly Rhodesia, where the best-quality tobacco could be grown. The empire as a whole was the natural field for adventure and colony-planning. New Zealand had made advances to settlers of nearly £9,000,000 in 1904 alone. The gift of land, and the chance to make something of it was essential, as the Robinson Crusoe myth implied. They and Haggard (unlike the Jesuits) declared their faith in "the magic of property," quoting a phrase of Arthur Young.

The Salvation Army derived its popularity, and also incurred resistance because it was so clearly an application of the adventure movement to social problems. In the Imperialist period, when so many people

5. H. Rider Haggard, *The Poor and the Land*, 11.

believed in adventure, it seemed hopeful to direct those energies back up on religion and economics and sociology. That is why Haggard and Roosevelt, and Kipling and Buchan, were so sympathetic to General Booth, and why the Marxist socialists were so unsympathetic.

In *Regeneration* (1910), Haggard wrote an account of the Salvation Army as a whole, at the request of founder General William Booth, saying that the ordinary person of fashion or leisure thinks of the Army as a fraud for the benefit of the founder. Needless to say, Haggard takes an opposite point of view. By 1910 the Army was established in fifty-six countries and colonies, with 16,000 officers and seventy-four periodicals with a total circulation of one million. It had 149 "Slum Stations," and homes for criminals, drunkards, women, and children. Booth believed the government should support the Army, especially in its work with criminals. His was an attempt to save society by an exchange between its rotten center and its periphery, by bringing the virtues of the frontier more into play.

The Dutch government apparently did support the Army, both in Holland and in Java. Australia had Salvation Army men run boys' reformatories, New Zealand paid them to work with drunkards, and Canada let them run a prison. They also did a lot of work in India, where the soldiers in the Army wore Indian dress. They worked with criminal tribes and, anticipating Gandhi, devised a new hand loom.

Another man of letters who helped the Army was W. T. Stead, editor of the *Pall Mall Gazette*. He helped General Booth write his 1890 book, *In Darkest England and the Way Out*. Stead was a friend of Cecil Rhodes, although he bitterly opposed Britain's part in the Anglo-Boer War.

Opposition to the Salvation Army came from, among others, the Labour party, who called Booth "the Prince of sweaters" because he did not pay those who worked for him the trade union rate for their labor. Of course, late nineteenth-century socialist theory would always be hostile to the organization's religious and philanthropic affiliations.

The Salvation Army cooperated with the Barnardo Homes for Orphans, the two representing a different sort of social activism from the Labour party. The Barnardo Homes took boys up to the age of sixteen and sent the older ones on to the Army. (Kipling wrote stories about the Barnardo Homes, as he did about the Boy Scouts.) The colonies, like frontier communities, apparently preferred single men, and Haggard describes a shipload of five hundred (their wives left behind) that the

Army sent to Canada. In seven years, 50,000 men went, primarily to Canada, 10,000 of them paid for by the Army. According to him, only one percent returned. The Army wanted to see an imperial emigration board set up.

"Why do not the writers of naturalistic novels study Salvation Army Shelters?" Haggard asks.[6] It is indeed at first sight a paradox, this alliance of the Army with the adventure novelist rather than with the exposé-writer, but only at first. The adventure novelist and the muckraker contrasted with each other the way that mythical images contrasted with naturalist treatments of the same material. It is perhaps no accident that Haggard should declare Booth a great man, a great adventurer, like Napoleon or Muhammad, but one willing to help, not harm, others (p. 209). Haggard said President Roosevelt shared his admiration for Booth. On the other hand, the writers of naturalistic novels were likely to be natural allies of the Labour party, insofar as they dealt with existent reality, gave life to the statistics of official reports, and analyzed the forces that maintained an unjust status quo. They would not invoke Napoleon or Muhammad, and they wanted to solve social problems on the spot. The Salvation Army wanted to solve them by going abroad.

The missionaries were not so sympathetic to the native cultures they met as some of the other official adventurers were. Thomas Haweis, one of the founders of the London Missionary Society, had been inspired to do such work originally by Cook's *Voyages,* but he later repudiated Cook's picture of the islands as being too idyllic to be authentic. Haweis preached to the Society in 1795 about "whole societies of men and women who live promiscuously, and murder every infant born among them."[7]

Even a poet like Coleridge came to believe the missionaries instead of Cook, saying that the latter had done immense harm and that some of those societies were detestably licentious.[8] This change of sympathy was culturally and morally conservative, or reactionary. The adventure of becoming a missionary began to look more dangerous, though also more heroic, than before.

After 1820, some of the editions of Cook and other voyages were "evangelized," in the sense that the illustrations depicting natives made them darker and squatter, and the effect of the pictures became more

6. H. Rider Haggard, *Regeneration,* 173.
7. Bernard Smith, *European Vision and the South Pacific,* 2d ed., 144.
8. Ibid., 147.

racially emotive. For instance, in one, Webber's picture entitled *Human Sacrifice at Tahiti* was included. And in W.H.G. Kingston's edition of Cook a picture of a potbellied, pigeon-toed New Zealand idol was introduced.

A much-reproduced print was G. Baxter's *Massacre of the Lamented Missionary, the Reverend John Williams*, depicting his assassination on Erromanga. This antinative propaganda is one reason that contemporary scholars (such as C. H. Grattan, in his *South-West Pacific to 1900*) often take a hostile or condescending attitude toward the missionaries. They were indeed tradesmen of small schooling who had no contact with the world of taste and learning and had few cultural or anthropological interests.[9] But they had true adventurers among them.

If adventure was a part of religion in the nineteenth century, it was also a form of therapy, both physical and psychological. Sometimes this took the mild form of a cruise or a journey around the world. Sometimes it took the much more drastic form of sailing before the mast, like Richard Henry Dana; or of crossing the American prairies to observe Indian tribes at war, like Francis Parkman; or of running a ranch in the Dakotas, like Theodore Roosevelt. These were all varieties of masculine and outdoors therapy, on horseback or in the rigging, as opposed to the indoors therapy, recumbent and passive, offered to women by doctors like S. Weir Mitchell and (mutatis mutandis) Sigmund Freud. On the whole, the latter has triumphed, at least in the world of ideas. We haven't heard much of the former in the last few decades, though it is interesting that a recent mystery novel (Bruce Zimmerman's *Blood Under the Bridge,* 1989) offers us as hero a practitioner of "outdoors psychology" in the nineteenth-century sense.

Dana's last chapter from *Two Years Before the Mast* gives us an example of the way the Western landscape, and the journey west, was thought able to invigorate East Coast Americans in the middle of the nineteenth century. In San Francisco in 1850, Dana met a man he had known fifteen years earlier as a strict and formal deacon of the Congregational church in New England. "He was a deacon still, in San Francisco, a leader in all pious works, devoted to his denomination and to total abstinence—the same internally, but externally, what a change! Gone was the downcast eye, the bated breath, the solemn, non-natural voice, the watchful gait, stepping as though he felt himself responsible

9. C. H. Grattan, *The South-West Pacific to 1900*, 196–97.

for the balance of the moral universe. He walked with a stride, an uplifted, open countenance, his face covered with beard, whiskers, and moustache, his voice strong and natural—and, in short, he had put off the New England deacon and become a human being."[10] The adventurous life of the West has redeemed him. (Perhaps the most imaginative detail is the sprouting of beard, whiskers, and mustache, as a symbol of a new vitality.)

Ned Warren, the Bostonian collector of classical antiquities, found his own salvation by going east, to England, as so many American aesthetes did at the end of the nineteenth century. Among his friends were Bernard Berenson and George Santayana. But he writes of another Harvard friend and classmate (Class of 1883) who had gone to Texas and who wrote Ned exultantly to say he'd never known a man could be so healthy and so dirty. Those were the two escapes, toward the east and toward the west, and of the two it was the second that had more clearly the character of adventure therapy. (Ned Warren's life story is told in my *Mount Vernon Street Warrens*.)

In Russia a cure for consumption was to go to the eastern frontier, where Russia bordered on the tribal lands of Central Asia, and to live with the tribal peoples there and drink kumys, the milk of the wild mares, fermented. Tolstoy's father took that cure—the symbolic meaning of which is obvious—and in due time so did the novelist himself.

Tolstoy established a second home in the province of Samara, where his neighbors were Bashkiri tribesmen, in 1871. He bought 3,600 acres (paid for with his literary earnings) on a trip he took with his brother-in-law Stephen Bers. Tolstoy developed a ranch. His land was divided into twelve "fields," two of which were sown with wheat; the others were pasture. (Samara had essentially a single-crop economy.) Oxen pulled the plows, but Samara was above all a land of horses. Tolstoy wrote to his wife about the magnificent spectacle of thousands of horses—the mares and foals separate from the stallions—coming down from the mountains to the steppe. He bred Bashkir mares with English and Russian trotters, and by 1877 had 150 horses on his farm. He rode Bashkir-style, using Bashkir wooden stirrups.

This was not so much farming as ranching in the American sense, and for Russians it carried the same elements of wildness and adventure as it carried for Americans in their national myth. The oldest son, Sergei

10. Richard Henry Dana, *Two Years Before the Mast*, 314.

Tolstoy, tells us he rode semi-trained horses across the steppes and watched wild horses being tamed for the first time. The herd was guarded by stallions trained to bite and kill horse thieves. When some Kirghiz stole forty of the Tolstoy horses, a Tolstoy party pursued them, and there was a fight with whips. The Kirghiz were planning to drive the horses into a literal limen, a no-man's-land beyond the Urals, two hundred versts away. And in 1876 Tolstoy got to know a merchant in nearby Orenburg who traded in tiger skins with Turkestan and whose grandfather had lived by selling Russian girls as slaves to the markets of Central Asia.

The life was primitive. There was no wood on the steppe, and the Tolstoys burned bricks of manure. They ate mutton and drank kumys almost exclusively. A Muslim Bashkir, Muhammad Shah, brought his tents, his family, and ten milking mares to live beside the Tolstoys and talked to the novelist of the old Bashkir ways. Because serfdom had never been established in Samara, he shook hands as an equal with the Russian count, free from peasant deference. On the other hand, his wife and daughter-in-law did all the work and took no part in social life; Sonia Tolstoy was indignant on their behalf.

The Tolstoys lived in local housing, a felt-covered hemispheric cage of wood. The family went there first in 1873, and the eldest daughter, Tania, recorded the strangeness of the landscape and the life. There were no ponds, woods, rivers, or mushrooms, as at home, but instead eagles, buzzards, tarantulas, wolves. Tolstoy wrote to his wife: "We've just been riding after buzzards, and only scared them away as usual, and then we came on a wolf's litter, and a Bashkir caught a cub there."[11] In these letters he evoked the legend of the Swiss Family Robinson, and in his diary said that part two of his new novel would have a Robinson Crusoe figure who "starts an entirely new life, made up of only the most indispensable factors of existence."[12]

It is clear that this idea of returning to the human or societal origin stayed with Tolstoy a long time as a subject to write about. In his diary for June 19, 1896, we read: "The picture of life in Samara stands out very clearly before me: the steppes, the fight of the nomadic, patriarchal principle with the agricultural-civilized one. It draws me very much."[13] Sonia, on the other hand, disliked not only the primitive conditions of

11. *Tolstoy's Letters,* 164.
12. Quoted in Sophia Tolstoy, *The Diary of Tolstoy's Wife,* 67.
13. *The Journal of Leo Tolstoy,* 58.

life in Samara but also the Robinson Crusoe idea itself. In 1884 she wrote to him from Moscow that she knew he had stayed behind alone in Yasnaya Polyana not to do intellectual work, the most important thing in the world to her, but to play at some Robinson Crusoe game. For her, Samara was primarily a business investment, and there were many bitter quarrels between husband and wife over his inefficiency in managing it. (In the family the Samara estate became known as "the Eastern Question" because of these quarrels.)

The Bashkir tribes were an incarnation of wildness. They had taken part in Pugachev's revolt against Catherine the Great in the eighteenth century and had been exiled to the Samaran steppe thereafter. Marc Raeff says Pugachev's rebellion was directed against Peter the Great's modernization of Russia. They hated and raided Russian factories and the city of Orenburg, which represented all Russian cities to them (Tolstoy's estate was only 120 versts from Orenburg). But they also represented nonhistorical or prehistorical forces. They led a pastoral nomadic life on land where nothing but silvery feather grass grew for hundreds of miles. In the winters they lived in primitive villages, but every spring they moved out to wander the steppe.

The kumys cure included, besides the diet, a great deal of riding, living in a tent, sleeping on the ground, and generally entering into the Bashkir lifestyle. Tolstoy, for instance, wrestled with the tribesmen and no doubt felt their virtue pass into him with their sweat. The cure was one of the ways a revolt against civilization could be built into the culture and transformed into a renewal of the civilizing race's vocation.

Tolstoy's friend Sergei Aksakov, who wrote *A Russian Gentleman*, came from a family that bought land from the Bashkirs. Aksakov's mother took the kumys cure, and his father bought 7,000 desyatinas very cheap, thirty versts from Ufa. According to Aksakov, his grandfather was a true patriarch; he wore homespun and had two servants who slept on the floor of his room. He had purchased his land direct from the Bashkirs; he *was* a Crusoe of the steppe, or perhaps a Swiss Family Robinson. "How wonderful in those days was that region, with its wild and virginal freshness!" says Aksakov. "Both steppe and forest were filled beyond belief with wild creatures. In a word, the place was, and still is a paradise for the sportsman."[14]

14. Sergei Aksakov, *A Russian Gentleman*, 8.

A Russian sportsman could thus own Nature, although Aksakov felt the pathos of his own destructiveness. "But man is the sworn foe of Nature, and she can never withstand his treacherous warfare against her beauty" (p. 14). As in America, in Russia some of the settlers imitated the tribes they met; Aksakov's uncle, Karataev, wandered the steppe with a tribe all through the summers, speaking their language, shooting with bow and arrow, drinking their mead, singing their songs, growing bowlegged from his days in the saddle.

Tolstoy's great disciple, Gandhi, developed a kind of nonhunting adventure therapy in South Africa. His most notable establishment he called Tolstoy Farm, though it was not like the Samara estate just described. Gandhi's was a venture in the Simple Life, which he combined with a refuge for the families of those imprisoned for their part in civil disobedience. But it was similar in its effects to Tolstoy's. "The weak became strong on Tolstoy Farm and labor proved to be a tonic for all."[15]

In June 1910, Gandhi's friend Hermann Kallenbach gave his farm at Lawley, near Johannesburg, to the satyagraha cause and announced its new name. Gandhi told his readers that Kallenbach was going to retire from architecture and live in poverty with the Indians. They had no servants, and the descriptions in Gandhi's letters are full of zest in the physical work—chopping and sawing wood, fetching water and doing laundry, rolling stones for a foundation. "I for one am a farmer and I wish you all to become farmers," he wrote to his nephew Maganlal in August of that year. "My way of life has completely changed here. The whole day is spent in digging the land and other manual labor instead of in writing and explaining things to people. I prefer this work and consider this alone to be my duty. . . . I regard the Kaffirs, with whom I constantly work these days, as superior to us. What they do in their ignorance we have to do knowingly. In outward appearance we should look just like the Kaffirs."[16]

These were the Robinson Crusoe pleasures, here renewed. "Having founded a sort of village," wrote Gandhi, "we needed all manner of things large and small, from benches to boxes, and we made them all ourselves."[17] And the reduction to simplicity produced an exaltation of spirit. The experience was profoundly and permanently important to

---

15. M. Gandhi, *Satyagraha in South Africa*, 217.
16. Gandhi, *Collected Works*, 10:308.
17. Gandhi, *Satyagraha in South Africa*, 241.

Gandhi. "My faith and courage were at their highest in Tolstoy Farm. I have been praying to God to permit me to re-attain that height."[18]

Gandhi wrote a series of articles on health that endorsed the simple life, in diet and labor and clothing, even to the point of nudity. On July 15, 1911, he wrote: "A moment's thought ought to convince our friends that a nation cannot be built out of clerks or even merchants. 'Back to the land' is General Botha's advice even to the Europeans who, after all, do follow many useful occupations. The world lives on its farmers and those who are indispensable to farmers, e.g. carpenters. . . . We all live upon the great industry of the Natives and Indians engaged in useful occupations in this country. In this sense they are more civilized than any of us."[19]

The idea of adventure of a new life at the frontiers of the settlements, potent enough to reanimate exhausted nerves and diseased bodies, was therefore a manifold presence in all white countries in the nineteenth century. So, for some, was the religious idea of missionary work and even martyrdom as a supreme Christian adventure.

18. Ibid., 244.
19. Gandhi, Collected Works, 11:124.

14

Caste and Empire

The most important single way in which the cult of adventure inspired or justified a political idea, and the rhetoric of adventure ornamented or disguised it, had to do with empire. At the end of the nineteenth century, the activities of imperial governors and soldiers were habitually described to readers, and were known to the participants themselves, in one of the dialects of adventure. In the adventure language we can distinguish more than one vocabulary suited to exciting action, to awe-inspiring landscape, to the grandeur of a court, or to the pathos and triumph of the hero, but notably a set of words connected with the aristo-military caste. So the talk of adventure and empire then often implied a preference for a warrior caste or for an aristocracy.

We find this language in Nietzsche and Kipling and Rider Haggard. As early as *King Solomon's Mines,* Haggard is discussing the crucial quality of being a gentleman, which Zulu warriors have and white clerks lack. (In his very first book, *Cetywayo and His White Neighbours,* he denies the character of gentleman to the Boers.) But we find this language also in those who took the opposite political attitudes, such as Tolstoy and Shaw and J. A. Hobson. In *Imperialism* the latter sets words like "glory," "adventure," and "empire" together, and when he talks about "the upper classes" and "the upper middle classes," he could as well talk of castes. Tolstoy and Shaw do speak of the military, or aristo-military caste.

We can take from the introduction to General Gordon's journals an example of one military-adventure and solitary-hero perspective in which imperial politics were often seen and described: "Thus he avenged defeat, drew in stores and guns, and held the enemy at bay. So that for eleven long months, spite of mutiny, cowardice, and treachery within, and the constant attacks from the enemy without, he held his own, and to spare. . . . How his time was passed till we should come, how he viewed our chances of success, and how he proposed to act if we at last did arrive, this is a story which the *Journals* tell themselves."[1]

John Buchan's *History of the Great War* (1923) used similar lofty language. Describing one of his friends, Raymond Asquith, who had died in the war, he said: "His aloofness from the facile acquaintanceships of the modern world made him incomprehensible to many, and his high fastidiousness gave him a certain air of coldness. Most noble in presence, and with every grace of voice and manner, he moved among men like a being of another race, . . . a type of his country at its best. . . . Debonair and brilliant and brave, he is now part of that immortal England which knows not age or weariness or defeat."[2] Buchan uses another variety of the same rhetoric for the U.S. Army in Europe: "Those who watched the first American soldiers on the continent of Europe—grave young men with lean, shaven faces, a quick, springy walk, and superb bodily fitness—found their memories returning to Gettysburg and the Wilderness, where the same stock had shown an endurance and heroism not surpassed in the history of mankind."[3] Seeing people in these terms obviously means selecting certain "noble" features to focus on and staying blind to others.

The introduction to the American edition of Buchan's book was written by an American officer in the same epic language—not exactly that of adventure narrative, but the language of adventure celebration, the painting of a grand mural-mosaic background to particular exploits. (Kipling was the most remarkable writer who employed this language.) "To the great outpouring from her island homes, . . . her absent sons came rallying from many a tropic isle and distant strand. Our own gallant neighbour, Canada, with the men of the sweeping Western

1. Introduction to Gordon, *Journals of Major-General C. G. Gordon*, xxv.
2. John Buchan, *The History of the Great War*, 3:197.
3. Ibid., 552.

plains; the Boers, Basutos, and Barotoes, children of the African veldt; the brave Anzacs from Australia and New Zealand; black men from the West Indies; the proud old races of lands from Burma to beyond the Khyber Pass. . . . No such pageant of the legions had ever before been mustered under the colors of a reigning sovereign."[4]

This rhetoric reaches a natural climax in the image and concept of kingship, as does the quite different rhetoric of Kipling in his story "The Man Who Would Be King." It would of course be easy to show, by citing dozens of autobiographies, that Englishmen in India and Africa *did* feel they were royal, far more often than they admitted (and when they did use the word, they masked their admission with irony). But the same seems to have been true of the other white nations.

In American literature, even when the theme and setting seem as far as possible from the British Empire model, the language of kingship is used in a way that seems to point to an archaizing nostalgia for royalty. You find that in stories of Americans ruling South Sea islands by Richard Harding Davis, for example, but more strikingly in O. E. Roelvaag's *Giants in the Earth* (1927), dealing with Norwegian immigrants in the Midwest forty years earlier; we find that book two is subtitled "Finding the Kingdom." The migrant hero, Per Hansa, sees himself as a king. Indeed, as he handles the grain or looks at his baby son, he is a *god*, a creator, and the fact that he is always also a man only connects together and strengthens those other, more extravagant and fanciful identities. And Mark Twain again, in his paradoxical way, bears testimony to the lust for kingship by giving us such characters as the Duke and the Dauphin, and all his other claimants to noble birth and great estate.

In *Reappraisals in British Imperial History*, Ronald Hyam and Ged Martin suggest that the empire was important all through British history. The continuity of imperial action during the successive periods is more striking than the gaps: Palmerston was as much the imperialist as Disraeli. No great change came over England in 1870 (when Disraeli began to speak of the Empire).[5] Martin also believes that the export of surplus emotional energy, not economic greed, was the basic dynamic of expansion and empire (p. 1). This theory corroborates the importance attributed to adventure as a historical force within the growth of empire. It was what such famous imperialists as Frederick Lugard and John

---

4. Ibid., 1:xxvi.

5. Ronald Hyam and Ged Martin, introduction to *Reappraisals in British Imperial History*, 14.

Buchan had said, although modern historians stress the social-fear component of that dynamic: "If Tudor England lived in fear of the beggar, the England of the 1780s was equally fearful of the untransported convict."[6] But it was still in some sense an emotional dynamic. Thus, according to Martin, "imperial history should treat of power—its nature and use, its location, devolution, and transfer."[7]

Hyam and Martin also link imperialism, and therefore adventure, to the upper classes. They remind us that in 1836 Richard Cobden listed colonies with the army, the navy, the church, and the Corn Laws as "merely accessories to our aristocratic government."[8] The Chartist Bronterre O'Brien said, "Our aristocracy and merchants possess colonies all over the world, but the people of England—the real, veritable people of England do not possess a sod of ground in their own country—much less colonies in any other."[9]

Lewis Feuer tries to make a case for the benefits brought by empire and "to reopen the question of the basic character of imperialism."[10] He suggests that imperialism is a universal theme of history and that "anti-imperialist literature has perhaps beclouded the great fact that the world's advances have been associated with the eras of progressive imperialism. [The latter concept he defines as] . . . one in which energies are liberated for the advancement of civilization and creative activity" (p. 1). His examples of progressive imperialism are Athens, Rome, Napoleonic France, Victorian England, and modern America. The opposite, regressive imperialism, is to be seen in the Mongols, the Nazis, and Renaissance Spain. In progressive empires—for instance, in Rome—Feuer says, people of various colors participated in the empire and could rise high in the imperial structure. Regressive imperialism, on the other hand, extended the political relations of forcible domination into economics, as in Spanish America (p. 6).

Enthusiasm for adventure is naturally involved in any defense of this progressive imperialism, and Feuer uses an adventure vocabulary to take the curse of disapproval off empire. "A people with a sense of vigorous energies, with zest, adventure, and creativity, and endowed with a capacity for leadership, will experience an imperialist calling. There will

6. G. Martin, "The Founding of Botany Bay," in ibid., 47.
7. Hyam and Martin, Introduction, 17, 18.
8. G. Martin, " 'Anti-imperialism' in the Mid-Nineteenth Century," in ibid., 95.
9. Quoted in ibid., 101.
10. Lewis Feuer, *Imperialism and the Anti-Imperialist Mind*, 1.

be the merchant's pursuit of profit, the miner's quest for ores, the soldier's taste for glory, but there will also be the schoolmaster's mission to educate, the scientist's venture to find fresh wonders of fact, the doctor's desire to battle disease, the missionary's conviction that he brings a higher morality" (p. 13). (The social categories begin to sound like castes, in this description.) Nearly all these phrases will ring false in the ears of those who adhere to the antiadventure ethos of today, but we should not be so ready to disagree that we cannot consider what is said.

Feuer quotes French and English testimony on his side from the age of conscious imperialism. For instance, the French Socialist statesman Jean Jaurès said: "The law of expansion and conquest to which all peoples yield seems as irresistible as a natural law; and even though we denounce eloquently all the villainies, all the corruptions, all the cruelties of the colonial movement, we shall not stop it."[11] Bergson, at much the same time, said, "Imperialism is, as it were, inherent in the vital urge. It is at the bottom of the soul of individuals as well as the soul of nations."[12] Bertrand Russell said something similar in his *Why Men Fight* (1917). He speaks of a creative impulse that finds various expressions, some socially approved, others not. "Some few people are able to satisfy this desire; some happy men can create an Empire, a science, a poem, or a picture."[13] Imperialism is thus a form of creativity. Can one have expansion of the kind we want without the kind of expansion we disapprove?

Can we have even democracy without empire? Adams and Jefferson, Feuer says, founded an imperial republic. He quotes Adams writing to the other man on November 15, 1813: "Our pure, virtuous, public-spirited federative republic will last for ever, govern the globe, and introduce the perfection of man."[14]

For a long time, at least, the British Empire thought itself quite unlike other empires, and Gandhi believed its account of itself. He thought the British Empire was an expression of the Englishman's love of adventure. It is less surprising that believers in the empire did the same. Elspeth Huxley's *White Man's Country* shows us Lord Delamere's imperial work in Kenya as inspired by the sense of adventure. "Here, indeed, he must have thought, was a promised land, the realization of a Rider

11. Quoted in ibid., 24.
12. Quoted in ibid., 25.
13. Quoted in ibid., 122.
14. Ibid., 215.

Haggard dream of a rich and fertile country hidden beyond impenetrable deserts and mountains. Here was a modern Eldorado, waiting only for recognition. . . . [To him] . . . the East African settlers were historical successors to the sailors who crept in their battered boats up the inlets of Virginia, the men who walked by their wagons into the south-west interior of America."[15]

Another white woman novelist in East Africa, Isak Dinesen, gives us a more aesthetic sense of the same thing: "Here at last one was in a position not to give a damn for all conventions, here was a new kind of freedom which until then one only found in dreams. It was like beginning to swim where one could stretch out in all directions, it was like beginning to fly where one seemed to have left the law of gravity behind. . . . It was glorious, intoxicating."[16] There was extraordinary height, endless space, and a peculiar kind of air on her farm. "It was Africa distilled up through six thousand feet, like the strong and refined essence of a continent."[17] Hers is a landscape of adventure, and the socioeconomic lifestyle it supported was of course aristocratic: "Life out there was rather like 18th century England: one might often be hard up for cash, but life was still rich in many ways, with the lovely landscape, dozens of horses and dogs and a multitude of servants."[18]

This is perceptibly the same historical and geographical excitement Kipling distills for us in, for instance, *Kim*. And the natural partner to that landscape is the caste philosophy Kipling works out. The English in India saw themselves as belonging to castes there, not only in the superiority that separated them from the Indians but also among themselves, in the difference between the civil and military services, with their code of service and their self-image of the Roman Empire, and the "box wallahs," the merely commercial English, the traveling salesmen. Kipling often used the point of view of an Indian and the language of caste to express the critical detachment from English civilization at home, especially the liberal philosophy of that civilization, which he felt.

Thus, in "The Eyes of Asia" Kipling has a Rajput write home from London, "It is not true there is no caste in England." He goes on to describe the castes: "The high castes are forbidden to show curiosity, appetite, or fear in public places. In this respect they resemble troops on

---

15. Elspeth Huxley, *White Man's Country*, 1:54, 131.
16. Quoted in Donald Hannah, *Isak Dinesen and Karen Blixen*, 29.
17. Isak Dinesen, *Out of Africa*, 3.
18. Dinesen, interview, in *Writers at Work*, ed. George Plimpton, 10.

parade. Their male children are beaten from their ninth year to their seventeenth year, by men with sticks. Their women are counted equal with their men. The nature of the young men of high caste is as the nature of us Rajputs. They do not use opium, but they delight in horses, and sport and women, and are perpetually in debt to the moneylender. . . . They belittle their own and the achievements of their friend, so long as that friend faces them. In his absence they extol his deeds."[19] Here caste is the crystallization, in seemingly immemorial and immortal forms, of certain psychological options, in opposition to the liberal philosophy of constant progress.

Some of Kipling's most interesting work follows that pattern—for instance, his playful essays on the origins of contemporary phenomena. In the *Just So Stories* we have "How the Alphabet Was Made" and "How the First Letter Was Written." In 1917 he gave a talk to the Guards Cadet Corps on "The Magic Square," on the origins of military drill, and in 1918 he gave one to the junior naval officers on the origins of ships and sailing called "The First Sailor." The sense of origins, and the virtue of staying true to those origins, is essential in Kipling and in many other adventure writers, and Kipling had his "scientific" allies in Karl Pearson and the other eugenicists. (Pearson wanted a socialist state but with a warrior chieftain to head it.)

The opposite is true of Kipling's liberal enemies, who believed that civilized men should be ashamed of staying primitive. Hobson wrote of "interests which appeal to the lusts of quantitative acquisitiveness and of forceful domination, surviving in a nation from early centuries of ancient struggle for existence, . . . a deliberate renunciation of [that] culture of the higher inner qualities."[20]

Kipling's tone about Englishmen at home could be aimed at Hobson, as when he complains, in this passage from "Letters on Leave," about a man who "knows all about the aggressive militarism of you and your friends; he isn't quite sure of the necessity of an Army; he is certain that colonial expansion is nonsense."[21] Kipling's representative declares, "You mustn't treat any man like a machine in this country, but you can't get any work out of a man until he has learned to work like a machine. . . . I honestly believe that the average Englishman would faint if you told him it was lawful to use up human life for any purpose

19. Kipling, *The War and the Fleet in Being*, 150–51.
20. Hobson, *Imperialism*, 368.
21. Kipling, *Uncollected Prose*, 185.

whatever. He believes that it has to be developed and made beautiful for the possessor" (p. 190). This vein of thought—Kipling's most interesting but most shocking—is again expressed in "Drums of the Fore and Aft," his 1888 story about a green regiment that broke under fire and how two drummer boys rallied it by playing "The British Grenadiers." "Wherefore the soldier, and the soldier of today more particularly, should not be blamed for falling back. He should be shot or hanged afterwards—to encourage the others—but he should not be vilified in newspapers, for that is want of tact and waste of space. . . . Speaking roughly, you must employ either blackguards or gentlemen, or, best of all, blackguards commanded by gentlemen, to do butchers' work with efficiency and despatch."[22]

If we discount the moral bravura of Kipling's cynicism, we may be struck with a similarity between his attitude and that of someone we usually count his archenemy—Gandhi. Both of them believed that the right cause was justified in using up human life; neither of them attributed supreme value to the idea of "making life beautiful for the individual possessor." Gandhi would have been much closer to Kipling in his attitude to, say, the Scout movement, than most men of letters would be.

Kipling does not often write adventure narratives, but he writes adventure landscape, adventure philosophy, and adventure politics, all of which are linked to his idea of caste. At its most intensely felt, as in *Kim,* his caste philosophy is very like what one Hindu tradition finds in the Bhagavad Gita. The values of Kim and the Lama are so profoundly different that they are incompatible, and the apparent similarity of their "quests," for instance, is often little more than a pun. But Kipling gives such intense appreciation to each, and so balances his sympathies, one against the other, that we feel the two harmonizing. At its most deeply felt, this is not incomparable with the teaching of the great religious classic and its balancing of our sympathies, first with Arjuna's recoil from his calling as a soldier called on to slay members of his own family, and then with Krishna's summons to him to stay loyal to that calling. The soldier caste and the Brahmin support each other, despite their irreconcilable differences.

This is part of the pathos of adventure, the pathos and paradox that attend adventure's insertion into the social contract and the city. The values of adventure are categorically incompatible with those of social

---

22. Kipling, *A Kipling Pageant,* 101.

piety. And yet the adventurer wants to be forgiven for his sins against the community, and the fathers of the state want to forgive him. He must see himself as called to the life of violence *for them,* and as performing the deeds of war while remaining true, in some inoperative way, to peace and law-abidingness.

Caste thinking seems to go naturally with adventure, even where there is no connection with India. We find it in the writing of American adventure authors, such as Washington Irving, James Fenimore Cooper, and Francis Parkman. In *Astoria,* for instance, Irving takes a strong anthropological interest in the trappers, merchants, and Indians engaged in the fur trade. Thus, the merchant at his trading post "had a little world of self-indulgence and misrule around him, . . . his harem of Indian beauties, and his troop of half-breed children; nor was there ever wanting a loutish train of Indians."[23] When in New York these men bought lavishly at the goldsmith's, showing a "gorgeous prodigality, such as was often to be noticed in former times in Southern planters, and West Indian Creoles, when flush with the profits of their planta- tions" (p. 11). In Montreal, he tells us, the merchants cleared a 200 percent profit from the naked Indians who sold them their furs, and he quotes La Hontan on the extravagance of the Coureurs de Bois: "The bachelors act just as our East India men and pirates are wont to do; for they lavish, eat, drink, and play all away as long as the goods hold out."[24] Back in the woods, they lived like Indians, or worse, and impeded the influence of the missionaries, who teach opposite values.

These picturesque terms are not trivial in their significance, nor are they merely dated. They signify a social theory we meet often in later adventures, an intellectually challenging theory that modern readers are likely to overlook because it is so unlike the social theories we now take seriously. Irving sees a nation, we might say, in terms of its castes—as a mosaic of social contrasts—as incompatible but complementary types, and he rejoices in their incompatibility in a way that is implicitly treacherous to the democratic faith. The contrasting types Irving sees as making up the nation have conflicting interests. He does not take seriously the egalitarian populism that is the proclaimed political piety of the modern world-system. He believes in the nation rather than in democracy, and so he believes in the caste system, which is the organic

23. Washington Irving, *Astoria,* 8.
24. Ibid., 7.

structure of a nation. He sees his fellow Americans as soldiers or merchants or robbers or priests, fundamentally unlike each other, and he rejoices in each equally. That is why the American scene often sounds, in his descriptions, like a medieval principality or a city in the Orient. He borrows his rhetoric from Sir Walter Scott, who employed it as part of his adventure fiction.

Irving tells us, for example, that after the Northwest Company was founded in Canada in the 1780s two opposite social types emerged: the clerks and the partners. The former came mostly from the lowlands of Scotland and were full of perseverance, thrift, and fidelity—the mercantile virtues. But the partners "ascended the rivers in great state, like sovereigns making a progress; or rather, like highland chiefs navigating their subject lakes. They were wrapped in rich furs . . . [and they brought] cooks and bakers, together with delicacies of every kind." They liked to entertain English aristocrats as their guests. They held councils in as much state as the House of Lords in London, and "these grave and weighty councils were alternated by huge feasts and revels like some of the old feasts described in the highland castles. . . . While the chiefs thus revelled in hall, and made the rafters resound, . . . their merriment was echoed, and prolonged, by a mongrel legion of retainers."[25]

In *Astoria,* Irving tells us that John Jacob Astor much regretted that "the true nature and extent of his enterprise and its national character and importance had never been understood. . . . [He wanted the world to know] . . . of the fur-trade; of its remote and adventurous enterprises, and of the various people, and tribes and castes and characters, civilized and savage, [that] affected it operations."[26] The word "caste" there is the key to much that recurs in the narrative. Irving describes the Canadian voyageurs as "one of those distinct and strongly marked castes or orders of people, springing up in this vast continent, out of geographical circumstances" (p. 28). The word obviously implies that these groups are identified each by a way of life so idiosyncratic that its members are separated from their fellow citizens; less obviously, perhaps, it implies that the writer rejoices in these picturesque separations and likes to see society in caste terms.

Irving characterizes the American castes with an almost theatrical vividness that so stresses difference as to subvert the ordinariness, the

25. Ibid., 12–13.
26. Ibid., 3.

generic humanity, valued by pure democrats. Thus, he tells us that in the streets of St. Louis you could see "the hectoring, extravagant, bragging boatmen of the Missouri, with the gay, grimacing, singing, good-humoured Canadian voyageurs; vagrant Indians of various tribes loitered about the streets; now and then a stark Kentucky hunter" (pp. 92–93). These groups lived each according to its own ethos, which is radically unlike the others.

These types are presented as being distant in either time or space from the speaker, but this is not necessarily so. The distance is a rhetorical device that allows the reader to combine his ordinary pieties with this opposing value. An interesting case of the ethos of caste thinking, and of its connection with adventure, is the survival of the duel into late nineteenth- and even twentieth-century France and Germany. Both Karl Marx and Max Weber challenged individual opponents to duels, and so did Marcel Proust. A related institution was the feud, which has inspired a good deal of modern fiction (for instance, stories about the Mafia), but the duel is especially interesting because of its survival even among men of intellect.

Caste thinking is also capable of sustaining politically radical meanings. Ruskin's late political thinking analyzes nineteenth-century England in the terms of the medieval estate: the knight, the priest, the merchant, the peasant, and their mutual and complementary duties. And when Gandhi was given a copy of *Unto This Last*, in South Africa, and immediately started to put its ideas into practice, part of its appeal for him must have been its recourse to the familiar language of the caste system.

The traditional uses of adventure words, in relation to empire and caste, recur again and again, in all sorts of contexts, and we must acknowledge that though this is an archaizing mode of thought, it is not necessarily archaic in the sense of being irrelevant to contemporary life.

Part

4

ADVENTURE AND ART

WE COME BACK TO ART and its treatment of adventure—though not to the adventure tale—because art supplies such a range of vivid examples and because in that field I can point more confidently and reinterpret more radically.

The antagonism between literature and adventure is something my three books on adventure have examined at length and found to be quite important. But equally striking is something almost opposite: the *link* that exists, as of consanguinity, between adventure and aestheticism, in literature and the other arts.

If set in a old-fashioned moral perspective, the category that links them could be called the pride of life. In the language I have used to this point, both would be said to defy the social contract; in yet another language, fashionable today, both are excesses or transgressions. The adventurer claims at least to be independent of what the ordinary citizen needs to have society provide him with, and most often he claims to embody all the guilty splendor of forbidden violence. The aesthete claims to subsume all the moral, political, and religious kinds of experience under the names of beauty, charm, boredom, ugliness, and to move free from obligations that constrain others. They are both types that have waxed fat and kick.

It is no accident that both types became prominent in the West at the end of the nineteenth century—that is, in the age of conscious imperialism. The adventure tales of Stevenson and Haggard, echoed in more fragmentary but more sonorous form by Kipling, were clearly imperialist in sympathy. The aestheticism of Wilde and Diaghilev had no such close links to the empire-builders, in England or in Russia, but there can be no mistaking the significance of the way their work differs from that of their great nineteenth-century predecessors (from, say, George Eliot and Tolstoy). The new art was strikingly more sumptuous, sensual, provocative, splendid. It was an art of opera and ballet and art galleries, not of books, an art of marble and gold and music and dance and exoticism, bringing together all the art forms of all the world, past and present, East and West, primitive and futurist.

Other periods could be looked at, such as the Elizabethan age in England, when the heroic adventurers like Raleigh and Drake were matched by brilliant poets like Spenser and Shakespeare and by male costumes of extraordinary colorfulness and cost. (It is no accident that these periods of adventure and aestheticism are also periods of dandyism.)

The late nineteenth-century period is, however, the most interesting, because in reaction against it we see defining themselves two men who were the great spokesmen for the opposite option and who are still today our teachers or challengers. Tolstoy and Gandhi have been the great denouncers of both adventurism and aestheticism, seeing both in their relation to empire. And although modernism has gone through its own development and self-differentiation and now scorns any link to the adventure tale, our own art is still from this point of view the child of aestheticism.

Hence, this last section of the book consists of one chapter on the aestheticism of that late nineteenth-century period and another chapter on more wide-ranging examples of art's sense of its social and moral limits and the itch to transgress against them.

15

The Aesthetics of Adventure

The societies we usually call "imperial" (of course, nearly all are imperial to some degree) have taken up a number of different attitudes toward adventure and to art and to the combining of the two. These attitudes are quite various and centrifugal, and even in the world of art are expressed in a variety of aesthetics. In *The World Encompassed* G. V. Scammell describes several societies in the sequence of Western development from this point of view. The Icelandic sagas were the product of "a society organized for, and largely devoted to, war, in which strife was a major theme of literature, and where the virtues most highly esteemed were those of the warrior."[1] Those sagas have inspired many artists of later generations and distant lands. On the other hand, the commercial empire of the Hanseatic cities was not much interested in art or science, and their merchant culture lacked the heroic style of both missionary and soldier.

Most comparable to the age of imperial adventure in England, Venice became, "as did no other dying imperial power, pre-eminent in the arts" in the years between 1500 and 1650.[2] Venice inherited via Byzantium

1. G. V. Scammell, *The World Encompassed,* 11.
2. Ibid., 152.

the aspiration to be another Rome. We think primarily, Scammell says, of the painters: Titian, Veronese, and so on. "The vast and voluptuously coloured canvases of Veronese" expressed the self-esteem of Venice's rulers the way the art of Elgar and Kipling expressed that of the ruling class of Edwardian England (p. 210). But we should also think of Palladio, Monteverdi, and Galileo, of the civic buildings commissioned, and of the collections of voyages printed, for the adventures of travel and trade, and of war against the national enemy, the Turks, held the same place in Venetian culture as the adventures of Drake, Sidney, Raleigh, and the defeat of the Spanish Armada did in Elizabethan England. These last remained proud themes of English culture as long as there was an Empire.

In the period of conscious imperialism in England, adventure challenged the criteria of high art, the criteria by which adventure was excluded and held inferior. Adventure claimed admittance into the aesthetic preserve, and, insofar as it succeeded, in the work of Stevenson and Kipling (and for a quarter of a century it did seem to have triumphed), it changed the laws of aesthetics, the rules of art, in all sorts of ways. Ambitious new writers set out to be something quite different from their parental precursors—in England, different from the great Victorian humanists, such as George Eliot. These were differences not only in topic and theme but also in aesthetics itself.

One way to sum up those changes is to say that the new masters offered themselves as being artists not of truth but of trick. What truth means in such a context—the context suggested by naming George Eliot—is moral realism and an ethos of severe judgment blended with compassion. What trickery means—in a context suggested by the name of Kipling—is technical mastery backed on occasion by abrasive cynicism and flamboyant aestheticism. (It was Kipling's special vocation to combine that cynical aestheticism with a social and moral conservatism that satisfied an audience that was in some ways quite philistine and sentimental.) I offer "trick" as a center for a group of words that also includes "game," "joke," and "play," and it is no accident that we now return to the idea of play that concerned us at the beginning of this argument.

To compare the two generations of writers in this way is not, however, simply to condemn the Kipling group. Indeed, in our present climate of critical opinion their renunciation of the truth claim should count as a mark of grace. Moreover, writers who thus inveigle their readers into interaction with them are likely to act on those readers' minds at least as powerfully as those who stand at a distance, absorbed in the picture they are painting. Kipling's readers played at being Kim and the Lama; Joyce's readers did not (I assume) play at being Stephen and Bloom. The latter, these days, work much harder at their reading, but the former, then, played at it.

In England all this happened at the level of aesthetic practice rather than theory, and in popular rather than avant-garde forms. Artists took to themselves the freedom to play and invited the audience to become counterplayers, as we shall see if we look at Kipling, Stevenson, and Barrie. But the age of conscious imperialism, the age of Kipling, was succeeded by another, the age of modernism, which distorted and erased its predecessor's meaning more completely than is usually the case. And we are still living in that age.

Thus, because of the revulsion the world of letters expressed against this age of Kipling, and the displacement of the latter by a "modernism" with more international and intellectual sponsors, these writers have not been recognized for what they were. Their art and their aesthetic has not been appraised or taken seriously. In fact, however, they initiated a long-lasting development, the contemporary climax of which is magic realism.

Kipling, Stevenson, and Barrie used the adventure material (and comparable though lesser claims can be made for some other writers of the time) with admitted brilliance, but in what we have been told is a straightforward manner. However, the three magic realists most famous today (Grass, Marquez, Rushdie) write for—and above all are read by—an "intellectual" or socially alienated audience. As the label "magic realism" suggests, the new materials and modes have ostensibly more to do with fantasy and the fairy tale. The age of Kipling dealt brilliantly in those forms too, and adventure joins them as an important part of the novels of the three moderns. Indeed, in this context, adventure is to be thought of not as an ally of imperialism but as something continuous with fantasy and fairy tale.

Thus, adventure was welcomed into sacred precincts that had been forbidden to it, but that was only one feature of what we can call the aesthetic movement. The great figures of that movement in Kipling's time were quite unlike him (as the names of Proust and Diaghilev will suffice to remind us), artists with no interest in adventure. We can associate that movement in its English origins with the name of Swinburne and

the immoralist themes of pain and sin; with the artists of the Pre-
Raphaelite movement and the amoralist themes of sensual brilliance and
color; and with the name of William Morris and the forms of romance.
Given these aesthetic dispositions, the great themes of empire, including
its guilt and shame, were irresistible, as were also the great forms of
adventure, including its audience of boys and boyish men.

If we look at the introductory material Stevenson wrote for *Treasure
Island*, or Kipling for the *Jungle Books*, or Barrie for *Peter Pan*, we see
many layers of playfulness. And as we enter into each story, we are asked
to understand what we are told in a number of ambivalent ways and to
play a complicated game with the author, in which he will try to charm
and amuse us, surprise or outwit us, again and again. That, we gradually
realize, is his primary purpose. The artist is a *fils de joie*, Stevenson said,
twin brother to the courtesan, the *fille de joie*. An artist of truth, like
George Eliot or D. H. Lawrence, will of course use language and
narrative suggestively and seductively, and in some ways ambivalently,
but it will all be offered as being in the service of truth. An artist of
trick, such as Stevenson, Barrie, and Kipling, offers himself or herself
primarily as a master of veils, illusions, and prestidigitation.

It is worth pointing to the likeness between these writers and a lesser
contemporary, Arthur Conan Doyle, because Doyle's tricky dealings
with the reader are so obvious. Author and reader compete against each
other to conceal/uncover the mystery. Has the writer played fair? Has he
given clues enough so we might have solved the problem? The trickery
extends into the subject-matter. The Sherlock Holmes stories are closely
related to the Kipling of *Kim*—for instance, in the stress on observation
and disguise and enigmas and clues. They are also crucially related to
the London that was the capital of the empire (the crimes that come to
solution in Holmes's London often have their origin on a frontier of
empire), and that city is presented to us as a gigantic enigma, all fogs
and broken cries, appearances and disappearances. After such reading,
one felt, when literally walking through the literal city, that one was
taking part in a work of art, in something that can be understood in
aesthetic terms. It is no accident that Sherlock Holmes is an aesthete or
that an early Holmes story was entitled *A Study in Scarlet*.

In Kipling's autobiographical novel, *The Light That Failed*, the setting
is another version of that same London. In this story the artist Dick
Heldar paints a portrait of "Melancolia," his masterpiece. His friend
Torpenhow looks at the paiting and says there is a mysteriously murder-

ous suggestion in the poise of the head. Dick chuckles with delight at being completely understood and replies, "It's a French trick, and you wouldn't understand; but it's got at by slewing round the head a trifle, and a tiny, tiny foreshortening of one side of the face from the angle of the chin to the top of the left ear. That, and deepening the shadow under the lobe of the left ear. It was flagrant trick-work; but, having the notion fixed, I felt entitled to play with it. —Oh, you beauty!"[3] And in his autobiography Kipling talks of his own writing in similar terms of esoteric expertise and deceptive trickery—the cult of craftsmanship.

Sometimes Kipling implies there is no truth to be found; "the world" or "life" is inherently deceptive and disappointing. Most often we know that he *is* interested in truth, as much as most of us, but he does not present himself as a dealer in truths, as a truth-teller primarily. The truth makes itself felt despite and through the writer's lies. He talks through a megaphone and pulls levers to release clouds of colored smoke. He is a Wizard of Oz.

In writing *Treasure Island*, Stevenson began, he says, with conscious inventions, with the map he drew to entertain his stepson and with the incidents and settings taken from previously existing books. He was turning away from more "serious" efforts at writing. In the essay "My First Book," which was published together with *Treasure Island*, he begins: "It was far indeed from being my first book, for I am not a novelist alone. But I am well aware that my paymaster, the great public, regards what else I have written with indifference, if not aversion."[4] (Kipling also speaks of his public as his paymaster.)

Besides the flirtatious protest to his adoring public, we notice Stevenson's stress on the difficulty of the novel-form. He goes on to tell us that from childhood he has felt driven ("bound") to write in that form but could never manage it. Over fifteen years he had made ten or twelve efforts to write a novel but always failed (p. xx). Each story went for a while and then stopped inexorably, like a schoolboy's watch, he says. "It is the length that kills." He looked on a three-volume novel as a feat of physical and moral endurance (p. xxi).

Of course, we don't believe exactly that. We know the novel-form was difficult for Stevenson (and for Kipling) because it was realistic—by virtue of what the great realistic writers had made of it—because of its

---

3. Rudyard Kipling, *The Light That Failed*, 145–46.
4. R. L. Stevenson, *Treasure Island*, xix.

claim to be *responsible*. It claims to tell the whole truth, especially about personal relations between adults and about life in a real city or real village. His difficulty was, at least in part, not length but substance, something intrinsic to the novel-material. When he hits on the idea of *Treasure Island* and can write his full-length book, it is because he has a new kind of material—and a new audience: "It was to be a story for boys. Women were excluded" (p. xxiv). This was not a literal boyhood: Stevenson's father was one of those who listened to the story enthralled, becoming a boy as he did so; but it was certainly a new reading audience.

Women had been an essential part of the audience for fiction as George Eliot and Henry James wrote it. In beginning *Treasure Island*, Stevenson had escaped the constraints that a mixed audience and mature themes put on a novel. He says that a writer must give up something of moral dignity. No doubt he is not entirely serious in so saying, but that ambiguity is part of the same amoralism.

In *Peter Pan* we find something not unlike some of the Night-Town scene in *Ulysses* or the magic realism of a modern writer such as Nabokov. Metaphors turn into pseudo-realities and back again; aspects of characters, embodiments of ideas, or wish fulfillments assume names and bodies and then disavow them. What makes this conjunction seem incongruous (and the larger conjunction I am proposing, too) is almost exclusively a matter of the enormously expanded eroticism of the modern writers. When the latter are dealing with children, the resemblance is comparatively easy to see. In his prose style and playfulness, of structure as well as manner, Barrie must remind us of several others, not all of them magic realists. (In certain stories, such as "The Laughing Man" and "For Esmé with Love and Squalor," J. D. Salinger can remind us of Barrie, and Salinger stands in a relationship to America's Belle Epoque of the 1950s, like Barrie's relations to his England.)

In Kipling we also find the same incapacity to write a novel in the traditional sense, which he discusses at length in his autobiography. And *The Light That Failed* is indeed a fictional failure, in a number of obvious and major ways, because Kipling could not develop major female characters or an autobiographical character in a mature love relationship—just as Stevenson could not. The significant relationships are with landscape, machinery, or other men.

Kipling, moreover, developed further Stevenson's stress on the paymaster, the reading public. Dick Heldar and his friend Torpenhow talk about the public's fathomless folly, but when Dick plans to sell a bad painting that will please them, his friend puts his boot through it, saying, "No man born of woman is strong enough to take liberties with his public. . . . They are your masters. . . . You aren't strong enough to trifle with them—or with yourself, which is more important."[5] Cynicism is a dreadful temptation, ever-present to Kipling, which must be resisted at all costs. These are aesthetic movement themes.

This is the artist's conscience speaking, but, characteristically for Kipling's art, it claims to be cynical. It denies every link, except paradox, to other moral or rational discourse, just as in him the vocation of artist denied every link to that profound and humane discourse of the Victorian novelists and essayists. What did stir Kipling and activate his talent was what stirred his autobiographical character, Dick: the sight of the Paris night mail, the sound of a ship at sea, the idea of tropical islands, the spectacle of war, the romance of machinery. This is all adventure material, and Kipling could handle it marvelously in more than one form—but not in the novel, which was, at least in England then, incompatible with that material.

Barrie of course fantasized his adventure, deprived it of all claims to our belief. The adventure part of *Peter Pan* was quite important to him, as his long introductory dedication shows, but the fantasy was more important, in what he offered the public. The distinction between the two, as literary forms, is indispensable for the study of adventure; in fantasy, the assertion and retraction "It was so and it was not so" is insisted on at every page. And though fantasy is as distinct from moral realism as adventure, it has proved less alien to men of letters, easier to combine with the values of serious literature. The price adventure had to pay for being taken up into art was to be treated as fantasy.

An eloquent expression of that comes in H. G. Wells's *Mr. Polly* (1910). In this novel, Wells, like other authors then, built a story around a Cockney clerk whose brain had been addled by the reading of adventure, which was the wrong imaginative fare for men of his caste. "He would read tales about hunters and explorers, and imagine himself riding mustangs as fleet as the wind across the prairies of Western America, or coming as a conquering and adored white man into the swarming villages of central Africa. . . . He was beloved by queens in

5. Kipling, *The Light That Failed*, 45.

barbaric lands, and reconciled whole nations to the Christian faith. . . .
He explored the Amazon, and found, newly exposed by the fall of a
great tree, a rock of gold."[6] He has, we deduce, been reading stories by
Stevenson, Jules Verne, Conan Doyle, and lesser names.

Mr. Polly presumably read these books as adventures and therefore
believed in what he was reading, but Wells presents them to us as
fantasies, so that we do not believe in them or in our own reading of
that kind. For the individual reader of Wells and for a whole reading
public, what had been adventure is now fantasy.

This fantasy life was the result of Mr. Polly's boyhood reading of
fiction. Later he read the nonfiction travels of, for instance, the French
explorer La Pérouse. Then he delighted in "the frankest revelations of
the ways of the 18th century sailorman, homely, adventurous, drunken,
incontinent, and delightful" (p. 128). Wells tells us that adventure, plus
a few "licentious" authors like Boccaccio and Rabelais, constituted
literature for Mr. Polly. All the edifying authors of English literature
seem to have been forgotten. "Mr. Polly had been drinking at the
poisoned fountains of English literature, fountains so unsuited to the
needs of a decent clerk or shopman, fountains charged with the dangerous suggestion that it becomes a man of gaiety and spirit to make love
gallantly and rather carelessly" (p. 80).

Thus, not only adventure but also all literature is assumed to belong
to the aristo-military caste and not to "the decent clerk or shopman." It
belongs to the adventurous castes and is only "borrowed"—and at their
own risk—by other people. But this was only true during the age of
Kipling. When that came to an end, during the Great War, literature was
reclaimed by the Brahmin caste through its various spokespersons,
whether T. S. Eliot and F. R. Leavis, or Virginia Woolf and Bloomsbury.

The aesthetic movement ingredients of adventure and fantasy, however, have continued to be mixed, at different times during this century,
in various ways that have had various powers to please—and to challenge
the hegemony of the Great Tradition. One striking literary phenomenon
of the 1960s was the serious (not intellectually but spiritually serious)
popularity of J.R.R. Tolkien's fantasy *The Lord of the Rings*. This
popularity was explained in the 1970s by Peter S. Beagle, himself a
writer of fantasy, on the grounds that that decade of revolution was the
time when millions of people became aware that the industrial society

6. H. G. Wells, *The History of Mr. Polly*, 10.

had become paradoxically unlivable, incalculably immoral, and ultimately deadly. It was when the word "progress" lost its ancient holiness, and escape stopped being comically obscene. In other words, the Enlightenment idea, and the realistic art that is its natural counterpart, lost authority. It is no coincidence that Tolkien's fiction, and that of Hermann Hesse, became so popular at the same time as Jungian psychology. Tolkien's popularity, Beagle says, thus represented an important shift in the orientation of our imaginations. We realized that we were raised to honor all the wrong explorers and discoverers—thieves planting flags, murderers carrying crosses. Let us at last praise the colonizers of dreams. This turn from adventure to fantasy was, as we have seen before, a turn from outside to inside.

In *The Lord of the Rings* Tolkien's story world was, in one sense of that ambiguous term, more *realistic* than fantasy and adventure usually are. His Hobbits are cozy, reliable English-peasant figures having their teas and smoking their pipes in a well-ordered and well-farmed countryside. The Hobbits of Eastfarthing were "rather large and heavy-legged, and they wore dwarf-boots in muddy weather."[7] But this is a matter not so much of moral realism as of antiadventurousness, which in fact amounts to adding a tincture of conventional and cozy humor. The humor of the magic realists is wilder, more abrasive, more shocking, and that is one reason why their mixing of fantasy and adventure has more authority.

Meanwhile, realism is the aesthetic we associate most often with homeland politics, insofar as the mood of readers and writers is—as usual—liberal and left-wing by intention. Thus new, reformed societies usually call for a new and more realistic art. We see an instance of that in the effort to found a new literature after a revolution in twentieth-century China. In *Etchings of a Tormented Age* Hsia Chien describes the efforts of Dr. Hu-Shih to bring a new literature into being from about 1920. The new writing would be for the people, avoiding the aristocratic elegance of the old literature and being simple, plain, and expressive; it would be realistic, avoiding classical stereotypes and monotony; it would be plain-spoken, avoiding the pedantry and obscurantism of the reclusive scholar.

In 1904 the imperial examinations were abolished, which affected literature because novels in China had hitherto been written by failed or

7. J.R.R. Tolkien, *The Fellowship of the Rings,* 27.

exiled scholars. Thereafter, our novelists were "social reformers at heart."[8] "The 19th century had become a nightmare to us. It was a period filled with humiliation from abroad and corruption at home, accompanied by poverty, illiteracy, contagious diseases, all the poisons of a decayed empire" (p. 12). This has a familiar ring, even for those of us who know little about Chinese literature.

Nor is this aesthetic limited to times of revolution. Scammell tells us that at the time of Venice's triumph Genoa was the culture more like England the homeland (nonimperial England), a culture of free trade and free enterprise. This made for a moderate and realistic art in both places. Thus, William Cowper says in "The Task" (1784):

> Blest he, though undistinguished from the crowd
> By wealth or dignity, who dwells secure
> Where man, by nature fierce, has laid aside
> His fierceness. (lines 592–95).

This is the opposite, Cowper tells us, of the adventurous landscape of "remote / And barb'rous climes, where violence prevails, / And strength is lord of all."

We hear the same voice in Freneau's "American Village" (1776), where the poet asks his muse to sing of the peaceful side of village life (lines 14–19):

> O muse, forget to paint her ancient woes,
> Her Indian battles and her Gallic foes,
> Resume the pleasures of the rural scene,
> Describe the village rising on the green,
> Its harmless people, born to small command,
> Lost in the bosom of this Western land.

This affiliation of art to peace, its alienation from war, is a recurrent sentiment, though scholars are usually shy of declaring it. But they are even more reluctant to admit the opposite affiliation of art with war. Thus, Arthur Quinn, said of adventure writer Jack London in *American Fiction* (1936) that London's vogue was passing, as it inexorably must, because "there is something impermanent in the very nature of the literature of violence."[9] That proposition is easy to refute with a

---

8. Hsia Chien, *Etchings of a Tormented Age*, 12.
9. Arthur H. Quinn, *American Fiction*, 542.

reference to Homer or to *War and Peace,* but it is nevertheless deeply and widely felt.

Men and women of letters take largely for granted this opposition between truth-telling in art and the celebration of adventure, empire, glory, and so on. Such an opposition exists, but it overlies and obscures a certain linkage, as I have suggested. Lionel Trilling drew attention to that in his essay on Henry James's *Princess Casamassima,* the hero of which novel is a political radical who finds his earlier narrower conviction overwhelmed by the love of art when he comes to know things of beauty. He finds, as Trilling puts it, that he now wants rather to fight for art and for what art suggests of glorious life. Trilling relates this to James's own development:

> In Chapter XXV of *A Small Boy and Others,* his first autobiographic volume, James tells us how he was initiated into a knowledge of style in the Galérie d'Apollon in the Louvre. As James represents the event, the varieties of style in that gallery assailed him so intensely that their impact quite transcended aesthetic experience. For they seemed to speak to him not visually at all but in some "complicated sound" and as a "deafening chorus"; they gave him what he calls a "general sense of glory." About this sense of glory he is quite explicit. "The glory meant ever so many things at once, not only beauty and art and supreme design, but history and fame and power, the world in fine raised to the richest and noblest expression."[10]

Thus James, one of the great aesthetes of the age of conscious imperialism, perceived art to be connected to empire and to a form of potestas.

The English essayist Hazlitt, Trilling continues, "said that 'the language of poetry naturally falls in with the language of power,' and goes on to develop an elaborate comparison between the processes of the imagination and the processes of autocratic rule."

> He is not merely indulging in a flight of fancy or a fashion of speaking; no stancher radical democrat ever lived than Hazlitt and no greater lover of imaginative literature, yet he believed that poetry has an affinity with political power in its autocratic and

10. Lionel Trilling, *The Liberal Imagination,* 81.

aristocratic form and that it is not a friend of the democratic virtues. We are likely not to want to agree with Hazlitt; we prefer to speak of art as if it lived in a white bungalow with a garden, had a wife and two children, and were harmless and quiet and cooperative. But James is of Hazlitt's opinion; his first great revelation of art came as an analogy with the triumphs of the world; art spoke to him of the imperious will, with the music of an army with banners. Perhaps it is to the point that James's final act of imagination, as he lay dying, was to call his secretary and give her as his last dictation what purported to be an autobiographical memoir by Napoleon Bonaparte (pp. 81–82).

Trilling's suggestion clearly is that the novelist had something of the overweening ambition of the Emperor—the great adventurer. Trilling goes on to tell us of a nightmare James had that involved him in a situation of terror in the same Louvre gallery and that James himself retold in writing and interpreted for the reader as a fantasy of guilt. "Having experienced art as 'history and fame and power,' his arrogation seemed a guilty one and represented itself as great fear" (pp. 82–83).

Art, therefore, is not to be set in simple opposition to empire, as a form of innocence in opposition to guilt: art is a field of fierce and worldly ambition, a kind of adventure. This, then, is yet another aesthetic of the age of Kipling, and again significantly linked to the cult of adventure.

16

Serious Art and Adventure

I use the adjective "serious" here to refer to the best of modern literature, in a sense of "modern" that will become clear, and to raise one last time the vexed questions of art and adventure and empire.

England supplies some of the best examples. England today is one of the postimperial countries of the world. Economically and culturally, that world is still dominated by the white empire, of course, and England continues to profit from that domination, but still its position is quite inferior to what it was a hundred years ago. It is not surprising, then, that we see in England's writers a reaction against adventure and empire, a reaction so strong, according to Seamus Heaney, that it turns writers' minds socially or nationally inward.

Heaney's *Preoccupations* contains an essay on Ted Hughes, Geoffrey Hill, and Philip Larkin entitled "Englands of the Mind." "I think that sense of an ending has driven all three of these writers into a kind of piety towards their local origins, has made them look in, rather than up, to England. The loss of imperial power, the failure of economic nerve, the diminished influence of Britain inside Europe, all this has led to a new sense of the shires [the title of a volume by Donald Davie], a new valuing of the native English experience."[1]

1. Seamus Heaney, *Preoccupations*, 169.

No doubt Heaney is right about these English poets, and the same would apply to other European writers. But not all of them have reacted to the postimperial or postcolonial situation in this way. If we take account also of, say, Salman Rushdie and Martin Amis, and the magic realist novelists outside England, we shall see the heritage of empire—embodied in the imperialist writers—being differently accepted. This sort of writing is a dominant literary phenomenon of our time, and magic realism is closer to imperialist writers like Kipling than to, say, E. M. Forster, even though the latter is acclaimed (properly) as the hero of the liberal imagination and postcolonialism.

We might take Forster as a precursor of the modern British mood. *Howards End* (1910) is of special interest to us because it is recognizably an attack on Kipling and Kiplingism, a recapturing of the novel form for women readers after its abduction by adventure writers Kipling and Stevenson. But Forster set himself to reconcile cultural opposites, such as "the prose and the passion" and the two families, reconciling the feminine and cultured Schlegels with the masculine and imperialist Wilcoxes.

Margaret Schlegel likes Mr. Wilcox, despite all that make them opponents. She is ready to marry him, and she tells him why, using the terms of adventure. She begins by explaining to him that she also likes the young Cockney, Leonard Bast, first because he cares for " 'physical adventure, just as you do. . . . [You care for] motoring and shooting; he would like to go camping out. Secondly, he cares for something special *in* adventure. It is quickest to call that special something poetry. . . . Yes, that's what I am trying to say. He's a real man.' "[2] She means that he and Mr. Wilcox are brave. (A book about the Spanish romances of the fifteenth century, which were written in some sense for the Spanish knights, is entitled *Books of the Brave*, and I have pointed out how inconceivable such a title would be for a book about twentieth-century fiction.)

We can say quite confidently that Margaret speaks for Forster there and that he would have liked the idea of *Books of the Brave*. We are told that Margaret's brother, Tibby Schlegel, who probably represents Forster's own self-criticism, "had never known young-manliness, that quality which warms the heart till death, and gives Mr. Wilcox an imperishable charm" (p. 260). Tibby is, we are told, not a boy who cares for men (p.

2. E. M. Forster, *Howards End,* 137, 139.

130). He is not an adventure hero or even a hero's follower; Tibby cannot be imagined as inhabiting the landscape of adventure at all.

Usually, however, serious writers like Forster, when they rebelled against Kipling, did not concede so much value to adventure and young-manliness—as we see when we turn from *Howards End* to a book very similar in its themes and also an attack on Kipling but bolder in its art and thought: D. H. Lawrence's *Women in Love.* In this story Gerald Crich, who comes to disaster, is an adventure hero; Rupert Birkin, who represents the author, is not. (Gerald is a kind of Wilcox—he resembles Mr. Wilcox's son Charles—while Rupert is a much more boldly asserted Tibby.)

Let me now consider the phenomenon of Forster's other brilliant novel, *Passage to India* (1924), which is parallel in its attack on Kipling and adventure. In doing this I shall return the reader's attention to the Anglo-Indian writers with which I began this book: Duncan, Diver, Scott. What Forster did in *Passage,* by way of discomfiting Kipling and his admirers, was deny his Anglo-Indian characters any share in the romance and magic of India, and even in the power and guilt of empire, the themes that these Anglo-Indian writers and Kipling himself made their topic. Forster made the Turtons and their friends seem, above all, *dull* people and limited minds.

In the historical record there is plenty of evidence that (as Duncan declared in the passage I quoted) the Anglo-Indians were in many ways bolder and freer than the English at home. Their lives had more of adventure in them. And Kipling had implied, as Paul Scott later said in so many words, that the crucial history of England was enacted on its overseas frontiers, not at home. That is what Forster—just as implicitly—denied.

So much for the postcolonial mood. In what we call the literature of the ancient past, empire and adventure traditionally held an honored place as the source of stories and topics of discourse—of tragedy, triumph, or eulogy. And even those who reject contemporary adventure often accept that decorum in discussing the literature of the past. The dichotomy or enmity we are discussing is conventionally seen as a matter of the modern period.

For instance, C. S. Lewis's *Allegory of Love* discusses *The Song of Roland* and other such premodern works in Kipling-like adventure terms. "The deepest of worldly emotions in this period is the love of man for man, the mutual love of warriors who die together fighting against odds and the affection between vassal and lord. [To understand such emotions] we must think rather of a small boy's feeling for some hero in the sixth form."[3]

In Renaissance England too, the writers were close to the adventurers. Michael Nerlich points out that Milton wrote the history of the Merchant Adventurers in Moscow, of whom Sebastian Cabot, one of the great Bristol adventurer brothers, was the first governor.[4] Henry Sidney greeted the new company with a speech that ennobled sea travel, exploration, and exploitation as manly, courageous, and patriotic (p. 129). Sir Philip Sidney and Edmund Spenser were poets who encouraged the nobles who (like the Icelandic Sagamen long before) hoped to find in colonizing a return to feudal independence (p. 130).

On the other hand, for many modern critics, when they discuss poetry, and literature in general, this linkage of art and adventure is not acceptable. The mutual love of warriors, the affection between vassal and lord, and the theme of glory are all incompatible with the true purpose of art. At least we assume that when dealing with white people.

The recent movie *Glory*, about the regiment of black soldiers who fought in the Civil War, could affirm the values of glory, but only because it was dealing with black people. American radicals, visiting Castro's Cuba in its early days, were disconcerted to hear the exaltation of military virtues but accepted their appropriateness there. In the early days of satyagraha in South Africa, Gandhi talked enthusiastically not only of the Indians' manliness and pride but also of adventure and war.

But among the possessor nations, the adventure virtues, even courage, have long been unpopular with the men and women of letters. The unpopularity is not unremitting. In times of war, things are different, as they are in periods like the age of Kipling. But the unpopularity is recurrent, and it seems to derive from something in literature itself. It is strong today. We shall see that Harold Bloom marks a profound difference that has come over literature, distinguishing between ancient and modern, when he analyzes the case of Wordsworth.

In the world of letters, there is something of a split over this matter. What I have just said is true of scholars and critics, rather than of novelists. For instance, in real life D. H. Lawrence wanted to acquire the adventurer's strengths himself. Henry Miller is not totally misleading

---

3. C. S. Lewis, *The Allegory of Love*, 9–10.
4. Michael Nerlich, *The Ideology of Adventure*, 127.

when he says that Blaise Cendrars was the man Lawrence wanted to be. Norman Mailer has always espoused a philosophy and aesthetic of adventure; courage is still a major virtue for him, even in literature. (He says we could not respond to Hemingway's prose as we do if we knew the author to be a physical coward.) In *The Presidential Papers* he writes, "Since the first World War Americans have been leading a double life, and our history has moved on two rivers, one visible, the other underground: there has been the history of politics which is concrete, factual, practical, and unbelievably dull if not for the consequences of the actions of some of these men; and there is a subterranean river of untapped, ferocious, lonely and romantic desires, that concentration of ecstacy and violence which is the dream life of the nation."[5] He also says, in the same book, that every American dreams that "each of us was born to be free, to wander, to have adventure and to grow on the wave of the violent, the perfumed, and the unexpected" (p. 39).

The archetype of such characters in Mailer's fiction is a bullfighter named Sergius O'Shaughnessy, about whom he has more than once woven fictions. And in the story "The Man Who Studied Yoga" in *Advertisements for Myself,* he depicts O'Shaughnessy as a figure dreamed by Sam Slovoda, a part-Jewish man who "seeks to live in such a way as to avoid pain, and succeeds merely in avoiding pleasure."[6] Adventure, then, is individually a dream and socially a transgression, and because of their character of willful fantasy Mailer's stories always mix something else (more psychological or philosophical) with their adventures. Adventure is nevertheless at their core.

This must recall Henry James's idea of art, expounded by Trilling. We would hesitate to apply this idea equally to all artists, even of this century, but it would be difficult not to apply it to Mailer, and he must, because of his talents and his courage, count as in some ways representative of his generation. He has certainly experienced his own art as history and fame and power and has told his public in so many words about his ambitions.

He has talked of his self-affiliation with Hemingway and Faulkner, and one could draw other parallels between Mailer and *their* father, Kipling. (Rhetorically, for instance, Mailer is often very like Kipling, and his politics have a certain similarity.) In terms of political career, one

5. Norman Mailer, *The Presidential Papers,* 38.
6. Norman Mailer, *Advertisements for Myself,* 175.

might compare him with Jack London, who intervened on public issues and ran for mayor of his city, as Mailer did. It is among these men, and not among the great nineteenth-century novelists of England or America, that Mailer finds his forebears.

A more recent and playful example of a turning toward but then away from adventure is found in Anthony Burgess's novel, *Napoleon Symphony* (1974), which was first inspired by the figure of perhaps the greatest adventurer of modern history. (Napoleon is a much more challenging figure than Scott's Adventurer, Bonnie Prince Charlie.) But Burgess sums up his book's themes in verse at the end: his hero has not been Napoleon, after all, but Beethoven:

> My Ogre, though heroic, is grotesque,
> A sort of essay in the picaresque,
> Who robs and rapes and lies and kills in fun
> And does no lasting harm to anyone.
> Standing behind him, though, or to one side,
> Another, bigger hero is implied,
> Not comic and not tragic but divine,
> Tugging Napoleon's strings and also mine,
> Controlling form, the story's ebb and flow—
> Beethoven, yes: this you already know.[7]

The French emperor therefore shrinks into historical insignificance beside the German composer. Beethoven matters, Bonaparte doesn't. This summing up has the character of a fate overcoming this novel at its end, a defeat overcoming the novelist: we feared, we foreknew, that the world of art, the world of novelists and composers, was almost bound to triumph ("This you already know"). The enterprise was bound to come to rest in some such truism. But Burgess is too lively-minded to be comfortable there, as his uncomfortable phrasing suggests (Napoleon "did no lasting harm to anyone?"). He wrote his book because, in the course of composing the symphony, Beethoven had angrily substituted Prometheus for Napoleon in the last two movements—had replaced history with myth, taking an artist's revenge. So Burgess had originally believed he must restore that "bad Colossus" to the symphonic program, must reevoke Napoleon's presence—a quite interesting idea if he could

7. Anthony Burgess, *Napoleon Symphony*, 362.

have pulled it off. But in the long run he found he could only imagine Napoleon as picaresque and harmless.

But then even Tolstoy, after all, did little better, in portraying Napoleon in *War and Peace*. Why this strange impotence, obliquity, eccentricity, in the literary mind? Why is the violence of history beyond our reach? That is a question toward which all this book's argument tends. Contemporary critical theory offers us an interesting explanation, relative to the Romantic poets and the way they differed from their precursors, the new direction they gave to their art. For instance, in "Home at Grasmere" Wordsworth wrote about himself as being in love with violent adventure as a boy:

> While yet an innocent little one, with a heart
> That doubtless wanted not its tender moods,
> I breathed (for this I better recollect)
> Among wild appetites and blind desires,
> Motions of savage instinct my delight
> And exaltation.

By itself this is a recognizable and undisturbing exaltation of natural vitality, familiar to us in Romanticism in general, even if the vitality is surprisingly set in opposition to tender moods.

> Nothing at that time
> So welcome, no temptation half so dear
> As that which urged me to a daring feat,
> Deep pools, tall trees, black chasm and dizzy crags,
> And tottering towers: I loved to stand and read
> Their looks forbidding, read and disobey,
> Sometimes in act, and evermore in thought.

But perhaps we are somewhat surprised to find, in Wordsworth, this praise of unregenerate nature linked to standard patriotic images of historical and military adventure:

> With impulses, that scarcely were by these
> Surpassed in strength, I heard of danger met
> Or sought with courage; enterprise forlorn
> By one, sole keeper of his own intent,

> Or by a resolute few, who for the sake
> Of glory fronted multitudes in arms.
> Yea, to this hour I cannot read a Tale
> Of two brave vessels matched in deadly fight,
> And fighting to the death, but I am pleased
> More than a wise man ought to be; I wish,
> Fret, burn, and struggle, and in soul am there.

But then he renounces, turns away from that excitement:

> But me hath Nature tamed, and bade to seek
> For other agitations, or be calm.

He credits Nature with this, and so sets a high value on this "calm," but the verb "tamed" inevitably suggests regret and the sense of something lost.

> That which in stealth by Nature was performed
> Hath Reason sanctioned; her deliberate Voice
> Hath said; be mild, and cleave to gentle things,
> Thy glory and thy happiness be there. . . .
> All that inflamed thy infant heart, the love,
> The longing, the contempt, the undaunted quest,
> All shall survive.

This renunciation and reconciliation is fully endorsed, has poetic authority, but, as Harold Bloom observes, we are asked to note that a sacrifice has been made, and we, at least (perhaps the same would not be true of Wordsworth's intended readers), are bound to believe that regretted sacrifice to be the essential message of the poem. Wordsworth continues:

> Then farewell to the Warrior's Schemes, farewell
> The forwardness of soul which looks that way
> Upon a less incitement than the Cause
> Of Liberty endangered, and farewell
> That other hope, long mine, the hope to fill
> The heroic trumpet with the Muse's breath.

Bloom says that we here see Wordsworth giving up the intention to be the kind of poet "who would have had a subject beyond that of his own subjectivity." An enormous curtailment made Wordsworth the inventor of modern poetry, which is, Bloom says, a poetry significantly more sublimated than that which went before it, from Homer to Milton.[8] What was left out or renounced or undeveloped in modern poetry includes what I have been discussing as the adventure-material.

Homer, Virgil, Dante, Shakespeare, and Milton offered partly narrative pronouncements on the history and destiny of their societies, made partly in the name of, the voice of, the participants in that destiny. That involved them in endorsing national adventure. But for the period after Milton, English departments neglect the equivalent texts, though they were still being written, in Britain by Defoe, Scott, and Kipling, the adventure writers. English departments concentrate on quite different authors, those who dissent from their society and differ from the likes of Defoe, Scott, and Kipling. In their interpretations it is the "different" meanings that are accentuated. Thus, literature has come to mean "the literature of dissent," and even Jane Austen is treated as a social dissenter.

Of course, the heroic material did not entirely disappear, and the voice of adventure can still be heard in what is taught, despite the arrangement and orchestration the teachers have given it. Browning, for instance, was a major figure in nineteenth-century English poetry, and in Browning the excitement of adventure is reintroduced, under cover, into epistemology and into poetry. When J. Hillis Miller, in *The Disappearance of God*, discusses Browning, he says:

Along with self-awareness and the power to expand goes

"a principle of restlessness
Which would be all, have, see, know, taste, feel all—"

Miller continues, "No lines in Browning better express the expansive energy of his soul, the violent instinct of self-aggrandizement which would know all things, and, knowing them, become them. . . . His restlessness will not be appeased until it has swallowed up 'all' that is."[9] This is the sort of language that would apply well to Mailer.

8. Harold Bloom, *The Anxiety of Influence*, 125.
9. J. Hillis Miller, *The Disappearance of God*, 91.

It was, after all, from Browning that Kipling took that conception of the artist which he adapted to his own work as bard of empire. In his autobiography he saw himself as a son of Fra Lippo Lippi, as Browning presented the latter in his dramatic monologue. And in *Brideshead Revisited* Evelyn Waugh makes a similar allusion to Browning as the man who gave Charles Ryder his enthusiasm for the "creative" passion of art. For Browning, Kipling, and Waugh, Fra Lippo Lippi is the Renaissance artist-figure—adventurer and lawbreaker.

We can then take Lippi as a kind of disguised version of "the poet," and so of Browning himself. In *Poets of Reality* Miller says of poets like the latter that in them "Man as subjective ego opposes himself to everything else" and "The isolated ego faces the other dimensions of existence across an empty space," phrasing that suggests imperial conquest and despoilment."[10] These propositions gain rather than lose if we translate them into more concrete historical propositions, to refer to, say, Robinson Crusoe and the WASP entrepreneur. Thus, we might change "man" in what follows to "white man." "When everything exists only as reflected in the ego, then man has drunk up the sea. If man is defined as subject, everything else turns into object" (p. 3). This suggests that the source of this aesthetics lies in modern capitalist and imperialist activity.

However, there are other ways of understanding literature, found outside our culture, schemes that give a different explanation for the division between the different periods and the different kinds of literature and take the focus off Western entrepreneurialism—for instance, classical Tamil poetry, as explained by A. K. Ramanujan. In *The Interior Landscape* Ramanujan tells us that this literature, written in the remote past, was divided by scholars into two kinds of thematic material— "poems of *akam* (the 'inner part' or the Interior) and poems of *puram* (the 'outer part' or the Exterior)."

> *Akam* poems are love poems; *puram* poems are all other kinds of poems, usually about good and evil, action, community, kingdom; it [this latter] is the "public poetry" of the ancient Tamils, celebrating the ferocity and glory of kings, lamenting the death of heroes, the poverty of poets. . . . Unlike *akam* poems, *puram* poems may mention explicitly the names of kings and poets and

10. J. Hillis Miller, *Poets of Reality*, 1, 2.

places. The poem is placed in a real society and given a context of real history. . . . [On the other hand,] *akam* poetry is directly about experience, not action; it is a poetry of the "inner world." . . . The love of man and woman is taken as the ideal expression of the "inner world."[11]

This division, so familiar to us in our own literature, occurred in all South Dravidian literatures, Ramanujan says. Tamil literature was written in the first three centuries of the Christian era, and for a society very unlike our own, but we recognize in it the same organizing division that is in our own literature. The difference is that in Tamil the adventure and cognate themes apparently were not regarded as material categorically suited only to inferior writers and readers (but then that was not true for us in the earlier centuries of our culture). The two genres, Ramanujan tells us, complemented each other; they contrasted in theme, mood, and structure but were unified in imagery. "Together, they make the classical, 'bardic,' Tamil world."[12]

That Tamil world was unlike our own in many ways. If we try to compare our own culture with something more similar, with the other great empires, we find they have nationalist adventure stories. We sometimes see them taken over and reinterpreted by priestly castes in a way that can remind us of the conflict between the adventure and literature in our own case. At least this is obvious in the Indian epic of the *Mahabharata* and its most important section, the Bhagavad Gita, where one sees adventure and epic overlaid by allegory and art. In the poetry, as in the doctrine, the claims of the Brahmin and the Kshatriya come into perfect (perfectly ambiguous) stasis. Arjuna must fight and kill, even his kinfolk, because he is a warrior and that is his moral duty, but he must do so in perfect detachment and dispassion, regarding the medium of action as a whole as *maya,* illusion. Just so, the story is tribal and national adventure, but it is also purely symbolic.

Chinese literature gives us some even more interesting cases. In one episode of the picaresque novel *Monkey* the Buddhist devotee Tripitaka, traveling to India in pious pilgrimage, is saved from a tiger by a hunter, and the opposite social types confront each other.[13] "You are a veritable

11. A. K. Ramanujan, *Interior Landscapes,* 101, 103, 104.
12. A. K. Ramanujan, *Poems of Love and War,* 256.
13. Hsi Yu Chi, *Monkey,* 122.

god of the mountains, sir," the Buddhist says politely. When offered some tiger meat to eat, Tripitaka must explain that he is a vegetarian. The hunter himself sits down to eat that wild meat (and the flesh of a fox and a serpent) at a little distance from the Buddhist. A humble man, Tripitaka says grace over the other's savage meal, despite his own feelings of revulsion, but the grace is so alien to the hunter's feelings and beliefs it disturbs his meal. Then the former is taken to a room that contains weapons and trophies of the hunt—bows and arrows, and fetid and bloody tiger skins—intolerable to his sensibility. He hurries out, ill at ease (p. 123). However, his prayers, incense, and scripture readings procure for the hunter's household a vision in which his dead father says his evil karma has been wiped out, and so the women are grateful to Tripitaka. Clearly we are being shown a balancing of accounts between the adventurous ethos of the hunter and warrior, and the contemplative ethos of the scholar.

In Ming China (1368–1644) we find some great adventure narratives that correspond to the history of the great Chinese empire. Kuan-Chung Lo's *Three Kingdoms* is about the end of the Han dynasty, which ruled from 206 B.C., to A.D. 220, after which China broke up into three parts or kingdoms and a long period of civil strife began. Lo, who lived from about 1330 to 1400 and wrote this just before he died, collected and transformed old national legends much the same way Shakespeare did.[14] This story begins with three friends, Liu Pei, Kuan Yu, and Chang Fei, swearing the Peach Garden Oath, to be loyal brothers to each other always. Ts'aa Ts'aa, the imperial chancellor, though Liu's patron, is (to use Western terms) a Cardinal Richelieu figure who stands partially opposed to these three Chinese Musketeers.

The brotherhood of heroes is presented as a higher value than the morality of clan rule and dynastic interest and imperial diplomacy. "Liu Pei and I are brothers even more than friends," says Kuan Yu. But Liu is also presented as a Confucian moral hero (who sees the king's duty to his people, and the destructiveness of all war), and at the end of their lives kings and warriors alike know that they have sinned.

The story also acknowledges a conflict between Confucian ethics, with their strong sense of the social contract, and Taoism, with its independence of society. Kuan Yu is a spiritually transcendent Taoist and gets

14. Introduction to Kuan-Chung Lo, *The Three Kingdoms*, xx.

killed just for that reason. Other Taoists retreat to the mountains and declare themselves "disengaged men" who cannot take up public employment in so evil an age. These conflicts between loyalty to public values and loyalty to private ones are the themes of imperial adventure everywhere.

Kuan-Chung Lo may also be the author of another famous story, *The Water Margin* or *All Men Are Brothers,* set in the thirteenth century, the period just before the Mongols took over. Men were then driven (by unjust officials, bad conditions, bad government) to flee from society to a mountain in a lake surrounded by a reedy marsh. The community includes thirty-six chief robbers who lead a Robin Hood existence. Three of them compare the bond between them to the bond between the legendary three of *The Three Kingdoms,* and their mutual devotion becomes so famous that it wins over an enemy.[15] There is much detail about military costume, weapons, strength, fights, tactics; some famous highway robberies are described; and there is much comedy when the fierce Lu Ta puts on a priest's robes.

Volume two ends with a great adventure celebration. All the heroes assemble in their hall on the mountain, to make a joint vow: "One hundred and eight of us, each face differing from the other, yet each face noble in its way; one hundred and eight of us, each with his separate heart, yet each heart pure as a star; in joy we shall be one, in sorrow one; our hour of birth was not one, but we will die together." Then, "when Sung Chiang had thus vowed, all the host together shouted assent and they said, 'We would but meet again, life after life, generation after generation, forever undecided, even as we are this day!' On that day did they all mingle blood with wine and drink it and when they had drunk themselves to mighty drunkenness, they parted."[16] This climax to the novel is close in spirit to the sagas of European nationalism and imperialism.

As we saw before, the authorship of Chinese novels was usually concealed, at least if the authors were "literocrats." The authors were not proud of their work. Apparently many of them loved these "vulgar" adventures in their boyhood and youth, turned to classical literature after their education, but turned back in old age to write such stories

15. Kuan-Chung Lo, *All Men Are Brothers,* 40.
16. Ibid., 1278–79.

themselves, in "the language of the streets." We are familiar with this conflict between the two kinds of literature, which with us is just as emphatic as it was in imperial China. We must learn to see beyond the conflict and its vested interests, but we cannot hope to transcend it permanently.

Conclusion

Thus, adventure is a powerful force in our intellectual lives, even if we sometimes judge it sinister, and it is a force more powerful than we usually admit. Moreover, it is also inextricably linked to other forces that we count as strengths and are unwilling to renounce.

This book has traced the presence of that idea in activities like travel and exploration; in institutions like the Boy Scouts; in enterprises like missionary work; in literature, philosophy, historiography, and capitalism; and in the way we apprehend diffusely and amorphously powerful experiences like sexuality and violence. If the idea can be found in such important places in our ideology and art, our individual and communal lives, it is surely wrong to neglect it or take it for granted, as we have done.

A number of ways to study adventure have been sketched in this book, but there are many others. For instance, I have focused on the gender link between adventure and men because that link has been so important in constituting the idea of manhood. However, the link between adventure and women may deserve study even more, as being both more hidden and more intricate—a love of adventure often involving women in crossing gender lines. The tomboy—the traditional term for an adventurous girl—is usually held to spice her feminity with a flavor of the masculine, while the corresponding figure of the sissy, the boy who is *not* adventurous, loses his masculinity without gaining any feminine virtue to compensate. The relationship of the two ideas, woman and adventure, therefore seems to be dialectical.

There have certainly been women adventurers in all the fields I have investigated, and nowadays many books are being written about such figures. They have been exceptional, but, just for that reason, influential figures. Ours has been to a significant degree a patriarchal culture, as the scholars of feminism have taught us to recognize. One consequence of that is that all its citizens, female as well as male, have participated in male ideas, including the cult of adventure.

Moreover, there are kinds of adventure particularly suited to women—there is women's adventure, just as there is women's fiction. In this book my approach has been masculinist. I made that choice deliberately, believing that the gender link had been so important in the past that we needed to acknowledge it. (Besides, we cannot turn impatiently away from gender-biased phenomena, or we would have to abandon cultural studies; and we cannot cherish exclusively the hitherto neglected, or we shall create more gender bias.) Finally, the first step toward a study of women-and-adventure, I think, is a book like this, which suggests points for comparison and contrast. But adventure will be, and already has been, a feminine idea too—and just as powerful and dangerous a force when women appropriate it as when men do.

Seen in the broadest perspective, of the earth's different cultures, adventure is an idea we can see every human group appropriating on occasion. There are elements of adventure in all the folktales the anthropologists have brought to us, from even the smallest tribal cultures. But that does not cancel, and should not obscure, the special power-link between adventure and the culture of the West—European and American culture. Historically, adventure has been a white idea as well as a male idea; it has been the means by which the people of one particular culture have taken possession of most of the globe, and that history has left behind it a multiform responsibility.

Adventure has fostered certain kinds of courage and skill and independence and enterprise that are part of the human heritage and attractive and valuable to people outside the West. Certainly it would be wrong summarily to reject the adventure idea on their behalf as well as our own, because of our sense of its dangers. But adventure *has* indeed been arrogant and cruel and blinkered and destructive. Our historical responsibility begins with the perception of all those sides to the adventure heritage.

Bibliography

Aksakov, Sergei. *A Russian Gentleman*. Translated by J. D. Duff. London: Edward Arnold, 1917.
Alexander, Christine, ed. *Early Writings of Charlotte Brontë*. Buffalo: Prometheus, 1983.
Ashleigh, Charles. *The Rambling Kid*. London: Faber & Faber, 1930.
Babel, Isaac. *Red Cavalry*. New York: Knopf, 1929.
Bacon, Margaret Hope. *The Mothers of Feminism*. New York: Harper & Row, 1986.
Baker, Samuel. *Albert N'Yanza*. Philadelphia: Macmillan, 1866.
Barthes, Roland. *The Grain of the Voice*. New York: Hill & Wang, 1985.
Bataille, Georges. *Erotism: Death and Sensuality*. Translated by Mary Dalwood. 1962. Reprint. San Francisco: City Lights, 1982.
Beaumont, Cyril W. *Flash-Back*. Introduction by Sacheverell Sitwell. London: C. W. Beaumont, 1931.
Beauvoir, Simone, de. *The Second Sex*. New York: Vintage, 1953.
Beeching, Jack. *An Open Path*, Santa Barbara, Calif.: Ross-Erikson, 1982.
Bloom, Harold. *The Anxiety of Influence*. London: Oxford University Press, 1973.
Brontë, Charlotte. *The Professor*. London: Smith, Elder & Co., 1889.
Buchan, Anna. *Unforgettable, Unforgotten*. London: Hodder & Stoughton, 1945.
Buchan, John. *The History of the Great War*. 4 vols. Boston: Little, Brown, 1923.
———. *The Last Secrets*. London: T. Nelson & Sons, 1920.
———. *Memory Hold the Door*. London: Hodder & Stoughton, 1940.
Bulloch, Andrew, and J. Drummond. *The Church in Victorian Scotland*. Edinburgh: St. Andrew, 1975.
Burgess, Anthony. *Napoleon Symphony*. New York: Random House, 1974.
Burton, Richard. *Zanzibar*. London: Tinsley Bros., 1872.

Carrington, C. E. *The Life of Kipling*. New York: Doubleday, 1956.
Cendrars, Blaise. *Rhum: L'aventure de Jean Galmont*. Paris: LaBaconnière, 1965.
Chien, Hsia. *Etchings of a Tormented Age*. London: Allen & Unwin, 1942.
Cooper, J. Fenimore. *The Saga of Leatherstocking*. Edited by Allan Nevins. New York: Pantheon, 1954.
Dana, Richard Henry. *Two Years Before the Mast*. 1840. Reprint. New York: Dutton, 1912.
Darwin, Charles. "A Naturalist's Voyage Round the World." In Dennis Porter, *Haunted Journeys*. Princeton: Princeton University Press, 1991.
Day, William Patrick. *In the Circles of Fear and Desire*. Chicago: University of Chicago, 1985.
Detienne, Marcel. *Dionysos Slain*. Baltimore: Johns Hopkins University, 1979.
Dekker, George, and J. P. McWilliams, eds. *Fenimore Cooper: The Critical Heritage*. London: Routledge & Kegan Paul, 1973.
Deutscher, Isaac. *The Non-Jewish Jew*. London: Oxford University Press, 1968.
Dinesen, Isak. *Out of Africa*. New York: Random House, 1938.
―――. In *Writers at Work*. Paris Review Interviews, 4th Series. Edited by George Plimpton. New York: Viking, 1976.
Diver, Maud. *Honoria Lawrence*. Boston: Houghton Mifflin, 1936.
Donovan, Josephine. *Feminist Theory*. Chicago: University of Chicago, 1985.
Doughty, Howard. *Francis Parkman*. Westport, Conn.: Greenwood Press, 1978.
Duncan, Sara Jeannette (Mrs. Everard Cotes). *The Pool in the Desert*. London: Methuen, 1903.
Farrington, Benjamin. *Centaurus*, vol. 1. Copenhagen: Munksgaard, 1951.
Feuer, Lewis. *Imperialism and the Anti-Imperialist Mind*. Buffalo, N.Y.: Prometheus, 1986.
Forster, E. M. *Howards End*. London: Penguin, 1941.
Gandhi, M. K. *The Collected Works of Mahatma Gandhi*. Ahmedabad: Navajivan, 1958–.
―――. *Satyagraha in South Africa*. Ahmedabad: Navajivan, 1928.
Gellner, Ernest. *Nations and Nationalism*. Ithaca, N.Y.: Cornell University Press, 1983.
Gilman, Charlotte Perkins. *The Man-Made World*. New York: Charlton, 1911.
Goncharov, Ivan. *The Frigate Pallada*. New York: St. Martin's, 1987.
―――. *Oblomov*. London: Penguin, 1954.
Gordon, Charles. *The Journals of Major-General C. G. Gordon, C.B., at Khartoum*. London: Kegan Paul, Trench & Co., 1888.
Grahn, Judy. *True-to-Life Adventure Stories*. Trumansburg, N.Y.: Crossing, 1978.
Gramsci, Antonio. *Selections from Cultural Writings*. Edited by D. Forgacs and G. Nowell-Smith. London: Lawrence & Wishart, 1985.
Grattan, C. H. *The South-West Pacific to 1900*. Ann Arbor: University of Michigan Press, 1963.
Guillet, Edwin C. *The Great Migration*. Toronto: University of Toronto Press, 1963.
Guttmann, Allen. *From Ritual to Record*. New York: Columbia University Press, 1978.
Haggard, H. Rider. *The Poor and the Land*. London: Longmans, 1905.
―――. *Regeneration*. London: Longmans, 1910.
Hannah, Donald. *Isak Dinesen and Karen Blixen*. New York: Putnam, 1971.
Hayes, E. Nelson. *Claude Lévi-Strauss: The Anthropologist as Hero*. Cambridge: MIT, 1970.

Hargreaves, Jennifer. *Sport, Culture, and Ideology*. London: Routledge & Kegan Paul, 1982.

Heaney, Seamus. *Preoccupations*. New York: Farrar, Strauss & Giroux, 1980.

Hemingway, Ernest. *Death in the Afternoon*. New York: Scribners, 1932.

Hsi yu chi. *Monkey*. Translated by Arthur Whaley. London: Allen & Unwin, 1956.

Hobbes, Thomas. *Leviathan*. Edited by J. Plamenatz. Cleveland: World Publishing, 1963.

Hoberman, John M. *Sport and Political Ideology*. Austin: University of Texas, 1984.

Hobson, J. A. *Imperialism*. Revised edition. London: Constable, 1905.

———. *The Psychology of Jingoism*. London: Grant Richards, 1901.

Hoy, D. C., ed. *Foucault: A Critical Reader*. Oxford: Basil Blackwell, 1986.

Humphrey, Richard D. *Georges Sorel*. Cambridge: Harvard University, 1951.

Huxley, Elspeth. *Out in the Midday Sun*. London: Chatto & Windus, 1985.

———. *White Man's Country*. 2 vols. London: Chatto & Windus, 1953.

Hyam, Ronald, and Ged Martin. *Reappraisals in British Imperial History*. London: Macmillan, 1975.

The Illustrated History of South Africa. Pleasantville, N.Y.: Reader's Digest Association, 1981.

Irving, Washington. *Astoria*. 1836. Reprint. Norman: University of Oklahoma, 1964.

Jefferies, Richard. *Bevis*. 1882. Reprint. London: J. M. Dent, 1930.

———. *The Story of My Heart*. 1883. Reprint. London: Duckworth & Co., 1912.

———. *Wood Magic*. 1881. Reprint. New York: Cassell, Petter & Galpin, 1874.

Joll, James. *Three Intellectuals in Politics*. New York: Parthenon, 1960.

Joyce, James. *Exiles*. London: Penguin, 1961.

Keller, Evelyn Fox. *Reflections on Science and Gender*. New Haven: Yale University, 1985.

Kipling, Rudyard. *A Kipling Pageant*. New York: Library Guild, 1935.

———. *The Light That Failed*. 1890. Reprint. New York: Airmont, 1969.

———. *Something of Myself*. New York: Doubleday, 1937.

———. *Stalky and Co.* 1899. Reprint. New York: Dell, 1968.

———. *Uncollected Prose*. New York: Doubleday, 1941.

———. *The War and the Fleet in Being*. New York: Doubleday, 1941.

Knox-Shaw, Peter. *The Explorer in English Fiction*. New York: St. Martin's, 1986.

Kornbluh, Joyce, ed. *Rebel Voices: An I.W.W. Anthology*. Ann Arbor: University of Michigan Press, 1964.

Kuan-Chung Lo. *The Three Kingdoms*. New York: Pantheon, 1976.

Lawrence, D. H. *Aaron's Rod*. 1921. Reprint. New York: Viking, 1961.

Leiris, Michel. *Manhood*. Translated by Richard Howard. New York: Grossmans, 1963.

Le Vaillant, François. *Travels in the Interior Parts of Africa, 1780–1785*. London: G. & J. Robinson, 1796.

Levin, David. *History as Romantic Art*. Palo Alto, Calif.: Stanford University, 1959.

Lewis, C. S. *The Allegory of Love*. London: Oxford University, 1938.

London, Jack. *John Barleycorn*. New York: Century, 1913.

———. *Revolution*. New York: Macmillan, 1910.

Lovey, J.-C. *La situation de Blaise Cendrars*. Paris: La Baconnière, 1965.

Lowell, Robert. *Life Studies*. New York: Noonday, 1959.

McIntosh, Peter. *Fair Play*. London: Heinemann, 1979.

MacKenzie, John M. *The Empire of Nature*. Manchester: University of Manchester, 1987.

MacKenzie, John M., ed. *Imperialism and Popular Culture*. Manchester: University of Manchester, 1986.
———. *Propaganda and Empire*. Manchester: University of Manchester, 1984.
Mailer, Norman. *Advertisements for Myself*. New York: Putnam, 1959.
———. *The Presidential Papers*. New York: Bantam, 1964.
Malchow, Howard C. *Population Pressures: Emigration and Government in Late Nineteenth-Century Britain*. Palo Alto, Calif.: Stanford University, 1979.
Mandell, R. D. *Sport: A Cultural History*. New York: Columbia University Press, 1984.
Mangan, J. A., and J. Walvin, eds. *Manliness and Morality*. Manchester: University of Manchester, 1987.
Mannoni, Octave. *Prospero and Caliban: The Psychology of Colonization*. New York: Praeger, 1956.
Mason, Philip. *Kipling: The Glass, the Shadow, and the Fire*. New York: Harper, 1975.
Masterman, C.F.G., ed. *The Heart of the Empire*. 1901. Reprint. New York: Barnes & Noble, 1973.
Merchant, Carolyn. *The Death of Nature*. New York: Harper & Row, 1983.
Michael, Maurice A. *Traveller's Quest*. Freeport, N.Y.: Books for Libraries, 1950.
Miller, Henry. *The Books in My Life*. New York: New Directions, 1969.
Miller, J. Hillis. *The Disappearance of God*. Cambridge: Harvard University, 1963.
———. *Poets of Reality*. Cambridge: Harvard University, 1965.
Moorehead, Alan. *The White Nile*. New York: Harper & Row, 1960.
Nairn, Tom. *The Break-Up of Britain*. London: New Left Books, 1977.
Nerlich, Michael. *The Ideology of Adventure*. Minneapolis: University of Minnesota, 1987.
———. *Kritik der Abenteuer Ideologie*. Berlin, 1977.
———. "The Unknown History of Our Modernity." *Occasional Papers 3*, Center for Humanistic Studies, University of Minnesota, 1986.
Nehru, Jawaharlal. *Glimpses of World History*. New York: L. Drummond, 1942.
Newman, Gerald. *The Rise of English Nationalism*. New York: St. Martin's, 1987.
Nietzsche, Friedrich. *On the Genealogy of Morals*. 1886. Reprint. New York: Vintage, 1969.
Norris, Margot. *Beasts of the Modern Imagination*. Baltimore: Johns Hopkins University, 1985.
Novak, Michael. *The Joy of Sports*. New York: Basic Books, 1976.
O'Connor, Richard. *Jack London*. Boston: Little, Brown, 1964.
Plamenatz, John, ed. *Leviathan* by Thomas Hobbes. Cleveland: World Publishing, 1963.
Pleck, Joseph. *The Myth of Masculinity*. Cambridge, Mass.: M.I.T., 1981.
Porter, Dennis. *Haunted Journeys*. Princeton: Princeton University Press, 1991.
Quinn, Arthur H. *American Fiction*. New York: Appleton Century, 1936.
Ramanujan, A. K. *Interior Landscapes*. Bloomington: Indiana University, 1975.
———. *Poems of Love and War*. New York: Columbia University Press, 1985.
Rosenthal, Michael. *The Character Factory*. New York: Pantheon, 1986.
Roth, J. J. *The Cult of Violence*. Berkeley and Los Angeles: University of California Press, 1980.
Roth, Philip. *The Counterlife*. New York: Farrar, Strauss & Giroux, 1987.
———. *Portnoy's Complaint*. New York: Random House, 1969.
Salmon, Edward. *Juvenile Literature as It Is*. London: H. J. Drane, 1888.

Samuel, Maurice. *The Gentleman and the Jew.* New York: Knopf, 1950.

Sartre, J.-P. *Saint Genet: Actor and Martyr.* Translated by Bernard Frechtman. New York: New American Library, 1964.

———. *The Words.* Translated by Bernard Frechtman. New York: Braziller, 1964.

Scammell, G. V. *The World Encompassed.* Berkeley and Los Angeles: University of California Press, 1981.

Scott, Paul. *A Division of the Spoils.* London: Granada, 1978.

Simmel, Georg. *On Individuality and Social Forms.* Chicago: University of Chicago Press, 1971.

Smith, Bernard. *European Vision and the South Pacific.* 2d ed. New Haven: Yale University Press, 1985.

Smout, T. C. *The History of the Scottish People.* New Haven: Yale University, 1986.

Sontag, Susan. *I, Etcetera.* New York: Vintage, 1979.

———. *Under the Sign of Saturn.* New York: Vintage, 1981.

Spengemann, William. *The Adventurous Muse.* New Haven: Yale University, 1977.

Spengler, Oswald. *The Decline of the West.* 1920. Reprint. New York: Holt Rinehart, 1970.

Stanley, Henry. *Through the Dark Continent.* New York: Harper Bros., 1878.

Stanley, J., ed. *From Georges Sorel.* New York: Transactions, 1976.

Stearns, Peter N. *Be a Man!* New York: Holmes & Meier, 1979.

Stevenson, R. L. *Memories and Portraits.* London: Chatto & Windus, 1888.

———. *Treasure Island.* 1881. Reprint. New York: Scribners, 1909.

Stokstad, M.; H. L. Snyder; and H. Orel, eds. *The Scottish World.* New York: Crown Publishers, 1986.

Symondson, A. *The Victorian Crisis of Faith.* London: SPCK, 1970.

Theroux, Paul. *Sunrise with Seamonsters.* Boston: Houghton Mifflin, 1985.

Thompson, H. P. *Into All Lands.* London: SPCK, 1951.

Tiger, Lionel. *Men in Groups.* New York: Vintage, 1970.

Tolkien, J.R.R. *The Fellowship of the Ring.* New York: Ballantine, 1982.

———. *The Lord of the Rings.* New York: Ballantine, 1974.

Tolstoy, Leo. *Father Sergius.* Moscow: Raduga Publishers, 1988.

———. *The Journal of Leo Tolstoy, 1895–1899.* New York: Knopf, 1917.

———. *Tolstoy's Letters.* Edited by Reginald Christian. New York: Scribners, 1978.

Tolstoy, Sonia. *The Diary of Tolstoy's Wife.* London: Gollancz, 1928.

Trilling, Lionel. *Beyond Culture.* New York: Harcourt Brace Jovanovich, 1965.

———. *The Liberal Imagination.* New York: Scribners, 1950.

Twain, Mark. *Roughing It.* 1872. Reprint. New York: New American Library, 1962.

Wagner, Gillian. *Children of the Empire.* London: Weidenfeld & Nicolson, 1982.

Waugh, Evelyn. *Brideshead Revisited.* 1948. Reprint. New York: Dell, 1962.

Wells, H. G. *The History of Mr. Polly.* 1910. Reprint. Boston: Houghton Mifflin, 1960.

White, Richard. *Inventing Australia.* London: Allen & Unwin, 1981.

Wurgaft, Lewis D. *The Activists.* American Philosophical Society Transactions 67, part 6, December 1977.

———. *The Imperial Imagination.* Middletown, Conn.: Wesleyan University, 1983.

Index